A Choice of Heroes

A Choice of Heroes

**The Changing Faces
of American Manhood**

Mark Gerzon

HOUGHTON MIFFLIN COMPANY
BOSTON   NEW YORK   LONDON

For information about permission to reproduce
selections from this book, write to
Permissions, Houghton Mifflin Company,
215 Park Avenue South,
New York, New York 10003.

Library of Congress Cataloging in Publication Data

Gerzon, Mark.
    A choice of heroes : the changing faces of
American manhood / Mark Gerzon.
        p.   cm.
    Includes bibliographical references.
    ISBN 0-395-61152-0
    1. Masculinity.   2. Sex role.   3. Role
expectation.   4. Heroes in literature.
5. Heroes — United States.   I. Title.
HQ1090.G47   1992
305.31 — dc20   91-42132
                            CIP

Printed in the United States of America
BBS   10   9   8   7   6   5   4   3   2   1

For my father, my brothers, and my sons

The truth about the need for heroism is not easy for anyone to admit . . . to become conscious of what one is doing to earn his feeling of heroism is the main self-analytic problem of life.

— Ernest Becker,
  The Denial of Death, 1973

Contents

Preface

NO STORY IS COMPLETE without a storyteller. Particularly when the subject is sexuality, the personal and the political merge. One's life history and history itself intersect, each infusing the other with its own crises and commitments.

My life is no exception, and this book reflects it. Three times I have approached the subject of this book.* But each time I veered off into pressing subjects — the generation gap, the social responsibility of parents, my own personal evolution — that demanded my concern and attention, both as a writer and as a man. Having waited for ten years to deal directly with the question of changing ideals of masculinity in America, I began writing a few years ago with the hope that I was at last ready. I wasn't.

I hesitated to begin this book. Like many men, I resist facing, much less sharing, my feelings about masculinity. I was afraid of what others would learn about me and perhaps of what I would learn about myself. And because sexuality had become so political — along with homosexuality, abortion, and women's rights, among the most aggressively disputed public controversies — I had many moments of doubt about whether to proceed.

Many commentators on masculinity are paragons of virility, superstars of sports, war, movies, or some other public arena. Others are symbols of anti-masculinity in the arts or the professions; they are gay. Others, known for being objective, discuss masculinity as social scientists, marshaling studies and statistics to prove their hypotheses. Currently, there are members of men's liberation movements, who can be identified by their cause.

---

* *The Whole World Is Watching: A Young Man Looks at Youth's Dissent* (New York, 1969); *A Childhood for Every Child: The Politics of Parenthood* (New York, 1973); "A Father's Birth," unpublished novel.

None of these labels fits me or the men whose portraits appear in these pages. My life is as complex and multifaceted as any man's. Each of the chapters in this book begins with a personal perspective, a glimpse into my life and the lives around me. I include this autobiographical book-within-a-book because I want to share some of the experiences out of which my observations have grown.

The terrain covered here is vast. It traverses centuries and subjects, explores the personal as well as the political, and races through material that often deserves more thorough examination. The sources cited in the notes therefore assume added importance as a ledger of my intellectual debts. Without the path-breaking work of these writers, I could never have explored this territory.

Intellectual assistance leaves tracks called footnotes, but personal assistance does not. Some of those who helped me are mentioned by name or pseudonym. They are the men and women who permitted me to draw their portraits. By opening their lives to me, they have enriched this book beyond measure.

For every person who appears in these pages, however, there are many others who participated in their composition. Scholars, writers, therapists, ministers, teachers, veterans, parents, and neighbors — all kinds of people have shared their thoughts with me. I particularly want to thank Peter Davison, Doris Kearns, James C. Thomson, Jim Robinson, Ruth Salinger, and Jeanette Gerzon.

Three people deserve my special gratitude. My agent, Don Cutler, offered criticism and encouragement in good proportion. The sensitivity and commitment of my editor, Gerard Van der Leun, was invaluable to me in reworking the final drafts. This is a better book because of both of them.

My wife, Shelley Kessler, shared with me her library and her love. Without her, I doubt there would have been a book at all.

A Choice of Heroes

Introduction

A man would never get the notion
of writing a book on the peculiar
situation of the human male.

— Simone de Beauvoir, *The Second Sex,* 1953

I HAVE WORKED for them and against them; I have been their friend
and their enemy. I have grown up, studied, worked, and lived with
them. I am one of them, yet I feel apart from them.

We are white, college-educated, heterosexual men. We hold
more than our share of power. If not yet at the top, we feel we still
might be. We are only a minority of America's population, but wherever the action is, we are the majority. If we are not in charge, we
work with those who are. From state legislatures to university faculties, among military as well as corporate top brass, within the big
banks and the political parties, we are there.

We have so much more than our share of power, in fact, that
others resent us. Working women envy our privileges. So do blacks
and other victims of discrimination. Minorities ranging from Indians
to gays claim that they are oppressed by us. They want to have the
power and the privileges of the white male club.

But we, the club's members, see ourselves differently. Although
others may think we have it made, we do not feel comfortable. Behind masks of self-assurance, we feel confused. We yearn for adventure, particularly involving feats of endurance and skill. But we lead
extraordinarily sedentary, mechanized lives. We are inexplicably
eager to move on — to switch lovers, cars, careers, channels, identities. But we nevertheless complain of feeling in a rut. We are frus-

trated by the deadening demands of our jobs and of our role as breadwinner, yet we are somehow threatened when our wives' careers take hold.

We claim to care about the strength and vitality of our bodies, but we are out of touch with them. We act as if we deeply value our buddies, although we rarely move beyond sarcasm and backslapping to share our deepest feelings. We are quick to talk about sex and slow to discuss intimacy. We pretend that nothing is more important than being "free" and refer to getting married as being "snared," "caught," or "tied down," as we marry (and divorce) in record numbers. We say easily that we want children "someday." But when someday comes, we try to avoid the responsibility for their daily care. We allude frequently to being real, red-blooded, all-American men, and sometimes we even make fun of "queers." We want America to be strong, a world leader, and to devote precious resources to military expansion. Yet we feel increasingly vulnerable.

This book is about us. It is about why we think and act the way we do. It includes glimpses behind the finely tailored suits and dashing uniforms of the American male. It is about choosing one's heroes — who are, after all, only reflections of ourselves.

IF NOT in the judgment of history, then in the eyes of a woman, every man wants to be a hero. Men may not boast about it. We may not even talk about it. In fact, we may not even be aware of it. Yet each of us tries to emulate models of manhood that to us seem heroic.

But who are our heroes? Do names and faces spring to mind of men who have succeeded in battle or in business, in politics or in sports, in literature or in religion? Or does no clear image crystallize? Behind the response of our conscious mind is much that remains unsaid. This question of heroism is, wrote Ernest Becker in his Pulitzer Prize–winning essay, *The Denial of Death*, "the most important that man can put to himself." Yet we do not dare face it squarely.

Whether in the faculty club or the officers' club, at a board meeting or in bed, we want to be seen as real men, whatever that may mean to us. This need is so strong, so primitive, that some of us will risk anything to satisfy it — our wealth, our health, even our lives.

Yet how conscious are we of what we are doing to earn this feeling of heroism? Men's behavior, both in private and in public, suggests that our images of heroism are largely unconscious. They are so much a part of our boyhood conditioning that we are barely aware of them. In the midst of our Clark Kent lives, we dream of being Superman.

In the portraits of masculinity that follow, no image of heroism is alluded to more often than John Wayne. Countless men, in recalling the kind of man they wanted to be, say they wanted to grow up to be like John Wayne. But none of these men actually knew Wayne himself. They did not know Marion Michael Morrison, the son of a druggist. They did not know the lanky lad who forfeited his name because, as he put it, it "didn't sound American enough." They did not know the man who late in his life told an interviewer, "I still don't recognize it when somebody calls me John." Nor did they know the man who slowly died of cancer, possibly contracted while filming at an old nuclear testing site in the Southwest.

No, these men knew only his image as it was captured on celluloid. The same is true for boys who invoke, not movie stars, but heroes from football, baseball, and other manly sports. The ones who say they wanted to be like Mickey Mantle or O. J. Simpson are not referring to the real men. They never knew the tired men who tore themselves away from their families week after week, who cursed their lives in countless hotel rooms, and who, by the age of forty, were managing restaurants or marketing rental cars. They knew only those figures in uniform who flickered across their television screens. And the ones who say they wanted to be like Elvis Presley knew only the glittering, sequined strutter on the stage beneath dazzling lights. They did not know the drug-addicted, obese man who died isolated and alone.

When men go crazy, however, the image often surfaces. Listen to Frank Barber, a Vietnam veteran, describe his mental breakdown and the crazed, demonic rage that overwhelmed him. "I was not Frank Barber," he said. "I was John Wayne, Steve McQueen, Clint Eastwood." After Frank returned home, the navy gave him medals. But what he really needed, he said, was to be held and comforted by his wife. Why couldn't he ask his own wife for solace? "I never saw John Wayne walk up to a woman and say, 'I need a hug.' "

Through therapy, Frank rediscovered himself. But other men lose their identity so completely that they *become* the image. A few months after John Hinckley, the privileged son of an oil magnate, shot and almost killed President Ronald Reagan, he explained why he did it. He said he wanted to impress actress Jodie Foster, whom he had seen in the intensely violent film *Taxi Driver*. When asked why he bought so many guns, Hinckley replied, "Ask Travis." Travis was the taxi driver in the movie, played by Robert de Niro.

A normal man in ordinary circumstances obviously does not succumb so irrationally to his unconscious images of manhood. He remembers his identity; he does not lose his own self and become someone else's. Nevertheless, our culture's images of manhood influence us more than we know. Through the course of this book, five archetypes of masculinity will be introduced: the Frontiersman, the Soldier, the Expert, the Breadwinner, and the Lord. These archetypes, or hero-images, influence our behavior whether we are aware of it or not. The stodgy word *archetype,* which means original model or first form, is appropriate because it suggests that these images of manhood cannot be dislodged simply by frenetic consciousness raising or alternative life-styles.

These archetypes of manhood exist because they were once useful. They promised survival and well-being. The Frontiersman explored new lands. The Soldier symbolized greater security. The Expert marshaled new knowledge. The Breadwinner fostered economic prosperity, both for his family and for the nation. And the Lord, a symbol of divinity, offered salvation and immortality. Such hero-images served vital purposes. They led men to protect their loved ones, to defend cherished values, and to enrich and expand their lives.

But are these symbols of manhood useful for men today? We are no longer certain. Our presidents, once they leave office, drift into obscurity. Our veterans, after returning from Vietnam, are unheralded. Our sports stars are overpaid, overpublicized, and often just overnight sensations. A biography of Gary Cooper is called *The Last Hero.* After the space shuttle *Columbia* returns to earth, the pilots are not treated as demigods the way Charles Lindbergh was. We remember the machine, not the men. Only superhumans, humanoids from other galaxies, and the bizarre products of surgical or chemical experimentation now thrill the young.

Traditionally, men have identified with images that were passed down from father to son, generation after generation. Embedded in myths and rituals with prehistoric origins, their images represented the core of early human cultures. But as modern technological societies emerge, change accelerates. As Susan Sontag pointed out in *On Photography*, "Society becomes modern when one of its chief activities becomes producing and consuming images [that] are in themselves coveted substitutes for firsthand experience." Thus men today consume certain images of manhood even though the world from which they are derived may have disappeared — if it ever existed.

To model oneself after another man is in itself problematic. But to model oneself after an image of a man, repackaged for the camera, is dangerous. In comparing themselves to the dashing figure riding off into the setting sun or racing across the goal line, ordinary men in everyday life cannot help but feel overshadowed.

Even in private, men no longer feel like heroes. A husband is no longer undisputed lord of the manor, a small-scale hero. To be the breadwinner is no longer a badge of honor. A man cannot assume that his wife will tend his house and raise his children, or even take his name. His wife may earn as much money as he does. If she doesn't, she may resent the disparity in their incomes (even as she spends his). Whether or not his wife calls herself a feminist, she will expect him to do more housework and child care than he was raised to expect. If the marriage fails, she is as likely to leave him as he is to leave her.

For many men, feminism has only compounded their confusion. Few men in America are unaware that a movement led by women wants us to liberate ourselves from old styles of masculine behavior. This women's liberation movement has been echoed by men's liberation, which is also dedicated to raising our consciousness. In academic studies, best-selling books, popular films, government legislation, lobbying organizations, nationwide coalitions — indeed, in virtually every aspect of American society — these movements are advocating new images of masculinity.

Beginning in the sixties, feminists traced the impact of sexuality on literature, art, science, government, philosophy, law, medicine, psychology, religion. They challenged the masculine world view. Few men stopped to listen; even those who did often pretended that the problem was merely a women's issue. They dismissed men's liberation as a mere adjunct of feminism and assumed that any man who questioned the prevailing images of masculinity must be of doubtful virility.

But as the women's movement matured and deepened through

the seventies, more men noticed. Our mothers and sisters, wives and girl friends, made us listen even if we would not learn. Books by men, with titles such as *The Liberated Male, Tenderness Is Strength,* and *The Myth of American Manhood,* questioned the archetypes of masculinity in our culture. Newsletters began to flourish: "Changing Men," "American Man," "Nurturing News." Scores of articles about masculinity appeared in the popular and student press.

Writing on men's liberation is often shallow, severed both from history and from the heart. Some writing is merely a response to feminism. Other writing suggests that we should change our masculinity, not to appease feminists, but to enjoy ourselves more. There is nothing wrong with pleasing feminists or with having fun, but neither touches the deeper forces that shape masculinity, and neither will motivate enough men to profound change. We cannot retire the old chauvinistic images of manhood and put them away in our psychic closet like winter clothes.

Inevitably, some who wish to redefine masculinity have put forward an image of a "liberated" man. They extol the new male without ever exploring why the old one has been with us for so long. They exhort us to transform ourselves without admitting that the old masculinity cannot be exorcised overnight. It still influences each of us. Whether we cook dinner or call cooking women's work, whether we call women Ms. or Mrs., the old images of manhood live within us. Our task, as Jung argues, is not to deny these images or archetypes but to become conscious of them. As Phil Donahue puts it later in this book, men must stop "sleepwalking."

The purpose of such reexamination is not to make us all suddenly fit the mold of the new male. Just the opposite: it will enable us to see that molds, whether liberated or macho, are dehumanizing. Thinking about our own masculinity will enable us to take responsibility for ourselves. We will not be so quick to blame our problems on the finite earth, on our ungrateful wives and children, on some subversive enemy at home or abroad, or on some other force apart from us. Instead, we will find the courage to tell the difference between existential dilemmas inherent in life and the unnecessary pain caused by our own, unexamined selves.

This is true heroism: the courage to explore oneself deeply and to act with self-awareness. In this sense, heroism is not dead; it is constantly evolving. Old models of masculinity are dying. But if we look carefully, we can discover new models emerging that are as vital to our survival as the earlier ones were to our forefathers. As the threats to human survival change, so does masculinity. Walter Cronkite told the Harvard class of 1980 at its graduation that their challenge is "to unseat the Four Modern Horsemen of the Apocalypse — the population explosion, pollution, scarce resources, and nuclear war." Faced with such threats, we should not be worried if masculinity is changing. We should be worried if it were not.

PART I

In Public

IN 1840, Thomas Carlyle's lecture series *On Heroes, Hero Worship, and the Heroic in History* profiled the heroes of Western civilization. (He mentioned no heroines.) Carlyle rhapsodized on the hero as divinity, as prophet, as poet, as priest, as man of letters, and finally as king. He did not propose that such hero types are equals, however; one above all was chosen as "the most important of Great Men."

"We come now to the last form of heroism," Carlyle opined in his final lecture, "that which we call Kingship. The Commander Over Men . . . is practically the summary of *all* the various figures of heroism." The unique purpose of such a man is "to *command* over us, to furnish us with constant practical teaching, to tell us for the day and hour what to *do*."

The presidency, our closest equivalent to Carlyle's Kingship, is reserved for men. Lower levels of leadership have been open to women. They may run hospitals and schools, be elected to Congress, serve on corporate boards of directors, become judges and priests, occasionally be elected mayors or governors, and, at least in one instance, be appointed a Supreme Court justice. At token levels, women now have access to all kinds of leadership, except one.

The President has another equally important title: commander in chief. He, not the Joint Chiefs of Staff, ultimately controls the armed forces. Military leadership is the final all-male preserve. Violence is the form of power that women do not and will not control. Men will allow them to have power of the dollar, of the vote, of the womb, even of the orgasm. But after these powers are shared, the patriarchy will retain the ultimate power for itself: the power to destroy.

Behind the King stands the Soldier, an image of masculinity that underlies all others. He is the Frontiersman of the most barren wilderness — the battlefield. He is the Provider of the most precious commodity — security. He is the Expert of that most manly profession — war making. He is the Lord who delivers us from the most terrifying evil — the enemy. Little wonder that free men give their

11

government the authority to force their sons to fight. To be a warrior means to be a man.

To stress a man's experience, maturity, or skill, one may call him a veteran surgeon or a veteran of many political campaigns. But if one simply says he is a veteran, the unstated profession is understood. The test of battle is the ultimate experience, the final arbiter of maturity, the life-or-death skill.

If we wish, then, to understand our images of manhood and how they influence our behavior, the image of the Soldier is critical. While it is true that fewer men spend fewer years on duty than on the job, war making is distinguished from all other masculine enterprises by one irrevocable reality: the stakes are higher. War can destroy everything achieved through other human endeavors. It can take away health, wealth, dignity, and life. It can assassinate civilization.

We may think more about our jobs or our families than about combat. But even if war is on the periphery of our daily experience, it remains central in men's consciousness. The history and future of masculinity is interwoven with the history and future of war.

1 The Frontiersman

Images of the Earth

Raised in the woods till he knew every tree,
Killed him a b'ar when he was only three.
Davy, Davy Crockett, King of the wild frontier.
— "The Ballad of Davy Crockett"

I don't feel we did wrong taking this great
country away from [the Indians]. Our so-called
stealing of this country from them was just a
matter of survival. There were great numbers
of people who needed new land, and the Indians
were selfishly trying to keep it for themselves.
— John Wayne, 1971

THE GREEN-LAWNED SUBURB of Indianapolis, Indiana, where I spent my boyhood was hardly the frontier. My father was a biochemist, not a woodsman. Men were commuters, not cowboys. I carried a tennis racket, not a rifle, and wore Arrow shirts, not buckskin. The only Mustangs and Colts I rode were made in Detroit. The only Indians I knew played baseball. Instead of wilderness, there were shopping malls. Dodge City was a cut-rate car lot.

Yet in my mind the frontier persisted. After school, we played cowboys and Indians. In the evening, the Wild West came alive. The Frontiersmen — Daniel Boone and Davy Crockett, Buffalo Bill and Kit Carson, Wild Bill Hickok and Wyatt Earp — returned. The Frontiersmen had been preserved, or rather re-created, on film, and almost every night they took me on adventures. I went with Davy Crockett to the Alamo, with Wyatt Earp to the OK Corral. Matt Dillon, Maverick, the Lone Ranger, Hopalong Cassidy, Roy

Rogers — they all let me come along. I was their silent sidekick, riding with them through my electronic time machine.

In this world according to Hollywood, I first learned about heroism. The hero was a white man. He might have a pal, like the Lone Ranger's Tonto, but mostly he traveled alone. Wives were uncommon: the hero was always on the move. He never reflected or questioned himself. He followed Davy Crockett's motto: "Be sure you're right, then go ahead." The hero was always right. Though he was constantly fighting, he was never at fault. It was always his enemy who attacked. He upheld the law, freedom, justice, peace, progress. His enemy was the outlaw, the tyrant, the bully, the savage redskin. He was always altruistic, never selfish. He had mastered the land and himself. Nothing made him cry.

For me the Frontiersman was the most vivid and inspiring example of what man should be. He seemed *real*, certainly more so than the men who drove off in their cars each morning to work I could not understand. I liked the Frontiersman because, no matter how arduous his day might be, he always took me along. No matter how great the danger, he would protect me. The Frontiersman always knew what to do.

Now I am an adult. When I feel helpless, overwhelmed, or confused, I think of the Frontiersman. I thought of him recently when, for the first time in years, I wept.

I started crying while reading a magazine. That a magazine article should make me cry is strange because at the time I was a magazine editor; I tended to see written words in my hands as clinically as a surgeon sees a heart in the operating room. It is doubly strange because I was not at home but on an international airline flight, not the sort of place a man would pick to break down.

The article was by a writer I had never heard of, about a town to which I have never been and a family I have never met. It told how eight-year-old Jimmy Archer died of leukemia and how his parents, John and Virginia, reacted to his death. It also told how Virginia Archer later learned that Jimmy was only one of six children to be struck down by leukemia in a ten-block area of their tree-lined neighborhood in Rutherford, a New Jersey suburb.

"Two cases wouldn't be outside the realm of chance," said Dr. Ronald Altman, chief epidemiologist of the New Jersey Health Department. "But when you go beyond three, it means it's very unlikely it happened by chance alone. And when something happens that's very unlikely, you look for something that causes it."

Virginia could not get Jimmy's death out of her mind. She had accepted it as much as anyone can accept the death of one's child — until she heard about the others. Too many children were dying. She began to wonder if something had caused it. Once a trusting person, she became agitated, nervous, suspicious. She doubted official statements about the danger and began to cast a wary eye on everything around her. When death took her son, it took something else. It took her peace of mind.

I too live in a town with tree-lined streets, and I have a son about Jimmy's age. Just yesterday our newspaper published a map showing the sites of toxic waste dumps in our state. They were everywhere, cancerous tumors just beneath the surface of the earth. Like Virginia, I too have wondered about invisible killers — in the water contaminated by chemical companies' refuse, in the air polluted by automobiles and factories, in the atmosphere bombarded by microwaves, in the food riddled by additives.

The doctors in the hospital where Jimmy spent most of the last months of his life knew more about the body than any men in human history. But the leukemia was too strong for them.

Hours before the end, John looked at his son, curled up in his hospital bed. Destroyed from within by cancer and from without by chemotherapy, Jimmy's body was emaciated. A boy who only a year earlier had pitched in Little League had been reduced to an invalid. Regressing, he began to suck his thumb. Jimmy was embarrassed. He knew eight-year-olds were not supposed to suck their thumbs, but close to death, it was the only comfort he could find.

"Don't worry," John said, recognizing his son's plight and cradling him in his arms. "I'll hold you so no one can see."

When I read this, I began to cry. I was overwhelmed by this father's helplessness. As much as he loved his son, he could do nothing to save him. He had found the best medical care in the world. But in the end his son died, and John could not find the killer.

Like other men, John Archer saw himself as the protector of his family. He was not afraid to fight — for his country, for his honor, for his family. And yet he could not help but wonder if he had failed to protect his son. What the leukemia did to Jimmy infuriated him, but he did not know how to express his fury. From whom could he seek revenge? He wanted an enemy he could see again, the kind he had been raised to expect. Then evil had a name. He could get *that* enemy in his sights, pull the trigger, and protect his loved ones. But this enemy — how could a man fight it? He was ready to fight, but he could not find his adversary.

Virginia continued to investigate. She organized other parents into a citizens' lobby called We Who Care. She persistently alerted state and federal health and environmental agencies to the unusually high cancer rate in their region. She was determined to stay in Rutherford in order to identify potential hazards and try to get rid of them. Staring out her kitchen window one day, she told a visitor, "You look at the kids and here they are. They're playing in the same rotten air. You look at them and can't help thinking to yourself, Which one of them is going to be next?"

She cried. And so did I. I was not mourning for Jimmy Archer but for my dreams. John Archer and I, we wanted to grow up to be heroes. We wanted to be masters of the land. Instead, we find ourselves afraid of it. We wanted to protect our families from the enemy. Instead, we do not even know who the enemy is.

What would you do now, Wild Bill? Would you still be sure you're right, Davy Crockett? If you are the master of the wilderness, Daniel Boone, will you tell me why today men are so afraid? What has happened to the virgin land you won, Frontiersmen? Where did it go?

ALWAYS, the earth is *she*. Sometimes inchoately, often vibrantly, the voices of human culture call our planet Woman.

For eons, the earth was Mother, sacred and revered, the source and symbol of life. We were her sons, and women were her daughters. The Great Mother lived before us, and after. Omnipotent, her fertility represented life; her barrenness, death. We worshiped her and feared her at the same time: she giveth, and she taketh away.

"The Earth is our mother," said the Indians of North America. "She nourishes us; that which we put into the ground she returns to us, and healing plants she gives us likewise." Echoed the Indians of South America: "From her are born mankind, the good black earth, the edible plants, the animals and all of nature." In the North, the Delaware Indians believed that men lived as embryos within the body of Mother Earth. On the other side of the continent, the Navajo called the earth Naëtsàn, the recumbent woman. Farther south, the Indians in Mexico had their Centeotl, the mother of all things: men, children, and food. As varied as these cultures were, the worship of the Great Mother was universal. He-man to she-earth: it is the most fundamental marriage of all.

While traveling through the French countryside a century ago, the Indian poet Rabindranath Tagore marveled at the harmonious, loving relationship between Western man and the land. He was impressed by the "continent flowing with richness under the age long attention of her chivalrous lover, western humanity." He praised our European forefathers for their "heroic love adventure" with earth's body. As one man to another, he complimented us for our "active wooing of the Earth."

When European settlers encountered the Indians of North America, they considered the red man's mystical reverence for the land impractical as well as heretical. From our perspective, the heathen pantheism of the Indians undermined the very premises of commerce. Since they did not own the land, since they had failed (in James Madison's telling phrase) "to appropriate it to themelves," we considered it ours for the taking.

We were not sons of the North American landscape; we were her suitors. Like any fertile and ripe woman, the land was a prize to be won. Just as men covet the virgin, so we coveted the virgin land. Every man wanted a piece of her, a piece that no other man before him had ever touched. We would win her, seed her, make her produce. We deserved her because we were man enough to take her.

"God has given the earth to those who will subdue and cultivate it," wrote the respected editor Horace Greeley, "and it is vain to struggle against his righteous decree." The Lord (an image that we examine in Chapter 14) had given us permission, indeed commanded us, to subdue and cultivate the Indian's land. It was God's will, a blessed matrimony between the most fertile, untainted land and the most aggressive, righteous men. One nineteenth-century congressman declared on the floor of the House of Representatives that no nation "has the right to hold soil, virgin and rich, yet unproducing." So we claimed all undeveloped land as our own.

Although we, the white men, were the newest arrivals on the continent, we quickly came to view ourselves as its rightful owners. "Shall this garden of beauty be suffered to lie dormant in its wild and useless luxuriance?" asked an Illinois newspaper editor in 1846, urging that California be quickly annexed. It was our responsibility, our duty, to expand. The land needed us. Without us, she would remain unproductive and unfulfilled. It was our calling to tame the wilderness.

The Indians resisted. They had lived for centuries on the hallowed grounds of their Motherland. They loved her and they would not move. When we told them that they did not deserve the land because they did not exploit her fully, they were shocked at our lack of respect.

"You ask me to plow the ground," Chief Smoholla said to the military authorities of the far Northwest. "Shall I take a knife and tear my mother's bosom? You ask me to dig for stone. Shall I dig under her skin and bones? . . . You ask me to cut grass and make hay and sell it, and be rich like the white men. But how dare I cut off my mother's hair?"

The Indian considered himself Mother Earth's son. We considered him the son of Father America. "Your father requests you to take a chair," said William Henry Harrison's interpreter to the Shawnee chief Tecumseh, as negotiations between the two men were about to begin. "My father!" replied the outraged chief. "The sun is my father, and the earth is my mother."

We told the Indians, in effect, that they were mere children, and that they should entrust themselves to "the care of our father, the President." In the end, that care resembled what today's native Americans call genocide. In no more than a century, white replaced red throughout the territory east of the Mississippi.

When America won its freedom from England, two thirds of its citizens still lived within fifty miles of the Atlantic Ocean. In the following half-century, four million Americans left this narrow coastline and moved westward. By 1850, the western regions had more people than did the original thirteen colonies. It was an extraordinary human migration, rivaled in magnitude only by the extraordinary disappearance of the Indian. By midcentury, few native Americans remained east of the Mississippi. A few scattered tribes remained in undeveloped regions, such as the area bordering Lake Superior. But the rest of their people had fled, starved, been forcibly removed, or killed.

"Where today is the Pequot?" asked a tired, embittered Tecumseh. "Where are the Narragansetts, the Mohawks, the Pokanoket, and many other powerful tribes of our people? They have vanished before the avarice and the oppression of the White Man, as snow before a summer sun."

Our view of the land turned us into warriors. For generations, we lived with violence and bloodshed. For generations, we pushed the Indians farther and farther west. And for generations, we portrayed the triumph of white over red as a validation of our national manhood.

All kinds of men moved west: farmers and trappers, adventurers and misfits, ministers and schoolteachers, soldiers and miners. But only one type of man became a national hero, only one became a cultural archetype that would embed itself in the masculine mind. No one today knows the names of the surveyors and the blacksmiths, the homesteaders and legislators. But even in the Space Age, the Frontiersmen — Daniel Boone, Kit Carson, Wild Bill Hickok, and of course Davy Crockett — are the stuff of boyhood dreams.

In 1869, the *New York Weekly* ran a series of articles on Buffalo Bill. It "was so accurate an expression of the demands of the popular imagination," writes the historian Henry Nash Smith, "that it proved powerful enough to shape an actual man in its own image."*

The image was perhaps first embodied by a man named Daniel Boone. "We have recently seen a single person go and decide on a settlement in Kentucky," wrote Thomas Jefferson of him, admiringly. "Though perpetually harassed by Indians, that settlement in the course of ten years has acquired 30,000 inhabitants." Here, according to Jefferson, was a model of manhood worthy of America. If other men were courageous enough to follow Boone's example, Jefferson estimated that America could claim the rest of the continent within two generations.

Conquest: this was the key to the image of the Frontiersman. He took the initiative, he was aggressive, he did not settle down. His propensity for and proficiency at violence was a vital part of his charac-

---

* Unlike most historians, Henry Nash Smith took note of the sexual dimension of American attitudes toward the land. He points out, for example, that the historian Francis Parkman habitually referred to the frontier as "she" while calling the eastern seaboard "it." Asked Smith provocatively: "Is it wholly meaningless that the West, the region close to nature, is feminine, while the East . . . is neuter?" But he fails, unfortunately, to explore his own question.

ter. He did not provoke violence, and yet he was inseparable from it. Rifle in hand, knife sheathed on his belt, he was a solitary, restless figure on the American landscape. Civilization, with all its cumbersome comforts and petty rules, arrived only after the Frontiersman had claimed the land and moved on.

As his name implies, he was obsessed with the frontier. Although in reality men on the frontier were hunter-husbandmen, the legends that emerged focused only on the former. We revered him not because of how he nurtured the land, but because of his mastery of it. The Frontiersman was not a farmer, but an explorer. He did not till the land, he took it.

Thanks to our frontier heroes, land became abundant. For Europeans, it was paradise: instead of too many people and too little land, the New World had few people and plenty of land. Compared to nineteenth-century England or the France that Tagore surveyed, America was the promised land. It had more territory than men had imagined possible. But when a scarce commodity is suddenly plentiful, its value plummets. The earth was no longer something sacred, the incarnation of life itself. It was a piece of property. "A nation is much to be pitied that is weighed down by the past," crowed James Fenimore Cooper's fictional hero Aristabulus Bragg. Convinced that an emotional attachment to the land was economically unsound, Bragg prided himself on his willingness to sell any piece of land he owned if the price was right.

Once the land had been won, it was treated like a fallen woman. Commerce replaced romance. The wilderness, once conquered, was no longer wild; the virgin land, once used, lost her innocence. The Frontiersman and his followers could win the land, use her, and then abandon her, leaving behind a commodity that other men would exploit until they too moved on. Instead of wooing the earth, we began to waste her.

"Wastefulness was in the frontier blood," wrote the historian Vernon Parrington, "and Davy Crockett was a true frontier wastrel." This coonskin-capped hero, whose immortality was ensured by Walt Disney, killed more than a hundred bear in one season. He shot six deer in a single day. He was only one of thousands, laments Parrington, "who were wasting the resources of the Inland Empire, destroying forest, skinning the land, slaughtering the . . . vast buffalo herds."

Were Tagore to visit America today, it is unlikely that he would praise us for our "active wooing of the earth." He would be more likely to conclude that we treat the land neither reverently, as our mother, nor chivalrously, as a virgin, but contemptuously, as if she were no better than a whore. We rape her. And when we are done, we leave her — and our wastes — behind.

Callousness has replaced chivalry. Our romance with the land has turned ugly. Although she bore us more wealth than our forefathers could have imagined, we have not cared for her. She has begun to spit back our wastes, turning our poisons back upon us.

Writing just a century after Tagore first penned his words, René Dubos returned to the relationship between man and earth and warned us against the excesses of the Frontiersman. "The outcome of wooing can be rich, satisfying and lastingly successful," wrote this wise old biologist, "only if our relationship to the earth is based on respect and love rather than domination."

How fitting that this advice should come from an eminent scientist rather than a poet. For it is the scientific view of the universe as mere matter, along with the economic view of the land as mere commodity, that bred in Western man such dangerous arrogance. "We talk of 'matter,'" Jung wrote. "But the word matter remains a dry, inhuman and purely intellectual concept, without any psychic significance for us. How different was the former image of matter — the Great Mother — that could encompass and express the profound emotional meaning of Mother Earth."

The modern world view is based on this denial of dependency, on a belief that when science has perfected itself, mankind will be self-made. It is an arrogance that surfaces in every dimension of life where masculine encounters feminine. It is the arrogance of the frontier, which, as Leonard Kriegel observed, "is still the essential masculine image for those who see American manhood as a history of imposing power upon others."

Those whom the Frontiersman overpowered have renewed their resistance. The native American is reasserting his identity, both culturally and politically. When Universal Pictures released a new feature-length film called *The Legend of the Lone Ranger* in 1981, Tonto was no longer the silent companion of the TV serial. Actor Michael Horse told the press that Westerns had distorted the Indian, portraying him "as a violent person," when, in fact, "we are a spiritual people, with much humor and respect for life." Tonto pointed out what few TV viewers ever knew: that in the original story, the Lone Ranger was raised as a child by Tonto's tribe, where he developed his passion for justice. Said Michael Horse of the new movie: "The Indian way of life is shown in a positive and peaceful light. It's this way of living that inspires the Lone Ranger as a child, and points the way to what he will become."

In books and films, the native American has had some notable success in reasserting his claim to manhood. But in real life, success has come harder. His attempt to reclaim his land has had only mixed results. In some areas of the country, he is now being forced to reenact his tragic encounter with the Frontiersman. The barren reservation lands, considered worthless at the time, into which we herded his forefathers are now estimated to have one third of the coal in the western states and one half of all the uranium in the United States. From Arizona's Black Mesa to New Mexico's Ambrosia Lake Region to South Dakota's Black Hills, the Frontiersman once again stands poised to take the earth's riches.

When Russell Means, cofounder of the American Indian Movement, addressed thousands of red and white Americans in the Black Hills in the summer of 1980 at an International Survival Gathering, he told them that they were standing "in what white society has designated as a National Sacrifice Area." Pointing to the surrounding hills, which several Indian tribes consider sacred grounds, Means concluded: "We are resisting being turned into a National Sacrifice Area. We are resisting being turned into a national sacrifice people. The costs of this industrial process are not acceptable to us. It is genocide."

The indictment of the Frontiersman's treatment of the land is echoed by contemporary feminists. Like Dubos, these women writers are acting as marriage counselors for a precarious couple: man and earth. Their advice is clear: we must redefine masculinity. We must replace our desire to dominate with a willingness to learn humility, respect, nurturance. The earth will continue to serve us, they warn, only if we learn to serve her.

But such humility is not, as the *New York Times* columnist Anthony Lewis once put it, "politically sexy." It does not sound heroic. Unlike a space race or nuclear power, it cannot be described in terms of conquest. "It does not," says Lewis, "make Presidents sound bold."

It sounds timid, ineffectual, like a young man after a date telling his buddies that he couldn't "get any." It sounds as if he had failed to master her, failed to overpower the earth and make her yield everything to us, now.

Today the archetype of the Frontiersman persists, but the frontier is no longer a piece of real estate. It is an unconscious image, a psychic photograph. The Frontiersman is the Marlboro man, riding across the western plains as mobile camera units capture the image. He is the urban cowboy, working in sterile offices and laboratories, who seeks from sports and sex and movies the thrill of conquest. He is the President of the United States clearing brush at his ranch clad in jeans and boots. He is the red-blooded, quick-fisted all-American, who sees himself as the peace-loving champion of freedom — and will kill to prove it.

2 **The Soldier**

Images of the Body

The mother does the knitting
The son fights the war
She finds this quite natural the mother
And the father what does he do the father?
He does business
His wife does knitting
His son the war.

　　　　　—Jacques Prévert

IN MY FRESHMAN YEAR at college I tried out for crew. My classmates who arrived at Harvard from prep schools had already had several years' experience at this demanding sport. I had none, so I trained with a vengeance. Months of pulling that crimson oar through the murky waters of the Charles River gave me a chest, shoulders, and arms that made me appear robust. When the final cuts were made, I and fifteen others remained.

But the taste of success was not sweet. No matter how hard I drove myself, I felt emotionally hollow. Far away from my Indiana home, confused by the cosmopolitan college community, and sorely missing my high school girl friend, I was depressed. Whether to fuel my straining muscles or to fill my emotional void, I ate voraciously. My stomach gave me constant pain. If circumstances had not changed, I would have developed ulcers.

Compared to the stories of the two men I am about to introduce, this is a minor tale about a minor ailment. But I think it is symbolic of men's relationship to their bodies. As I was becoming more mighty on the outside, I was wounding myself within. My strength was visible,

25

my vulnerability invisible. I told everyone about my success, no one about my pain.

During all the months Dan Conrad and I saw each other in the boathouse, I did not even know his name. He rowed varsity heavy-weight, and we called him simply the Hulk. His two-hundred-pound frame was solid muscle. He could lift more weight and run the two-mile circuit faster than anyone. He was the ideal oarsman.

A few years later, I passed a man on the sidewalk whose face resembled the Hulk's. But this man was slim, almost monklike. So different did he seem that I doubted that it was the same man. I said nothing and walked on.

"Whatever happened to the Hulk?" I asked one of his old friends at our tenth reunion.

"The Hulk?" For a moment he was puzzled. "Oh. You mean Dan Conrad. He quit the team and sort of, well, disappeared."

I laughed uncomfortably. What did he mean, "disappeared"?

"He just wasn't around anymore. Somebody said they saw him once . . . lost a lot of weight, spaced out. But I don't know for sure: I never saw him again."

Now that I knew Dan's real name, I called the university alumni office and traced him to a Washington address. When I phoned, his wife answered. I explained I was working on a book about masculinity and asked if she thought Dan would mind talking with me.

"On the contrary," Claudia Conrad replied. "He'd be eager to. It's a subject that's been on his mind lately."

We met a few weeks later. When Dan talked about our college years, his tone was somber. He did not like what he remembered. As he talked, he held Claudia's hand.

"I was afraid, insecure," Dan said quietly. "At the time, I think I had convinced myself that if I could only make myself strong enough — invulnerable — everything would work out. I was probably competing with my father. He's always been rather distant and I was still trying to prove to him that I was a *man*. I thought that all those muscles could prove it."

I said very little. I still could not believe that this reserved, reflective man was the charging bull I remembered.

"Finally I asked myself why . . . why was I beating my brains out for three hours every day? What was I trying to prove, and to whom? Why did I still feel so miserable inside my impregnable body?"

He seemed lost in thought for a moment. "I guess I realized that

I wasn't getting what I really wanted. To be loved. To be intimate. To be close. My constant effort to be stronger" — he said the word bitterly — "was not helping me experience this. It was preventing me."

Claudia got up, and Dan watched her leave the room before he spoke again. "For the next year or so, I was in a very self-destructive phase — necessary, but destructive. I lost a lot of weight, used drugs, became a vegetarian, lived totally alone off campus. I did all the things people did in those days to exorcise what they didn't like about themselves. I wanted to destroy my old self, but I didn't know how."

I told Dan that I had seen him one day but had barely recognized him.

"I'm not surprised," he said. "My outer shell, my Superman uniform, was gone. That was all most people knew. I peeled off layer after layer, hoping to find my authentic self, but I didn't know where to stop. In some ways, I suppose I went too far. I lost too much weight, became too isolated, too introspective. But I had a lot of balancing out to do. I needed to go through it in order to get where I am now."

When Claudia returned, they talked together about the meditation retreat they would attend that weekend. I watched Dan closely. His eyes were still piercing, but more open. He no longer wore the two-hundred-pound armor plating of his college days, but he was considerably more solid than the emaciated figure I had passed on the street. His physique, his face, seemed at last his own.

I thought of Dan again when I met Walter Norton. Dan and Walter are two of the strongest men I have ever met. As the son of a union organizer, Walter's life never took him even close to Harvard. It took him to Vietnam.

When I first met Walter, he was thirty-three years old. His chest and shoulders were as solid as a wrestler's. His arms and hands reminded me of pictures of Paul Bunyan, the legendary woodsman. Walter did not have to brag about how strong he was: his body and the way he moved said enough.

But half his lifetime ago, Walter's body looked quite different. At well over three hundred pounds, he was enormous. He was so fat that the other kids made fun of him and called him names. His father was so ashamed of him that when he introduced Walter, he would quickly add, "We've sold Walter to Notre Dame. He's gonna play tackle. And then he's going in the marines."

When Walter finished high school, he tried to fulfill at least part of his father's dream: he volunteered for the marines. They accepted him on the condition that he lose weight.

In early April 1968, he married; in late April he arrived at boot camp.

At Parris Island, Walter Norton lost one third of his body weight in thirty-seven days. "The military offered me a chance," said Walter, "to change my relationship to my body." And change he did. By the time he was ready for action, hard muscle had replaced fat. He looked and felt like a soldier.

"I thought different, acted different, even walked different, than I had a few months before. I was afraid of nothing. The marines had reduced me to just what they wanted and nothing more: an efficient fighting machine."

Although he was eager to get to Vietnam, Walter's unit was delayed by legal wrangles. A drill instructor had kicked a recruit to death (the autopsy had called it "bleeding ulcers"), and an investigation was under way. But when his unit finally reached the war zone, Walter was not disappointed. His corps was sent to Quang Tri province. Within forty-eight hours, he had been shelled twice and seen men die before his eyes.

"My training paid off. I was a survivor," he recalled. "On patrol, when the moment came to shoot, I did. I could shoot people and never think twice about it. Sometimes I even enjoyed it. It was a real adrenalin rush."

For a while Walter was assigned to taking soldiers who refused to fight to the military prison. "The marine guards would beat the shit out of them, not because they hated them or anything, but because that's how they were conditioned. They were programmed."

When his tour of duty ended, Walter believed that he had survived the war with no scars. But he was wrong.

On a Thursday in 1970, Walter left Vietnam. On Saturday he was with his wife and seven-month-old son. On Monday he reported for work. What happened during the following two years is now only a blur of pain: night classes and nightmares, a new child and a new ulcer, another fight and another affair, more therapy and more anger, all laced with Librium, Valium, Thorazine . . . and memories.

In April 1972 he collapsed. The ex-marine had a nervous breakdown. Soon afterward, Walter left his job at the town parks department and his wife got a job. Unable to deal with the outside world, he stayed home with his two preschool sons. By 1977 the marriage had disintegrated. Walter found a job as a gardener on a large estate and his children came to live with him. The fighting machine became a single parent.

Faced with primary responsibility for his two boys, Walter finally confronted himself. He saw a man who was prepared to fight, but not to love.

"I was the last of four kids," he told me, secure in his new job and new home. "My father spent little or no time with our family. He was always pushing us boys to compete, to be winners. But he would never just talk with us. The entire time I was in Vietnam he never wrote me a letter. He wanted us to be tough, to be marines ... but *he* suffered from Parkinson's disease. He wanted us to be strong to make up for his own feelings that he was weak."

Now Walter spends a lot of time with his boys, particularly playing sports. "But I don't put competition first," he clarified, eager to draw a distinction between himself and his father. "I want the boys to learn, to know their bodies, to tap into the physical, and to be aware of themselves and their own abilities. And I want to have open lines of communcation, so we can talk about anything. I want them to think for themselves."

Walter particularly wants them to know about war. He took them to see *Apocalypse Now* (not *The Deer Hunter,* though, because it would "fuck their heads too bad"). He also takes them with him when Vietnam vets get together. Active in the Agent Orange movement, Walter is determined that his boys "see the other side of war, the way it destroys people emotionally." Would he mind if they joined the marines one day? "More power to them, if that's what they want. But before they run off to any war, I'd be sure that they'd looked at it from *every* angle. I don't want them risking their lives for the almighty dollar. The government's going to have to declare a war, a real war, before I'd want them to go. But I wouldn't have to tell them all this. They're my sons. They'll know it themselves by then."

His boys, now eleven and nine, probably will. They fixed sandwiches in the kitchen as their dad sat with me in the living room.

"World War II had heroes," says Walter. "I watched them in the movies every Saturday when I was a kid. Even Korea had some heroes. But after Vietnam, the soldier wasn't a hero anymore. If people still gave us the 'awe status,' coming home would have been easier. We could have made the transition. But this country ignored us. They didn't want to see us. And so what we did over there returned to haunt us."

I could see anger in Walter's eyes as he spoke, and he seemed about to lose his temper. Instead, he got up from the couch and shouted to the boys, "Saddle up, you guys, or we'll be late for the movie." He was taking them to see *King of Hearts,* a French movie about the insanity of war.

Just before Christmas 1981, Walter Norton stood in front of several hundred students at his local high school. He had been invited to speak by a group of parents who had petitioned the school board to provide alternative information about the draft. These "Parents Against the Draft," as they call themselves, asked Walter to be part of a panel and to speak from his heart.

"Any person who lives in this society has a responsibility to this society," Walter told them. "The question is, How does a man shoulder this responsibility? If you feel the military will make you a man, then you are not thinking for yourself. You are still watching John Wayne in *The Sands of Iwo Jima.* You are making a choice through conditioning, not by your own free will."

At the end of his ten-minute speech, he added a special message to the young men in the audience: "You don't have to go to war to fight for your country. You don't have to go to war to prove you're a man. As I see it, you don't have to prove you are men at all. You already are!"

And they rose to their feet, whistling and clapping wildly. What made Walter feel particularly proud was seeing a particular young man who stood with the others. His name was Walter Norton, Jr.

THE SOLDIER, particularly since the Vietnam war, is frequently maligned. The veterans of that war were not welcomed home as heroes. Sometimes they were not even welcomed home at all. The Soldier now is often seen as a mere custodian of weapons systems, and both friends and foes of military spending openly criticize the intelligence and the morale of the men in the armed services.

Before we can understand the Soldier as a heroic image of masculinity, we must recall his original function. He was the protector, the man who made the difference between survival and annihilation. He was the man who defended his loved ones and the entire community. He symbolized security. He was the man who did not hide from danger, who did not give in to fear. The Soldier was willing to risk his own life in order to protect those he loved.

The Soldier was not only male, he was a certain kind of male. He symbolized strength, courage, responsibility. He was the man who inspired other men to act bravely, who rallied a community and enabled its members to defend their sovereignty. In virtually every cultural system, the Soldier was a hero because without him, that system could not endure.

Great sacrifices were required of the Soldier. Hardship and deprivation, fear and anxiety, were unavoidable. Injury, captivity, or death were constant possibilities. But the Soldier endured because, in exchange for his services, his culture conferred upon him a priceless gift. It considered him a man. If he performed his duty well, he was a hero. As James Fallows wrote, war is "life's most abhorrent activity," and yet it "has been, in many eyes, the ultimate manifestation of masculinity."

Although this image of heroic masculinity often led men to brutality, it nevertheless seemed vital to civilization. To embody courage under the most gruesome circumstances, the Soldier had to repress his fear. To embody strength, he had to repress his feelings of vulnerability. To embody toughness, he had to repress his sensitivity. To kill, he had to repress compassion. No alternative existed. So men through the ages have measured themselves against what seemed to be male destiny. Rather than deny it, we have embraced it. Those who have not, we called cowards. What war required was, by definition, manliness. The men who were the best soldiers were, in effect, the best men.

Under such circumstances, to call upon men to be more sensitive or compassionate, or to criticize them for being out of touch with their feelings or their bodies, would seem absurd to them. Facing Rommel in North Africa, an Allied tank commander was not concerned about anything except victory. Who would dare suggest that compassion or sensitivity could have disarmed the Third Reich? Clearly only brave soldiers could have defeated Hitler.

The postwar generation of American men grew up revering its heroes. Many of us believed that we, like our fathers, could prove our manhood through war. We wanted to become the ultimate man, the hero vanquishing the enemy. When Vietnam veterans recall what led them to Vietnam, what made them *want* and *need* to go, they do not speak of communism or domino theories or patriotism. They speak of John Wayne.

Ron Kovic, who grew up in the shadow of Yankee Stadium, remembers being reduced to tears by the Marine Corps hymn. "I loved the song so much, and every time I heard it I would think of John Wayne. I would think of him and cry," he said. "Like Mickey Mantle, John Wayne in *The Sands of Iwo Jima* became one of my heroes."

As a boy, Ron played in the woods near his home. "We turned the woods into a battlefield. We set ambushes, then led gallant attacks, storming over the top, bayoneting and shooting anyone who got in our way. Then we'd walk out of the woods like the heroes we knew we would become when we were men."

When the Marine Corps recruiters came to his high school, Kovic's response was preordained. It had been imprinted in his mind, and in the collective masculine unconscious, for centuries. "As I shook their hands and stared up into their eyes, I couldn't help but feel I was shaking hands with John Wayne and Audie Murphy," he recalled. "They told us that day that the Marine Corps built men — body, mind, and spirit." Since he wanted to be a man, he decided to become a marine. His introduction to manhood was a drill instructor shouting: "Awright, Ladies! . . . When are you people gonna learn? You came here to be marines!" And Ron became one.

Phil Caputo also imagined himself becoming the Soldier. He grew up outside Chicago in a safe, clean suburb. In the "virgin woodland" near his home, he would walk and "dream of that savage, heroic time . . . before America became a land of salesmen and shopping centers." Like so many white American males, he wanted "to find in a commonplace world the chance to live heroically." Although college bound, he yearned to enlist. "I saw myself charging up some distant beachhead, like John Wayne in *Sands of Iwo Jima,* and then coming home a suntanned warrior with medals on my chest." When a marine recruiting station was set up on his college campus, Caputo's response was the same as Kovic's, as he wrote:

> They were on a talent hunt for officer material and displayed a poster of a trim lieutenant who had one of those athletic, slightly cruel-looking faces considered handsome in the military. He looked like a cross between an All-American halfback and a Nazi tank commander.

Clear and resolute, his blue eyes seemed to stare at me in challenge. JOIN THE MARINES, read the slogan above his white cap. BE A LEADER OF MEN.

That's when Caputo realized that "the heroic experience I sought was war; war, the ultimate adventure; war, the ordinary man's most convenient means of escaping from the ordinary ... I was excited by the idea that I would be sailing off to dangerous and exotic places after college instead of riding the 7:45 to some office."

But it was not mere escape from the white-collar world that he sought. It was entry into manhood. He admits that the motive that pushed him to enlist was the one "that has pushed young men into armies ever since armies were invented: I needed to prove something — my courage, my toughness, my manhood, call it whatever you like." His parents considered him still a boy; he wanted to prove them wrong. He wanted to do "something that would demonstrate to them, and to myself as well, that I was a man after all."

Caputo's and Kovic's articulateness should not mislead us, since both have written books about their experiences. For most men, the self-questioning was inchoate. Perhaps typical is this army sergeant, struggling to explain in Robert Jay Lifton's *Home from the War* why he decided that becoming a soldier "was the way you proved your manhood":

> I remember questioning myself ... saying this can all be a pile of crap ... this stuff about patriotism, and yet because of this indecision ... this confusion within myself, I said ... I don't think I'll ever be able to live with myself unless I confront this, unless I find out, because if I do not I'll always wonder whether I was afraid to do it ... and the whole question of whether I was a man or not ... whether I was a coward.

Strictly speaking, the soldier was not unemotional. He had feelings, but they conformed to pattern. Harold Lyon, a graduate of West Point and an army officer, says that soldiers were trained "to guide their emotions into acceptable channels ... I excelled in this red, white, and blue school of callousness and went on to do graduate work in toughness by becoming a paratrooper, ranger, and counterguerilla-warfare instructor ... I cannot remember during those years ever considering or suspecting or wishing that there might be a tender aspect to me. My toughness was my strength, or so I thought, and tenderness was a weakness."

The John Wayne syndrome meant keeping emotions buried.

"You can't display emotion around here!" West Point upperclassmen would shout at plebes (freshmen) whose faces betrayed anger, fear, joy, sadness.

One plebe had a tendency to break down in tears when he was harassed beyond endurance. "I recall with shame and chagrin," said one of his tormentors, contrite in retrospect, "how we systematically ran him out of the Corps of Cadets [by] writing reports on his unsuitability as a potential officer with over- and undertones concerning masculinity and possible homosexuality of a cadet who cried or could not control his emotions."

Like the military tradition it represents, West Point's self-defense for hazing is unapologetically chauvinistic. It is, after all, preparing its cadets to lead men into combat, that ritual of organized aggression "where display of emotions could cause one to falter and fail." The abuse the soldier receives in training is justified, explained an army sergeant, on the ground that "they're doing it for a reason . . . They want to discipline us [to] function in the context of war."

This is the soldier's credo. The John Wayne syndrome is an explicit, if unwritten, code of conduct, a set of masculine traits we have been taught to revere since childhood. It means to be hard, tough, unemotional, ruthless, and competitive; to be, in Lifton's words, "a no-nonsense sexual conqueror for whom women were either inferior, inscrutable or at best weaker creatures."

The military fostered a certain kind of manhood for the same reason that parents did: masculinity's bottom line was written in blood. Parents turned little boys into soldiers because they wanted them to survive. "Supermasculinity prepares one for war," concluded Lifton bluntly, and every generation of Americans has had one, or expected and prepared for one. We have sacrificed other traits — gentleness, openness, softness — because they were liabilities, not assets, in war. We have left them to women.

Even if the old masculine archetype is unfulfilling, many men refuse to let it go. As critics of male chauvinism argue, it conditions us to be aggressive, unable to express our feelings, power-oriented rather than person-oriented, robotistic male machines. But what men's liberation advocates often fail to mention is that we were raised that way by our parents and our culture for a reason. We were raised that way in order to survive.

At least until the nuclear age, wars were considered virtually inevitable, so parents raised their sons to fight in wars. Just as they reinforced in their sons the virtues of war — aggressiveness, competitiveness, toughness, lack of emotion — they reinforced in their daughters counterbalancing traits — passivity, gentleness, expressiveness, nurturance. As long as men fight wars, or are prepared to do so, liberation will remain elusive.

The military promoted the supermasculinity that the women's and men's liberation movements of the seventies found so offensive. It promoted it on purpose. The epithets of drill instructors or fellow soldiers — "maggot," "faggot," "snuffy," "pussy," or simply "woman" — left no doubt that not becoming a soldier meant not being a man.

No wonder the men's and women's liberation exhortations still fall on deaf ears. The character structure they want us to abandon — toughness, aggressiveness, insensitivity — has been bred in us for generations. It is not some vague force called socialization, but the vicious imperative of war. From a military perspective, it is ideal that men are expected by most Americans to be "very aggressive," "not at all emotional," "very dominant," "competitive," "rough," "unaware of others' feelings." These traits are essential for survival.

The critics of male chauvinism are well versed in itemizing the sacrifices required by this kind of manhood. Perhaps it does make sex unfulfilling, marriage barren, friendships superficial, work stressful, and politics a ritualized cult of toughness. But before we can understand why men do not readily leave this hell of machismo for the heaven of liberation, we must understand why a woman whose son had just left for Vietnam could say, "Every man must have his war." We must ask the questions that too many manifestoes of liberation have overlooked. How does masculinity depend on war, and war depend on masculinity?

To answer this, we must remember that the Soldier is an ancient figure. His image as epitomized by John Wayne — whether against Indians (in innumerable films), Mexicans (in *The Alamo*), Viet Cong (in *The Green Berets*) or other more contemporary villains — is but the last in a long line of military heroes that have excited men's imaginations. The Soldier was defined long before America was even born.

More than two thousand years ago, Julius Caesar wrote in *The Conquest of Gaul* that the men who inhabited what is now France, Switzerland, and the Benelux nations "do not even pretend to compete with the Germans in bravery." After respectfully describing Gallic culture and customs, Caesar stressed that the less civilized Germans were completely different in that they spent their lives "in hunting and warlike pursuits." To this end, they prized chastity in men because they believed it made them better soldiers. They did not cultivate their own land but instead moved each year from place to place. The reason for this custom, Caesar believed, was that if men were permitted to settle they would "lose their warlike enthusiasms and take up agriculture instead." To raid and plunder other tribes was not forbidden by the Germans because they believed that such raids kept the men in shape and prevented them from "getting lazy."

For centuries Caesar's view prevailed. Man's inherent aggressiveness has been cited as proof that war is inevitable. "War is a biological necessity," wrote the German general Friedrich von Bernhardi. "It gives a biologically just decision, since its decisions rest on the very nature of things." In 1911, General von Bernhardi called on his countrymen to abandon hopes for peace, which he felt would "poison the soul of the nation." This was not a uniquely German viewpoint, but one common throughout European intellectual circles on the eve of the twentieth century. From Spain: "When a nation shows a civilized horror of war, it receives directly the punishment for its mistake. God changes its sex, despoils it of its common mark of virility, changes it into a feminine nation, and sends conquerors to ravish it of its honor." From Ireland: "Bloodshed is a cleansing and sanctifying rite and the nation which regards it as a final horror has *lost its manhood.*"

According to this masculine-militarist interpretation, violence is the principal catalyst of human evolution. The capacity to communicate or to cooperate — which, as the feminist biologist Ruth Hubbard points out, is also part of our evolutionary achievement — is considered secondary, if not irrelevant. Masculine aggressiveness is not considered a trait that should be redirected into nondestructive competition or even constructive achievement; it is a trait to be extolled and developed to the fullest. It is to be nurtured by training for war and brought to maturity by war itself.

The equation of masculinity with soldiering was readily adopted in America. We brought with us to the New World a military tradition that had changed relatively little since Caesar's time. When America was born, battle was still considered the most basic and universal rite of passage into manhood. Americans were trying to become manly by at last leaving, in John Adams's words, "mother Britain's lap" to make our fortune in the world as a mature and independent nation. We achieved maturity through violence, through a ritual called war. The self-made American man did not call himself a son of England, but a "son of a gun."

The Revolutionary War triggered a reverence for the man in uniform; he was the midwife of the new republic. "Oh, that I were a soldier," exclaimed John Adams in 1775, embroiled in the complexities of the Continental Congress. "Everybody must, will and shall be a soldier."

Adams's wish came true. America had been, and would continue to be, almost constantly at war. We were never a peaceful nation. There was King William's War (1689–1697), followed five years later by Queen Anne's War, then the war against the Spanish (1739–1743), against the French (1744–1748), and against the French again (1754–1763). Then, in the Revolutionary War, virtually every major town experienced attack or occupation by the British. The Revolution was soon followed by the War of 1812, the Mexican War, and the Civil War. To all this must be added the never-ending campaigns against the Indians. No generation came of age in America without war, or the threat of war, confronting it.

Before the Civil War, eleven of the men nominated or elected President were military figures. George Washington was the "Father of Our Country" because he gave birth to it through battle. Later presidents, even those with strong civilian identities like Zachary ("Old Rough and Ready") Taylor, portrayed themselves in full uniform on campaign posters. Heroism in warfare constituted, said one military historian, "an important claim to America's chief office."

Noting in his diary "the pernicious influence of military glory," Alexis de Tocqueville asked himself, "What determines the people's choice in favor of General Jackson, who . . . is a very mediocre man? What still guarantees him the votes of the people?" Concluded Tocqueville simply, "The battle of New Orleans." If given a choice, we wanted a man of heroic stature in the White House. It was by his uniform that we identified him. We assumed that the hero in war would be the hero in peace.

Unfortunately, heroism is more complex. Even in our own century, men have sometimes fought for the fuzziest reasons. On the battlefields of France in 1917, the American writer John Dos Passos experienced a "curious hankering after danger that takes hold of me." In the "drunken excitement of a good bombardment," Dos Passos admitted that he felt "more alive than ever before." Scores of other articulate men of letters jumped pell-mell into the fray. None could explain what attracted him.

"What an odd thing — to be in the Italian army," says a woman to the eager American lieutenant in Ernest Hemingway's *A Farewell to Arms.*

"It's not really the army," he replies. "It's only the ambulance."

"It's very odd though," she insists. "Why did you do it?"

"I don't know. There isn't always an explanation for everything."

This inarticulateness is typical. Frantically searching for the action, these American volunteers would speak of their desire to experience danger, their feeling that all else was insignificant, their fascination with courage and injury — and with heroism. "These," observed an expert on American writing after the Great War, "were for the most part the prevailing motives. In scarcely any case was there a clear, pure reason." Thoughtful, well-educated, middle-class American men rushed into the war because they "envisioned the battlefield as a proving ground where they could enact and repossess the manliness that modern American society had baffled."

A half-century later, young Americans would rush off to Vietnam with the same phrases rolling off their tongues. Many Vietnam vets were just as confused as Hemingway's lieutenant. "It is easy to look at the war in Vietnam and know why one should hate it," reflected a veteran in one of the many oral histories of the Vietnam war that began appearing in the early 1980s. "What is infinitely more difficult to articulate is why I loved it."

When John Bell, the hero of one of James Jones's war novels, *The Thin Red Line,* asks himself if all war is basically sexual, he is struggling with this puzzling connection between virility and violence. One of the obvious links between the two is the emotion of fear.

Behind the gleaming medals and starched uniforms is the terror of injury and death. This fact is at the heart of strategies of military leadership. The most critical element in military leadership, wrote Lord Moran in *The Anatomy of Courage,* is the "care and management of fear." Thoughtful military analysts, beginning with the nineteenth-century military historian du Picq, have all recognized that men fight out of fear — fear of punishment (as a consequence of not fighting) and fear of death (as a consequence of not fighting well). But what the American soldier fears above all, according to S. L. A. Marshall in *Men Against Fire,* is "losing the one thing he is likely to value more highly than life — his reputation *as a man among other men."* After interviewing two groups of infantrymen just returned from combat (against the Japanese in the Pacific and the Germans in Normandy), General Marshall concluded: "Whenever one surveys the forces on the battlefield, it is to see that fear is general among men, but to observe further that *men are loath that their fear will be expressed* in specific acts which their comrades will recognize as cowardice." His interviews also revealed that, even in infantry units with high morale and intense fighting, only one out of every four fighting soldiers ever used his weapons against the enemy. Marshall observed that

> [modern Western man] comes from a civilization in which aggression, connected with the taking of life, is prohibited and unacceptable. The teaching and ideals of that civilization are against killing, against taking advantage. The fear of aggression has been expressed to him so strongly and absorbed by him so deeply and pervadingly — practically with his mother's milk — that it is part of the normal man's emotional make-up. This is his greatest handicap when he enters combat.

To overcome this powerful, almost unconscious prohibition against violence, a civilized handicap that General Marshall correctly identified as a feminine influence, the military enterprise must create an equally powerful and unconscious prohibition against *avoiding* violence.

To lose one's "reputation as a man among men" means to be identified as a coward or, more explicitly, as a woman. In *The American Soldier,* his exhaustive and definitive study of the American soldier in World War II, Samuel Stouffer found that the fear of showing cowardice in battle stemmed from "the more central and strongly established fears of sex-typing." To lack the Soldier's qualities means to risk "not being a man. ('Whatsa matter, bud — got lace on your drawers?' 'Christ, he's acting like an old maid.')" According to Stouffer, in such cases "there was a strong likelihood of being branded a 'woman.'"

The fear of being considered a woman — or, as marine drill instructors still call their recruits, "faggots" — is the sexual underbelly of combat. The Soldier's ultimate epithet and his ultimate (professed) love are identical: woman. But this contradiction appears perfectly logical when set against the inherently contradictory military landscape. The first woman the Soldier loved — the one from whose womb he emerged, on whose breast he sucked, by whose hands he was bathed and clothed — is the same woman who bred in him commandments against violence, which he is now trained and paid to violate. To become the Soldier, the real leader for whom the armed services are so desperately advertising, the boy must reject his mother's voice ("Don't hit, Johnny!"), reject his (woman) teacher's voice ("Stop that fighting, boys!"), reject his (effeminate) minister's voice ("Thou shalt not kill!"), and identify with that all-male voice of the drill sergeant ("Kill! Kill! Kill!").

Only something as repugnant as being considered a woman or a faggot — which Stouffer, in the prose of the social scientist, calls "a dangerous threat to the contemporary male personality" — is sufficiently terrifying that men are willing to die to avoid it.

But what exactly does the epithet "woman" signify? When the Soldier blurts it out venomously, it means that he is without fear, while women are fear-ridden; that he is strong, while women are weak; that he has courage, while women are cowards.

This fear of our feminine side, the "anima" in Jungian terms, seems inextricably involved in triggering our capacity for destructiveness. It is as if war provides men with a periodic exorcism of the anima — a ritual cleansing and purification of masculinity. The anima is banished from the Soldier's consciousness because it disturbs, in Emma Jung's words, "a man's established ideal image of himself."

We encase ourselves in muscles, which symbolize manhood. When attacking, our body is a weapon; when defending, it is a shield. Some psychologists actually call this process "armoring," a primitive defensive reaction designed to protect the organism against external threats. We sacrifice sensuous pleasure on behalf of the only instinct that is stronger — survival.

Always on duty, the Soldier pays a price for his bodily armament. As we have seen, despite all our protection, men in America die much sooner than women. Women may openly suffer more emotionally. For example, six times as many women as men suffer from depression. But while they are feeling low, we are dying. Inside our armor, we degenerate. Like good soldiers, we keep on marching. We tell ourselves that we are well, and we numb ourselves to our deterioration. Ironically, it is often our heart that reveals our lies.

This paradox is reflected in the weekend TV football games that punctuate the fall and winter months. Covered with padding, crowned with helmets, bulging with muscles, and weighing over two hundred pounds, the armored men will die sooner than the scantily clad cheerleaders dancing on the sidelines. Put the two figures side by side and they are diametric opposites: the woman exposed, her erogenous zones accentuated and (to the degree the law allows) revealed; the man encased, vulnerable parts of his body insulated against injury. Yet a few decades later, the ranks of the protected will have lost more members than the ranks of the exposed.

If our bodies are so strong and women's so weak, it is paradoxical again that it is women who dare to be shown naked. Whether in film, on the stage, or in glossy, full-color photographs, our culture exhibits the naked female form far more often than the naked male's. Despite such late comers as *Playgirl* (with a mere fraction of *Playboy*'s circulation), the fact remains that the male-controlled media have been far more zealous in their portrayal of the soft and tender reaches of women's bodies than men's.

One of the most sexually explicit films to receive critical acclaim in the seventies was Bertolucci's *Last Tango in Paris*. A man, played by Marlon Brando, has anal intercourse with a young woman. Bertolucci languorously displays the woman's entire body, from every detail of her breasts to the finest strands of pubic hair, before the camera's unflinching eye. Although he is portrayed as the aggressive and dynamic lover, the Soldier on the battlefield of Eros, the man remains unexposed; his genitalia are invisible throughout. It is the woman who is expected to take her armor off. It is the woman who is exposed, not to enemy fire, but to the uncaring eyes of tens of millions of strangers. Asked why he left the shots of Brando's genitals on the cutting room floor, Bertolucci first claimed that he "cut it out for structural reasons, to shorten the film." Then he admitted, "It is also possible that I had so identified myself with Brando that I cut it out of shame for myself. To show him naked would have been like showing myself naked."

Our bravery, it seems, is as contradictory as our bodies. We have the courage to fight, but not to be naked. We have the kind of courage required to put on armor, but not the kind required to take it off.*

What happens to the Soldier's bravery when he is in bed, naked, with a woman? "I'm sorry they ever found out they could have orgasms too," laments the protagonist of Joseph Heller's *Something Happened*. As long as men were the only ones with sexual passions, our satisfaction was enough. But when women, too, are sexual beings, men are no longer the center of the sexual universe. Before sexual liberation, men fretted about women's lack of sexual appetite. Now, as Christopher Lasch points out, we fret about our capacity to satisfy it.

As Soldiers, our bodies have been devoted to combat. We have cultivated its toughness. The penis — called a tool, rod, prick, or pistol when our language turns coarse — becomes the sole repository of our sexuality. Through it we shall give pleasure; through it we shall receive. Trapped within these self-imposed limitations, the Soldier is virtually incapacitated when he meets women. We reduce our sexuality to an organ requiring periodic discharge. If women wish to be quickly overpowered, a shot of semen will suffice. But few if any women find such sexuality fulfilling. Women do not want to be targets in some sexual shooting range. They want to be lovers, held in a mutual embrace.

The Soldier assumes that whatever pleases him pleases women. If it doesn't, he assumes something is wrong with *them*. If women are not satisfied by our lovemaking, then they are frigid or oversexed. If they do not love the Soldier, then they are not real women. We want

---

* In 1969, a writer in *Cosmopolitan* argued that men suffer from a "John Wayne neurosis," an inability to express deep emotions with women. Such men want to be in control at all times. The man who models himself on the Duke is prepared at any moment to rush away on his horse (or drive away in his Mustang) to his more important business back in Marlboro country.

This traditional frontier image is being replaced by a more sophisticated, but equally repressed, modern urban image. As John Wayne symbolized the Cowboy, James Bond epitomizes the Playboy — "the old cowboy in modern dress." As sociologists Jack Balswick and Charles Peck described him, the Playboy wears a different kind of armor. He is a "skilled manipulator . . . knowing when to turn the lights down, what music to play on the stereo, which drinks to serve, and what topics of conversation to pursue." He specializes in love affairs. He shares his bed with women, but little more. The Playboy prides himself on his ability to move on — to have sex with different women without the complications of human emotions.

women to act like "women," even if they have to pretend, because we have forced ourselves to act like "men."

In Burke Davis's *Marine!*, one of an endless stream of books on military heroes, the legendary Colonel "Chesty" Puller is glorified. In one scene, Puller is talking with a shell-shocked marine. The young man is lying on a hospital bed, staring forlornly at a picture of his girl friend. After tasting battle, he is so frightened that he feels he cannot face it again.

> "Too bad you'll never see her again," the Colonel said.
> "What do you mean?"
> "Why, she'll never look at you again after this. She wouldn't spit on you."
> "She'll never know. How could she hear?"
> "Oh, she'll find out . . . She'll find out all right."

The colonel's strategy works. The marine returns to duty and is later decorated for bravery.

A man who is raised in body, mind, and soul to embody the conquering Soldier, always dominant and in control, cannot go to bed and take off his armor. We cannot extol victory over others in public and then make love with our wives in sensuous surrender in private. We cannot devote our bodies to erecting invulnerable defenses and then become tenderly vulnerable in bed.

Harold Lyon explains that even at the moment of orgasm, he kept his emotions under iron control. He would try "to emit bass-sounding groans — instead of the tender, uncontrolled cries which would naturally come from me." With considerable pain he recognized that for years he had been camouflaging his real self, which wanted to be vulnerable, behind a more "masculine" exterior. "I realized," he wrote, "that I had been afraid that my partner would think of me as a boy and not a man if my love cries sounded childlike. How incredible! Even at the moment of release, to be so controlled."

But our language is misleading. The Soldier is not in control. On the contrary, he is controlled by his conditioning. That is why he is so dangerous.

Every age, even (suicidal as it may be) the nuclear age, has its soldiers. It is not the uniform that identifies us but our masculine attraction to violence. We experience what Rollo May called a "joy in violence," an ecstasy that "takes the individual out of himself and pushes him toward something deeper and more powerful than anything he has previously experienced." As May described it, the experience is a form of transcendence: "The ego is dissolved . . . 'I' passes insensibly into 'we': 'my' becomes 'our' . . . *Through violence we overcome our self-centeredness.*" General George Patton called it "the cataclysmic ecstasy of violence."

But many men now repudiate the Soldier. Some men consider him not a hero but a fool. Most Western nations have not fought a war for nearly forty years; some, like Sweden, have not had a war for more than a century and a half. The wars since 1945 have not bred heroism. Neither Korea or Vietnam was a "real" war; neither was won and neither had heroes. All conflict now takes place under the shadow of a computerized network of strategic nuclear weapons that dwarf the actions of any individual pilot or infantryman. Consequently, the Soldier seems almost obsolete. In nuclear war, aggressiveness is no longer considered a virtue. It no longer implies survival but, rather, annihilation.

Young men who seek heroism through soldiering often return home today disillusioned. For Ron Kovic, the shock came with sudden brutality: a bullet ripped through his spinal cord. When he asked himself why, he had no answer. When he returned home from Vietnam, paralyzed for life, he began to question more. His questions took him to the 1972 Republican Convention, where, seated in his wheelchair, he shouted, "Stop the bombing! Stop the war!" until the police threw him out into the street.

Others returned from Vietnam with their bodies intact but their minds shattered. "I had thought there would be a parade with banners when I returned," said Eddie Graham, the son of a Boston factory worker. Eddie had served two tours of duty in the marines. "I thought confetti would be thrown . . . that's what I had dreamed about." Instead, venomous shouts of "murderer" and "fascist" greeted him as he stepped off the plane and onto the soil of the land he had been defending. He had been the Soldier, but he was no longer the hero.

When Vietnam veterans reminisce, they often mock themselves. They realize that they were emulating an age-old masculine archetype that has become obsolete. "Always," reported Robert Jay Lifton, who interviewed scores of Vietnam veterans for his book *Home from the War*, "the men came back to the John Wayne thing." They came back to it again and again because they knew that they — and we who never fought — must free ourselves from our identification with the Soldier. Eddie Graham, Phil Caputo, Ron Kovic, are men raised in a nuclear age yet still infatuated with pre-nuclear heroes. Our consciousness lags behind history, our self-awareness behind our weaponry.

Ultimately, this is what makes the nuclear age so dangerous. It has shifted the meaning of heroism. If we annihilate ourselves, it will not be because we were cowards. It will be because we were still trying to be yesterday's heroes.

3 War

Virility and Violence

The Army can really make you feel good about
yourself.
                    —U.S. Army advertisement, 1981

Washington, D.C., 1967

Secretary of Defense Robert Strange McNamara stands on the Pentagon's roof. He watches as fifty thousand Americans, including some of his former colleagues and some of his children's friends, march toward his five-sided fortress. The event is not merely a political confrontation. It is also personal or, as Norman Mailer later put it, "spiritual, physical, moral and existential."

As we leave downtown Washington for the Arlington Bridge, men heckle us. It strikes me, as it has at virtually every antiwar demonstration in which I have participated, that the jeers are sexual as well as political. Always I hear "faggots" or "queers" as often as "commies" or "cowards." Of course many of the marchers *are* gay. Any group of fifty thousand Americans is bound to include many homosexuals. But so what? What does that have to do with the war in Vietnam?

As we jam our way across the Potomac, I stand up on the bridge railing to scan my fellow marchers. I see almost as many women as men. I see tall, virile, athletic-looking men as well as thin, long-haired hippie types. A few wear army surplus jackets and motorcycle helmets, prepared for violence. What makes the hecklers call such a group "faggots"? Why do they mix sex up with politics? Why are masculinity and war so intimately intertwined?

46

Jerusalem, 1969

Accompanied by an Israeli woman, I take a bus to Hadassah Hospital, on the outskirts of Jerusalem, for minor surgery. While traveling in Asia several weeks earlier, the car I was riding in was struck by a bus. I was thrown out of the car onto the pavement and struck my head. The wound on my forehead was sewn up but, according to the Israeli doctor, blood has been trapped beneath the skin — a "localized hematoma."

At Hadassah, Israel's major medical facility, a surgeon performs the operation in minutes. He puts a gauze patch over the injured area and wraps a bandage around my head to hold it in place.

"You feel well enough to return by bus, don't you?" my Israeli friend asks me.

"Sure," I say, even though I don't.

The midafternoon bus is crowded with women shoppers. Although it is the same bus we rode before, it seems like a different country. The women on the bus all stare at me. Whether grandmothers or teenagers, they smile warmly. Their smiles are not the stiff acknowledgment of urban strangers but the sensual, affirming, nurturant beam of old friends, old lovers.

"Why are they looking at me like that?" I ask my friend.

"They think you are a wounded soldier," she replies.

They assume my injury was received in the recent Six-Day War. They think I was wounded while protecting them from Arabs and that I am just now leaving the hospital after convalescing. They are looking at me as if I am a hero.

For that twenty-minute ride, I am John Wayne. I feel what men must have felt for generations when they left for — or, if they were lucky, returned from — war. In those countless wars before my time, they went to war to protect their loved ones, and their loved ones revered them for it. The *real* men went to fight while everyone else stayed home. This badge of courage, this invisible medal of manhood, is not only military or political. It is sexual.

As I get off the bus, several women affectionately say good-bye and wish me well. I do not need to speak Hebrew to understand. They speak with their eyes, which say, We thank you for being a man. As I walk away, I remember the hecklers in Washington the year before, whose eyes said, We despise you for *not* being a man.

Bitburg Air Force Base, West Germany, 1978

I am standing at the foot of the runway. I am about to witness a "scramble," a drill simulating the U.S. Air Force's response to a Red Alert, an all-out attack by the Warsaw Pact forces. The pilots on duty must be prepared to be in the air in less than five minutes, the elapsed time between the alert of a Soviet missile attack and the onslaught itself.

The siren sounds. Inside, the four pilots on deck jump out of bed, already dressed. They step into their boots. They slide down the fireman's pole into the fortified hangars and start the engines. *Two minutes.* They warm the engines, check the controls, strap themselves in. The massive steel doors open and the planes edge down the runway. *Four minutes.* For a split second, the planes stand ready, poised like mighty eagles. The pilots rev the engines for takeoff. The air temperature rises. One by one, the F-15s scream into the air. *Five minutes.* My ears still ringing, I see four fiery meteors scribing arcs in the sky miles to the north and south of where we stand.

For more than a week, the journalists with whom I am touring NATO installations in Europe have been exposed to an emotional and intellectual sales pitch that could turn the most ardent Quaker into a missile-waving militarist. One day, for example, we were taken by helicopter to the East German border. Some of the journalists requested that the doors be left open, as if we were a combat platoon on maneuvers. The green valleys of the German countryside passed beneath us until we landed at the border. We looked across the barbed-wire and booby-trapped fence that separated us from the enemy. As we reboarded the choppers later that day, we were each presented with a hand-lettered parchment document making each of us Honorary Members of the Border Legion. Signed by the commanding colonel of the Eleventh Armored Cavalry, it praised us for "having successfully undergone the hazards of a journey to the border of West Germany and the Communist World."

In case this approach didn't succeed, we were also barraged with lectures. The top brass talked on and on about the F-15's unique performance characteristics, its "thrust-to-weight ratio," its "wing-loading," its extraordinary "play time." They briefed us repeatedly about NATO's strategic and tactical responses to Soviet aggression. They told us that Bitburg was America's front line of air defense against surprise attack. In a ten-minute bus ride just before the scramble, we passed seventy-two renovated hangars that protected seventy-two F-15s. We saw hundreds of millions of dollars' worth of hardware that was supposed to make us feel safe in our beds at home.

So obviously have the NATO chiefs tried to bring us to a pitch of excitement for this moment that I caution myself to remain unmoved. I am a journalist. I will describe what I see objectively.

But as the planes burst into flight, my heart leaps. There is a majesty about them. Their power is breathtaking. Not a man in our group watches dispassionately. To fly such machines seems heroic. The jets are cosmic chariots, and to be their pilots seems almost godlike.

As the planes streak toward their targets, faster than the eye can follow, I am enthralled, intoxicated by the power. I envy the pilots' extraordinary opportunity. The entire air base is organized for them: they are the stars. While other young men in their twenties are punching time clocks or sitting behind desks, these men are making history. Day after day, they live on the cutting edge of war.

But the exhilaration passes. After we board the bus, the planes return, as they always do. They have done nothing but burn fuel. Their celestial ballet, no matter how exquisitely performed, now strikes me as a dance of death. It is choreographed for holocaust. In future wars, these four F-15s would be mere flies in a nuclear hurricane. They would burn and shrivel like plastic knives in a campfire.

Boston, 1980

Just as I smash an overhead and win the point, Pete's beeper goes off.

"Must be a problem on my ward," says Pete glumly. "We'd better shower."

My squash partner is Dr. Peter Stone, an old friend from boyhood days in Indiana who is now a surgeon at Massachusetts General Hospital.

"How's your writing going?" Pete asks. "Something about masculinity, right?" He is dressing quickly, so I know he expects a short answer.

"Pretty well. I have been researching how certain images of manhood affect the way men think about themselves."

"Images? Like what?"

"Like the soldier."

"The soldier? I've never wanted to be a soldier."

It is the moment every author fears: when he must package his writing into small boxes of conversation. "What I mean, Pete, is that for generations men have been raised to be soldiers, to prove our manhood on the battlefield. I know it seems far away. But I still think it's left its mark on every man. Even you and me."

"Sounds pretty far-fetched to me." Pete stares intently into the mirror, straightening his tie. I can tell he is rushing to get back to the hospital, so I say nothing. I am not surprised by his skepticism. His work is repairing the human body. He is a life-saver, I think to myself, not a life-taker. But just then Pete turns from the mirror and looks at me, as if troubled.

"I just thought of the strangest thing. My parents just sent me a couple of boxes of stuff from when I was a kid. I was looking through them last week." He paused, clearly embarrassed. "One box — it had drawings from first grade. I didn't even think about it then. But it seems that all I ever drew were jet planes, trying to shoot each other down."

O NLY AN IDEOLOGUE would claim that the sole cause of war is masculinity. But only a fool would claim that there is no connection at all.

Since wars must be fought for reasons, men are quick to find them. Conservatives talk of defending the national interest. Marxists allude to imperialism and liberation. Political scientists talk of nationalism, of grand alliances. But hardly, if ever, do we talk about ourselves. We do not want to consider that the organized murder of an estimated sixty million human beings between 1820 and 1945 might somehow be connected with our own masculinity.

At the turn of the century, America was worried about its manhood and sounded as bellicose and war-loving as any nation. We fretted about the loss of the martial virtues.

"There is a strange thinness and femininity hovering over all America," wrote William James to his brother Henry in 1893. He found American culture "so different from the stoutness and masculinity of . . . everything in Switzerland and England."

Henry James was worried too. "The masculine tone is passing out of the world; it's a feminine, a nervous, hysterical, canting age," says the hero of *The Bostonians*.

By 1900, manliness was of great concern. It meant, not the opposite of childishness, but the opposite of femininity. Men were worried that life was being "feminized." Suffering from this masculine malaise, we needed a virile tonic and Theodore Roosevelt provided one.

Teddy Roosevelt espoused the "doctrine of the strenuous life, the life of toil and effort, of labor and strife." As he told a Chicago men's club on the eve of the twentieth century, he believed in "that highest form of success which comes, not to the man who desires mere easy peace, but to the man who does not shrink from danger, from hardship, or from bitter toil, and who out of these wins the splendid ultimate triumph."

It was rousing rhetoric, but hardly practical. Roosevelt and his Rough Riders could storm San Juan Hill to prove their manhood. But what about other American men, caught in a bureaucratic, corporate economy? "In such a world," asked the historian Peter Gabriel Filene, "what did it mean to 'be a man'? A roughrider galloping down cement sidewalks? A strenuous life within the rules of the Interstate Commerce Commission?"

Roosevelt resuscitated the frontier images of masculinity. To him, the Civil War was not a tragedy in which brother killed brother. It was a revitalizing experience, and "we are all, North and South, incalculably richer for its memories." Roosevelt did not shirk from war; he worshiped it. In prose worthy of the most bellicose German general, Roosevelt exclaimed: "The nation that has trained itself to a cancer of unwarlike and isolated ease is bound, in the end, to go down before other nations, which have not lost the manly and adventurous virtues." Many American men, eager to revive their ailing self-image, welcomed this call to arms. They also wanted to keep women in their traditional role.

Elizabeth and Joseph Pleck, describing the mood of this era in their introduction to *The American Man*, observed that "the 'new woman,' who rode a bicycle, loosened the lacing of her corset, and took a job before marriage, [was] deeply threatening to men."

So men fought back. One attempt to defend the male virtues against the feminine forces of civilization was the Boy Scouts. Established in 1910, the scouting movement had one overriding purpose: to make men. "The Wilderness is gone, the Buckskin Man is gone," observed Daniel Carter Beard in the 1914 annual report of the Boy Scouts of America. "The hardships and privations of pioneer life which did so much to develop sterling manhood are now but a legend in history, and we must depend upon the Boy Scout Movement to produce the MEN of the future." Only the most virile scoutmasters, of course, could build such men. So the Scouts called for volunteers who were "REAL, live men — red blooded and right-hearted men — BIG men."

Roosevelt, despite advice to the contrary, decided to run for the presidency again in 1912. After he lost, his friend William Allen White wrote to him that many of the votes he got were "Teddy votes — votes of men who had confidence in you personally without having any particular intelligent reason to give why; except that you were a masculine sort of person with extremely masculine virtues and palpably masculine faults." It seemed necessary to many citizens to have what a later age would call a macho leader. War was once again in the foreground. According to Roosevelt, "There is no place in the world for nations who have . . . lost their fiber of vigorous hardiness and masculinity."

With such rhetoric in the air, the decision to enter World War I — for what reasons and at what time — was not only political. It was also sexual. Raging against the pacifists, whom he called "the most evil influence at work in the United States for the last fifty years," Roosevelt's attacks were personal. His criticisms of President Woodrow Wilson for failing to join the fight during the first years of the war were not only about foreign policy. They were about manhood. Roosevelt charged that Wilson "has done more to emasculate American manhood and weaken its fiber than anyone else I can think of."

Gallantly referred to as "The Great War" by its enthusiasts, World War I brought the heroic myth of war to its zenith. The idea of combat was so infused with sexual energy that it became a romantic myth. Even the language reflected the fantasy. The four-legged beast was not a horse, but a steed. Our enemy was the foe. Danger became peril; warfare, strife. To conquer was to vanquish, and to charge was to assail. Soldiers (called warriors) never died; they perished or embraced their fate. To face the enemy was to be manly. One never said brave, which brought to mind its opposite, but rather gallant, staunch, or valorous.

The literary gimmick was quite simple; even the most pedestrian writer could master it. The trick was to make every feature of war heroic, as if the drama were unfolding on a cosmic stage. Everything concrete was abstracted, inflated with metaphysical significance. The worshipers of war did not lie; they merely shaded the truth. They never wrote of corpses, only of ashes and dust. Nor did they refer callously to the dead, but always to the fallen.

Recruiting posters blatantly exploited the romance of war. A sexy young woman poses seductively in a navy shirt; the caption read: "Gee! I wish I were a MAN. I'd join the NAVY."

In a later poster, a middle-aged man sits in his living room, his brow furrowed, pensive. His daughter sits on his lap, asking: "Daddy, what did YOU do in the Great War?" Can he answer with pride? Did he do his part? It is the moment of truth, the poster implied, a moment all men have to face. It is the test of whether you are a man or not, and your daughter, like all women, will be waiting to judge you. His son, meanwhile, is playing quietly at his father's feet, playing with toy soldiers and cannon. He is already training for the *next* war, which will give him a chance to prove *his* manhood.

"You are going into a big thing: a big war: a big army: standing for a big idea," wrote one father to his son in a letter published in the *Ladies' Home Journal* during World War I. "But don't forget that the biggest thing that a war can do is to bring out that man [in you]. That's really what you and the other chaps have gone over for: *to demonstrate the right kind of manhood.*"

To suggest that men should fight reluctantly in order to defend themselves was not enough. On the contrary, the true patriot claimed we should fight *to advance our development as men.* "Universal military training means more than national safety and defense," declared the chairman of the Committee on Public Information during World War I. "It means national health, national virility . . . There is not a weakness in American life that it would not strengthen."

If war rid the nation of its weaknesses and provided men with an essential education, it was not a tragedy but a necessity. No wonder George Patton said on the eve of World War I: "There may be no war. God forbid such an eventuality, however." For without war, man and nation would have lost their virility.

When the poet Joyce Kilmer died in World War I, he received this eulogy in a mass circulation magazine: "Kilmer was young, only thirty-two, and the scholarly type of man. One did not think of him as a warrior. And yet from the time he entered the war he could think of but one thing — that he must, with his own hand, strike a blow at the Hun. *He was a man!*"

The writer, and indeed his generation, still lived in an era of masculine unconsciousness. The questions that plague us (Was the scholarly type not a real man? Why is violence the mark of true manhood?) did not haunt his purposeful prose. Scarred by war, history had given him and the men of centuries past a simple and seemingly eternal definition of masculinity's martial virtues. We were soldiers to guarantee our survival, not simply as nations, but as men.

Every age wants sexuality to be simplified, and for a while, World War I did just that. It prolonged the life of anachronistic images of masculinity. It postponed the self-examination that later generations of men could not avoid. It gave American men — uprooted by industrialization, facing mechanized and bureaucratic jobs, confused about manhood — a chance to be heroes together. They could be "buddies" and compete, not against each other, as they had to in peacetime, but against the enemy. Instead of the competitiveness and individualism of peace, they found the camaraderie and union of war. "In the trenches of the First World War," wrote Thomas Pynchon in *Gravity's Rainbow,* "men came to love one another decently, without shame or make-believe, under the easy likelihoods of their sudden deaths. While Europe died meanly in its own wastes, men loved."

Tenderness, camaraderie, affection — all the emotions normally taboo between men were permitted, even respected, on the battlefield. Facing the foe, two men could hug each other, pledge everlasting loyalty, exchange keepsakes, even cry. And if one's comrade perished, one could cradle him in one's arms, kiss his face, and admit to deeper feelings (love?) that in peacetime were forbidden. In uniform, men felt secure in their masculinity. They were soldiers, weren't they? They could permit themselves to become conscious of feelings that were otherwise too threatening. One reviewer suggested that "war poetry has the subversive tendency to be our age's love poetry." As the romance of war died, romantic rhetoric replaced it.

But behind all the romance was an ugly truth. War was changing. Combat had begun to lose its heroic qualities. Some military historians point to the Civil War as the turning point: for the first time, firepower and machine power began to replace manpower. New weapons enabled men to kill each other at ever greater distances. When the caplock rifled musket raised the killing range from fifty to five hundred yards, a soldier could no longer see the face of the man he killed. His victim's blood was almost invisible. At the same time, new means of transportation were expanding the battlefield. Both North and South used railroad and steamboat to enlarge the zone of combat. With their capacity for rapid reinforcement and resupply, riverway and railway systems turned vast regions into extended battlefields.

During World War I, these technological developments took their toll. Compared to the battle of Waterloo only a century earlier, at which forty thousand dead bodies occupied an area of two square miles, this war represented a quantum leap toward total war. At the battle of the Somme in 1916, a battlefield of similar size became a cemetery for four hundred thousand British soldiers, two hundred thousand French, and five hundred thousand Germans — over *one million* men.

The battlefield became a borderless scene of carnage. Because war depended on factories, industry became a military target, and so did the civilians who worked in them. Armed with bombs that could be hurled tens of miles beyond what the eye could see, the soldier was no longer at war only with other soldiers. He was at war with populations he never saw, which included women.

The widening scope of destruction led some thoughtful men, such as the influential William James, to question their blind acceptance of the warrior image of manhood. James was no pacifist. "Until an equivalent discipline is organized," he wrote in 1911, "war must have its way." But as a psychologist, he recognized clearly the connection between militarism and masculinity. He wanted to separate them, but could not figure out how. "What we now need to discover in the social realm," wrote James, "is the moral equivalent of war. Something heroic that will speak to men as universally as war does and yet will be as compatible with their spiritual selves as war has proved itself to be incompatible."

James accepted the view of war as the glue of civilization. "War has been the only force that can discipline a whole community," he observed coolly, and so the goal must be to "preserve in the midst of a pacific civilization the manly virtues." Without these "martial virtues," a nation is vulnerable, "liable to invite attack whenever [a] military-minded enterprise gets formed anywhere in their neighborhood." Although he yearned for a future that would "inflame the *civic* temper as past history has inflamed the *military* temper," he did not believe it would arrive soon.

A few years later, Walter Lippmann echoed James's concern about the connection between masculinity and war. "Of all sneers none is so carelessly thrown as the charge of cowardice," he began a column in the *New Republic*. In less than a thousand words, Lippmann described the essentially fascist strategy by which a male political figure "bullies men into agreeing with him by playing on their fear of appearing cowardly." Lippmann hated the masculine game in which calling "a man a coward is almost to obliterate him from discussion." He mocked the fact that "the man who uses the term always implies that he himself, of course, is a brave man." Lippmann despised such demagoguery, and he exposed it as well as any journalist could. He admitted, however, "It is an old, old trick, but it works."

Lippmann was willing to risk his reputation to make the unpopular observation that, vile as the Germans may be, the decent American middle-class man also had an instinct for war that must be examined. But to examine this instinct required examining masculinity, and American men were not yet prepared to do so.

Swept up by the twenties only to be crushed by the Depression, Americans let the Great War drift into the past. A new generation, told about the valor but not the vomit, came of age. As the sons of World War I veterans reached the threshold of manhood, another war was ready to ignite. Many fathers were happy that their sons, too, could have their war.

"Farley, my lad, there's bloody big news! *The war is on!*" announced author Farley Mowat's father as he came home one fine fall day in 1939. He was excited that young Farley could serve in his old regiment. "Nothing official yet, but ... there'll be a place for you. You'll have to sweat a bit, of course, but if you keep your nose clean and work like hell ..." Farley Mowat remembers it all, a quarter-century later, with puzzlement. He remembers the hell of war, a war that plunged mankind into the horrors of Auschwitz and Hiroshima. Yet there stood his father, referring to it as the opportunity of a lifetime.

J. Glenn Gray spent four years as a soldier in Europe. As the war's end grew near, he wrote in his journal: "The purgative force of danger . . . will soon be lost and the first months of peace will make some of us yearn for the old days of conflict." Ten years later, Gray returned to Europe as a Fulbright scholar to study the war and the motivations of its participants. In *The Warriors: Reflections on Men in Battle,* he concluded that "many men both love and hate combat. They know why they hate it; it is harder to be articulate about why they love it." Despite the agonies and terrors, he continued, "many veterans who are honest with themselves will admit, I believe, that the experience of communal effort in battle, even under the altered conditions of modern war, has been a high point in their lives . . . which they would not want to have missed."

War requires this masculine enthusiasm. Without it, massive wars would be impossible. The Nazis had to mobilize it in order to advance the Third Reich. America had to mobilize it in order to stop them. To manipulate this masculine energy successfully, however, nations must perpetuate the myth of war. They cannot permit the mechanized, technological realities of war to destroy men's illusion that war is heroic. The brutal truth must be suppressed.

In Germany, such censorship was simple. The Fascists controlled the news and told their people only tales of conquest. In a democracy like America, censorship was more difficult. But, as John Huston's war documentaries illustrate, the American government censored whatever threatened the myth of heroic war. Huston made a series of films for the U.S. War Department that were officially withheld. *Battle of San Pietro* (1943–1944) showed the courageous efforts of ordinary foot soldiers to regain a few hills in Italy from the enemy. A brilliant film, it had one fault: it repeatedly showed dead young American men being pushed into body bags. To "preserve morale," it was not released until after V-E Day.

The full force of censorship was reserved for Huston's even more threatening movie, *Let There Be Light* (1945–1946). This documentary was filmed at a Long Island hospital, where the shell-shocked survivors of hundreds of San Pietros were sent to recover their sanity. Some had forgotten how to walk or talk. Others had lost their memory or their reason for living. An uplifting chronicle of their amazing recovery, the movie was praised by a handful of professional critics, then locked away in a Pentagon archive for almost thirty-five years. The Department of Defense refused to release the film until outside pressure forced it to do so in December 1980.

To the military mind, this short, simple film was subversive because it showed the other side of war — and the other side of masculinity. If the generations of men who came of age in the fifties and sixties had been permitted to see it, they might have been less easily led. Every time they saw John Wayne emerge from battle without a scratch, they might have remembered Huston's pitiful young veterans, who needed weeks of therapy, hypnosis, and group support before they could return home.

At issue is neither courage nor cowardice, but consciousness itself. If we must fight to defend ourselves against aggression, then of course we must do so with resolve. But as Lippmann said in his column, let us "do it sadly, and with as little bombast as possible." For if we need to fight in order to prove our manhood, if we go into battle in order to become heroes, then we are no different from the enemy. If in our hearts we need war, then no matter who fires the first shot, we are also the aggressor. If we, even unconsciously, yearn for combat so that we can validate our virility, then we are just like the young German who was overjoyed when World War I broke out. "I am not ashamed to say," the young man later wrote, "that, overwhelmed by impassionate enthusiasm, I fell on my knees and thanked heaven out of my overflowing heart that God had granted me the good fortune of witnessing the Great War."

The young man's name was Adolf Hitler.

4 **Genocide**

The Authoritarian Mind

> 52-year-old, pure Aryan physician, fighter at
> Tannenberg, wishing to settle down, desires male
> offspring through civil marriage with young,
> healthy virgin of pure Aryan stock, undemand-
> ing, suited to heavy work and thrifty . . .
>
> — Marriage advertisement,
>   *Münchener Neuests Nachrichten,* 1935

> What great nation today can be self-righteous
> about its past? Let Americans remember the In-
> dians. Let the British recall the blood spilled
> while amassing an empire; and the Russians, the
> millions murdered in the Ukraine. The list is
> long. Atrocity is a human, all too human, crime
> and not the sole franchise of Adolf Hitler. He is
> dead, as is Nazi Germany, but the atrocities con-
> tinue.
>
> — John Toland, 1982

It is 1952, a summer evening in Indiana. A church picnic is in
progress. Families are gathered around grills and the scent of ham-
burgers fills the air. Children, tired from playing tag and kickball, rejoin their parents. Suddenly the lights flicker and die. My family, and
the other family with whom we share a table, the Klausners, are mo-
mentarily lost in darkness.

My father, always resourceful, gets up to turn the car headlights
on. As he walks toward the car, he hears Mr. Klausner say, "It's the
lousy Jews again." My father is shocked. Is there nowhere that I am
safe? he asks himself.

It was not until years later, when he learned some American slang, that he realized his old friend Klausner had said "juice," not "Jews."

My father was raised as a Jew in his native Holland and was one of the few who escaped before Hitler closed the borders. In 1939, Holland had one hundred forty thousand Jews. In 1945, twenty thousand remained.

After seven years in the Dutch army, my father was accepted as a graduate student at Cornell University. My mother, a former schoolteacher and a devout Christian, went with him, carrying my older brother in her womb. Soon America had three new citizens, and a few years later I made it four.

In the New World, married to a Christian woman, my father joined the Presbyterian church. It was not until we were teenagers that he told my brother and me that he was born a Jew. He had hidden it from us, he said, so that we could "stand up tall" in this land of the free.

But children know more than their parents tell them. As a child, I had always sensed the ghosts of the dead. The house we lived in was even a posthumous gift from one of them. The money, it turned out, was from my father's aunt.

Aunt Paula had been a psychotherapist who had studied with Alfred Adler, and she was well known and highly respected in intellectual circles. When Hitler invaded the Netherlands, she and her husband, Felix, both Jewish, hid in the homes of Christian friends in Amsterdam. Finally they agreed that they could no longer jeopardize other people's safety. They felt they must escape. So Paula, Felix, and their two teenage sons rented a car and a driver, intending to make their way to Portugal. The driver, however, was a Nazi collaborator and drove them straight to the Gestapo. The four were sent to Auschwitz and murdered.

A decade after the war's end, the Dutch government passed a law permitting the estates of those who died without a trace to be passed on. This is why my father received a few thousand dollars and why I, who had never heard of Judaism much less of Auschwitz, moved into the house in which I grew to manhood.

Aunt Paula's spirit lived on in our house, in my father's hopes and fears. In his hopes, she symbolized thoughtful, spiritual, yet scientific humanism. In his fears, she embodied the fate of the victims of fascism.

As his son, I saw both. I recognized in my father a depth of intellect, tolerance, and compassion. I also recognized, but did not understand, his fear. Throughout my childhood he seemed inexplicably afraid (he said he was "apprehensive"). A tense uneasiness would afflict him that none of us, neither his children nor his wife, could grasp. The car registration would be misplaced. A waitress would bring the wrong dish. Driving on vacation, he would take a wrong turn. A man would make what seemed to us an innocuous remark. These and scores of other minor incidents would trigger fear, a fear that no one else could understand. He was always sensitive to the potential insult, always ready to dodge the dart of an anti-Semitic remark.

At the age of fifteen, I knew nothing of religious discrimination and considered his fear an Old World anachronism. Even when he showed me clippings from the newspaper about city policemen who wore Nazi symbols, or about Jews who had swastikas painted on their suburban homes, I was not fazed. The neo-Nazis were kooks, I would tell him. No one took them seriously. There would always be a few extremists parading around, aspiring to be the new Hitler. Why worry?

As a high school student, I managed to ignore the Vietnam war. It seemed far away. Who I was dating and whether I made the varsity were more important to me. When I ran for governor in a mock election, I never for a moment questioned my party's pro-war stand. Similarly, when I was chosen to represent my high school at Boys' State, a gathering at Indiana University sponsored by the American Legion, I never questioned whether to accept the honor. When a wiry old war veteran there told us that we were the best and the brightest young men in the state, I had no reason to doubt his judgment. He told us to ignore the handful of students outside the conference center who were passing out antiwar material. "They are aiding the enemy," he said in righteous anger, "and you should have nothing to do with them."

But of course my ardent colleagues could not restrain themselves. As I left the conference hall, Boys' Staters were pushing the antiwar activists into the bushes while others threw their leaflets to the wind. I did not stay to watch what happened next.

The seed of doubt was planted then, and it grew quickly when I went to college. I realized that the Jews in America might be safe, but that peasants in Vietnam were not. For the next decade of life, they were never far from my thoughts. When I noticed how many of my countrymen and how many of my college classmates could go on with their daily lives untroubled by the carnage, I thought of Aunt Paula.

O F ALL THE mysteries connected with the Hitler era, one of the most intriguing may be the intense, sustained interest of Americans in Nazi Germany," observed William Shirer, author of *The Rise and Fall of the Third Reich.* "It defies rational explanation." He was commenting on America, not in the forties, but in the eighties.

A half-dozen or more well-budgeted TV productions dealing with Nazi Germany were aired in the United States between 1980 and 1982. A full forty years since his *Berlin Diary* sold over a million hardcover copies, Shirer was astounded that "the strange American appetite for books and films about Hitler and his murderous regime" still continues.

"There is today a Hitler cult, a Nazi cult, among some of our young," which makes Shirer both "depressed and puzzled." Many letters from young people say such things as: "Gee, Hitler must have been a great guy," and ask Shirer if he has any Nazi memorabilia, such as a swastika flag, an SS pin, or something else they can hang on their wall or pin on their shirt. Shirer could not explain the continuing allure of Hitleriana. He has simply concluded that America's resurgent interest in the Nazi period "may tell us more about ourselves than about Adolf Hitler and the Third Reich."

What does it tell us about ourselves? A 1981 poll showed that one out of four Americans still holds anti-Semitic beliefs. But this was down from one out of three in the mid-sixties. Despite prejudice, the security and success the Jews have found in this country are almost unparalleled in history. As individuals, as a nation, and as a culture, America is a totally different society from the Third Reich. Except for a handful of self-proclaimed Nazis, Americans consider Hitler evil. We describe him as psychotic, deranged, or despotic. Second, as a nation, we are a democracy. No Führer can usurp power here. We elect our leaders, and every four years we are entitled (and lately, even eager) to banish them to memoir-writing. Anyone who strutted and squawked like Adolf Hitler would look ridiculous to the cold, close eye of the TV camera and would be quickly dismissed as a pompous rogue. Finally, as a culture, we are not struggling for *Lebensraum,* as the Germans were. America is a big and powerful country, bordered by oceans, and its citizens have no rational reason to suffer from any inferiority complex vis-à-vis other cultures.

Nevertheless, if contemporary America is so different from Nazi Germany, we must return to Shirer's question. To find an answer, we must look at what the Nazis did — not to the Jews, but to themselves. Even before the war ended, social scientists and psychologists were beginning to focus on the German character structure. In 1940 Otto Fenichel scrutinized anti-Semitism from a psychoanalytic perspective. Erich Fromm published *Escape from Freedom,* on the anatomy of authoritarianism, in 1941. The following year, in an effort to understand why the Nazi leadership could so successfully organize the nation's young, Erik Erikson published "Hitler's Imagery and German Youth." In his article "The Authoritarian Character Structure," Abraham Maslow continued the inquiry in 1943. Just after the war, Jean-Paul Sartre contributed his "portrait of the anti-Semite."

But it was not until 1950, after several years of extensive interviewing and research, that a group of social scientists was able to publish a clinical portrait of fascism. Called *The Authoritarian Personality,* it explained why some people were more likely than others to become adherents of fascist ideology. Using a scale to measure "antidemocratic trends," they found that some Americans scored high and others low. By analyzing the attitudes of the high scorers, the researchers reached certain tentative conclusions about the authoritarian personality.

For example, they found that the more authoritarian men were likely to have distant, stern fathers, while the more democratic men tended to have fathers who were warm and demonstrative. Similarly, authoritarian men were likely to come from homes that were father-dominated, where children struggled with a threatening, overpowering male figure. A man raised in such a family, according to the study, "can apparently never quite establish his personal and masculine identity; thus he has to look for it in a collective system where there is opportunity both for submission to the powerful and retaliation upon the powerless." Such a son develops a polarized personality. On the one hand, he tends toward "passive submission" to authority; on the other, he adopts the "idea of aggressive and rugged masculinity."

The men most susceptible to a Hitler type of authoritarian figure are characterized by pseudo-masculinity. They are quick to boast about their will power, decisiveness, energy, and determination. They find it nearly impossible to admit to any tendency toward softness, weakness, or passivity. Similarly, men who measure high in authoritarianism are likely to describe all relationships as hierarchical, with one person clearly above or below the other. It is difficult for them to imagine an egalitarian relationship.

Fortunately for such men, women who test high in authoritarianism do not expect to be considered as equals. Such women tended to describe their men, not in terms of emotional closeness, but in terms of the material security the men offered them. The mother's role was characterized as sacrificing, kind, and submissive. Both men and women who scored high on the authoritarianism scale were preoccupied with what the authors called the "dominance-submission, strong-weak, leader-follower dimension." Simply put, high-scoring women tended to be "authoritarian submissive," while men tended to be "authoritarian aggressive." The follower-leader syndrome was at the heart of sexuality. As the good Nazi followed his Führer, so the good wife followed her husband.

Almost a thousand pages long and filled with complicated charts and scientific jargon, *The Authoritarian Personality* was hardly a bestseller. But even if it had been more accessible, it is unlikely that it would have been popular, for its message was too troubling. It suggested that the enemy the Allies had just vanquished was not an alien creature from another planet but a part of our own culture. The authoritarian man and woman could be American as well as German.

Feminists in America did not fail to notice the connection between authoritarianism and what they called male chauvinism. In *Sexual Politics,* Kate Millett argued that the "overriding reason" for the character of the Nazi state was not primarily due to political or economic factors but to sexuality. Sympathetic male writers have agreed. Theodore Roszak called Nazism "the most barbarically masculine ideological movement of the twentieth century."

This psychological perspective on Nazism is threatening because it brings authoritarianism so close to home. It lifts Nazism out of the past and suggests that it is always potentially part of the present. One cannot listen to Nazi leaders talk without hearing in virtually every phrase a chillingly familiar distortion of human sexuality.

Nazism is inherently "a masculine movement," said the propaganda minister Joseph Goebbels. Politics "without qualification must be claimed by men." Women must be banned from public life "not because we want to dispense with them, but because we want to give them back their essential honor." In phrases no different from those being used by anti-feminists today, Goebbels proclaimed that the "outstanding and highest calling of women is always that of wife and mother." He added, "it would be an unthinkable misfortune if we allowed ourselves to be turned from this point of view."

From the beginning to the end of the Nazi movement in Germany, this point of view was never challenged. The first Nazi meeting, in 1921, passed a resolution that "a woman can never be accepted into the leadership of the party and the governing committee." The Nazis kept their promise: the *Führerlexicon*, a voluminous *Who's Who* of the Third Reich, did not list a single woman.

No one had a more rigid stereotype of masculinity and femininity than Hitler himself. "The world of the Aryan woman should be her husband, her family, her children, and her home," he wrote. "We do not find it right when the woman presses into the world of the man." Woman's role was to "uphold the nation." While she might have the "power of the soul," it was he alone who had the "strength of hardness."

Hardness was an obsession with Hitler and his companions. According to an OSS profile, Hitler once invited a young woman to his room. To impress her, he stuck out his arm in the Nazi salute. "I can hold my arm like that for two solid hours," he announced in a booming voice. "I never feel tired ... My arm is like granite — rigid and unbending. But Göring can't stand it. He has to drop his arm after half an hour of this salute. He's flabby, but I am hard."

"Mankind has grown great in eternal struggle," Hitler wrote in *Mein Kampf*, "and only in eternal peace does it perish." This is why a young man must harden himself: if he becomes too soft, he will fall prey to others. "Nature confers the Master's right on the strongest," Hitler continued. "They must dominate. They have the right to victory."

In the shadow of such masculinity, women had to be submissive. They could not be independent or strong. As Hitler's functionary for women's affairs proclaimed, the Aryan woman should devote herself to "the care of the man — soul, body, and mind ... from the first to the last moment of man's existence." Martin Bormann's wife, who had a "yearning for subjection and self-surrender," fit the mold perfectly.

"Oh, *Vaterchen*," she wrote to her husband late in the war, "every word which the Führer said in the years of our hardest struggle is going round and round in my head again." When Bormann boasted in a letter that he had succeeded in seducing a well-known actress, she wrote back that she was neither angry nor jealous; "I'm only worried whether you haven't given that poor girl a frightful shock with your impetuous ways."

Hitler shrewdly used this sexual dynamic to further his political aims. At large rallies, Hitler the public speaker reportedly had a powerful, almost hypnotic effect on women. He once said that he had to remain unmarried in order to maintain his extraordinary power over the German woman. In private, however, Hitler's intimate relations were tragic. There has always been much speculation about his impotence, homosexuality, and sexual perversion. But the facts say more than any rumor. Of the seven women with whom Hitler was intimate, six committed suicide.

Nothing so threatened the authoritarian mind as the notion that women might have their own strengths. "The German girl is a state subject," wrote Hitler. Since the Nazis represented the state, they felt entitled to define womanhood as passive virginity and nurturant motherhood. They flew into a rage, for example, when confronted by Käthe Kollwitz, a German artist whom Adrienne Rich has called the only artist who "has ever come close to evoking" the reality of motherhood.

Käthe Kollwitz was persona non grata in Nazi Germany. A major subject of her sculpture and drawing, the strength of woman, was deemed subversive. Her small bronze sculpture *Turm der Mütter* (*Tower of Mothers*) shows several women with outstretched arms encircling a terrified group of children, militantly protecting them against an unnamed threat. The Nazis removed *Turm der Mütter* from an exhibition of Kollwitz's work. "In the Third Reich it is not necessary for mothers to protect their children," said the Nazi art censor. "The state does it for them."

Another bronze sculpture, *Hovering Angel*, was seized by the Nazis and melted down as scrap metal. Of Kollwitz's *Mourning Mother*, the Nazi party's official newspaper, *Völkische Beobachter*, commented derisively: "Thank God a German mother does not look like this." The

Nazis did not want a woman mourning her dead child; they wanted her praising her Führer.

As in art, so in life. The Nazi fear of women's strength led them to attack the German women's movement. They infiltrated and finally dominated the women's federations, ultimately reducing them to an extension of the party apparatus. They excluded women from higher education, removed women representatives from the Reichstag, and prohibited them from serving as judges. They did not trust women in any position of power. Women were not hardened enough to do what had to be done. In fact, many Nazi men believed that the "woman problem" and the "Jewish problem" were intertwined.

"The message of women's emancipation is a message discovered solely by the Jewish intellect," asserted Hitler. As the Nazi propagandist Gottfried Feder put it: "The Jews have stolen women from us through the forms of sex democracy." He urged that Aryans "march out to kill the dragon so that we may again attain the most holy thing in the world, the woman as servant." Women who expressed resentment at being limited to *"Kinder, Küche, Kirche"* ("Children, kitchen, church") were therefore considered to be under the influence of Jewish thinking.

So terrified were the Nazis that their women might have physical contact with Jewish men that in 1935 they passed the Law for the Protection of German Blood and Honor, which prohibited sexual and social contact between Jews and Aryans. Goebbels justified forcing the Jews to wear the Star of David as a "prophylactic health measure."

The Jewish man symbolized everything about masculinity that the Nazi detested. The Third Reich glorified the martial virtues; most European Jews did not. The Aryan superhero was a tall, blond soldier willing to give his life for the fatherland: a simple man, but decent, hard working, moral, and clean. The stereotypical Jew was short and dark-haired. He was not only unpatriotic but "parasitical." He was part of "international financial Jewry," which sucked the blood of Germany. He would not defend the fatherland; he would exploit it. "Those who do not want to fight in this world do not deserve to live," wrote Hitler. Not given to soldiering, a manly profession, the Jews clustered around more cerebral callings. They trained their young, not as fighters, but as intellectuals and professionals. The Jew was the antithesis of the soldier: he was small of body and introspective of mind. Whichever stereotype the Nazis used — religious (the rabbi), academic (the scholar), commercial (the banker), or social (the cosmopolitan) — the Jew was always portrayed as cowardly and unmasculine.

The problem with such stereotypes is that they often collide with reality. Nothing posed a more insoluble dilemma for Nazi ideologues than Jewish war veterans. To the Nazi mind, this was the ultimate contradiction. If a Jew is dirty, cowardly, and self-seeking, how could he be a soldier? If one revered the soldier as the embodiment of manhood, and despised the Jew as its antithesis, what should one's policy be toward Jews who had been patriotic soldiers?

This issue was mentioned by President von Hindenburg in a letter to Chancellor Hitler in April 1933. It did not seem fair, von Hindenburg argued, to dismiss government officials of Jewish descent who were "wounded war veterans." If these Jewish men "were worthy of fighting and bleeding for Germany," then von Hindenburg believed that "they must be considered worthy of continuing to serve the fatherland in their professions." Although Hitler promised to give special consideration to Jews who had "served personally in the war," he ultimately did nothing on their behalf. To him, a Jew was a Jew, even in uniform.

There were many Germans, like von Hindenburg, who considered soldiering more basic than ethnicity. In Fred Uhlman's *Reunion*, a Jewish doctor finds a Nazi in party uniform posted outside his clinic. The Nazi carries the sign: "GERMANS, BEWARE. Avoid all Jews. Whoever has anything to do with them is defiled." The doctor

> put on his Army officer's uniform together with his decorations, including the Iron Cross, First Class, and took up his stand beside the Nazi. The Nazi got more and more embarrassed, and gradually quite a crowd collected. At first they stood in silence but as their numbers increased there were mutterings which finally broke into aggressive jeers.
>
> But it was at the Nazi that their hostility was aimed and it was the Nazi who before long packed up and made off.

The doctor did not try to hide that he was Jewish; he merely made it clear that he had been an army officer, and a valiant one.

It was his uniform, his medals, that gave him the courage to confront the Nazi. It was his "positive" identity as soldier that somehow made the crowd respect him and overlook his "negative" identity as Jew. In the Nazi world view, the former represented man at his best; the latter, man at his worst. And between these two masculine poles swung the Third Reich.

That ethnic prejudice is also sexual was reflected in the composition of many of the concentration camps. The only group generally treated as viciously as the Jews were the homosexuals. The epithets used for Jews (such as "scum of humanity") were also used for homosexuals, even those who were German and Aryan. The Jews wore yellow badges; the homosexuals wore pink ones. Together they occupied the lowest rung in the concentration camp hierarchy.

As the Nazis took control of Germany, discrimination against Jews went in hand in hand with the growing discrimination against homosexuals. Paragraph 175 of the criminal code, which made homosexuality a criminal offense, was rarely enforced before the Nazis came to power. In the three years from 1931 through 1933, only two thousand convictions were recorded. But by the years 1937 through 1939, the convictions numbered almost twenty-five thousand. According to Heinz Heger's *The Men with the Pink Triangle,* an account of one homosexual's six-year journey through the concentration camps, tens of thousands of homosexuals died in the camps. It was official Nazi policy: Heinrich Himmler announced that homosexuality was to be "eliminated." It was considered as serious a crime as miscegenation between the races.

Although never the centerpiece of Nazi ideology, the irrational hatred of homosexuals was an integral part of the authoritarian world view. The primary Nazi target was the Jew, but any man who dared to be different was also in danger.

Some Nazis, of course, claimed that they were never anti-Semitic, saying that they joined the Nazi movement innocently. As one Hitler Youth member recalled, they "were looking for a place where they could get together with other boys in exciting activities ... We weren't fully conscious of what we were doing ... we enjoyed ourselves and also felt important." They identified their own manhood with the vitality of Germany, and the Nazis appeared to offer them an opportunity to reaffirm both. As this young man himself admitted, many of the men who followed in Hitler's footsteps "weren't fully conscious." Mankind cannot afford to pay the price of such unconsciousness again.

Ironically, one of the reasons *The Authoritarian Personality* was ignored upon publication was that the American public was caught up in a political-sexual drama of its own in 1950. We too were conducting a witch hunt, not for Jews, but for communists. Fortunately, we did not permit McCarthyism to reach the same extreme. Within a few years, Joseph McCarthy was nothing more than a lonely alcoholic. But despite these unquestionable differences, this quasi-fascist episode deserves our attention.

According to Senator Joseph R. McCarthy, "pinks, punks, and perverts" were to be the targets of the House Un-American Activities Committee. In America's home-grown fascism, sexual and political slurs fed on each other. A McCarthyite did not hesitate to call the State Department "a veritable nest of Communists, fellow travelers, homosexuals, effete Ivy League intellectuals and traitors." Because the list was a potpourri of disconnected and anomalous innuendoes, the rhetoric was beyond rebuttal. It appealed, as Nazism had, to the unconscious needs of the authoritarian personality. McCarthy's campaign against "commie perverts" gave any man who wanted to bolster his manhood a blank check.

"You can hardly separate homosexuals and subversives," said Senator Kenneth S. Wherry. "Mind you, I don't say every homosexual is a subversive, and I don't say every subversive is a homosexual. But a man of low morality is a menace to government, whatever he is . . . and they are all tied up together."

Homosexuals were not merely different, they were fundamentally alien. They were subhuman and therefore excluded from basic rights. McCarthyites used the phrase "commie perverts" in the same way the Nazis used the word "Jews." By offering a convenient scapegoat to whom people could feel superior, McCarthy gave every non-communist heterosexual ego a boost. He considered his followers to be patriotic, right-thinking American men; his opponents were either effeminate or subversive or both. He would mock the "bleeding heart" liberals, for instance, by brushing his hand through his hair with a deliberately effeminate gesture.

As Jack Anderson pointed out in 1952, McCarthy had studied and admired *Mein Kampf.* His career began with his crusade, now almost forgotten, to defend German SS officers who had been convicted of war crimes. One who urged him to do so was McCarthy's pro-Nazi financial backer, Wisconsin industrialist Walter Harnischfeger, a man who distinguished himself by distributing copies of *Mein Kampf* to his colleagues as gifts. McCarthy felt that the SS men had been victimized. They had been given harsh sentences for their role in the Malmédy massacre, the cold-blooded machine-gun murder of one hundred fifty American soldiers and prisoners of war in December 1944. McCarthy defended the Germans because he sympathized with them. He despised softness, effeminacy, intellectuality. He wanted to eradicate what he disliked and feared, and the object of those fears was always, somehow, "feminine."

Even then, McCarthy's critics publicly challenged this sexual slander. Why single out homosexuals as security risks? they asked. Could not an alcoholic (of whom Congress had always had its share) also be blackmailed? Weren't men who were heterosexually promiscuous also particularly vulnerable to subversive influence? Were not men who had a penchant for gambling with borrowed money (as did Senator McCarthy) liable to violate security?

Every witch hunt, whether in medieval Europe, Nazi Germany, or in McCarthyite America, is sexual. We remember McCarthyism as a witch hunt against communists, but it was also rabidly against homosexuals. In April 1950, in a front-page *New York Times* article, "Perverts Called Government Peril," the national chairman of the Republican party was quoted as saying that sexual perverts "who have infiltrated our government in recent years" were as great a threat to American security as actual communists. In the following weeks, a Senate subcommittee was formally authorized to investigate reports that "about 3500 sex perverts hold federal jobs, some of them in the State Department."

These two threads, sex and politics, were interwoven throughout the Army-McCarthy hearings. First only McCarthy and his aides used sexual slurs, but soon their adversaries joined them. Senator Ralph E. Flanders of Vermont implied that McCarthy's "passionate anxiety" to retain one of his assistants who had been drafted was, in fact, rooted in their unnatural "personal relationship." Another critic wrote a column calling McCarthy a "disreputable pervert." Many implied privately that he was gay.

Why recall these ugly aspects of American sexual politics? Because they persist. Under different banners, with different leaders, they reemerge. "Again, Anti-Semitism" read the headline above an extensive article in *Newsweek*, published as this chapter was being written. It described the threefold increase in anti-Semitic incidents in the United States in 1980. In Richard Rubenstein's *After Auschwitz*, borrowed from the public library while I was researching this chapter, the following message was scribbled: "There should have been more Auschwitzes."

What can be done about this tenacious behavior we call authoritarianism? We certainly cannot banish it. We cannot pass laws prohibiting such attitudes. All we can do is to become more aware of ourselves, thereby reducing the chance that we can be manipulated. We should do so not for the sake of Jews or homosexuals. We should do it for our own survival.

There is a lesson from the concentration camps that every citizen of the nuclear age should learn. By the end of the war, the Nazi death camps had a mechanized system of mass murder that enabled the SS to remain distant from it. Himmler was well aware of the psychological toll of disposing of bodies covered with blood and feces. When he saw it, it made him sick, and he knew it would dehumanize his soldiers if they were knee-deep in corpses every day. So he and his technicians devised a system in which machines accomplished all the killing, and either machines or other inmates destroyed or buried the flesh and bones. In October 1933, Himmler told his top commanders that he knew "what it means when 100 corpses lie there, or when 500 corpses lie there, or when 1000 corpses lie there. To have gone through this and — apart from a few exceptions caused by human weakness — to have remained decent, that has made us great."

What Himmler meant was that it was a bureaucratic, systematic, efficient, orderly genocide. No one needed to feel responsible for this mechanized procedure, this killing of six million people. It was an extraordinary accomplishment: mankind was learning how to annihilate itself without a trace of guilt. Man made the machines, and the machines did our killing for us.

5 Holocaust

Battlefield Without Borders

We can no longer cure our madness with war.
— Franco Fornari, *The Psychoanalysis of War,* 1974

I AM WORKING as a consultant to an institute whose offices are in a building on First Avenue, directly across the street from the United Nations building in Manhattan. Several of us are in a meeting. Suddenly, an explosive boom shakes the room. Everyone jumps reflexively. Although the sound is many times louder than any sonic boom I have ever heard, the meeting continues. For the next several seconds, I cast nervous glances at the gleaming, glass-encased UN skyscraper. I scan it for any new reflections of red or yellow. But there is nothing. Not this time.

Why does the possibility of nuclear war haunt me? I was born in the year 4 A.H. (after Hiroshima). My generation was the first born with strontium 90 in its bones. Our air raid drills at school, conducted with such urgency, involved marching into the hallway and kneeling with one's head between one's knees. When finished with our lessons, my elementary school classmates and I were allowed to thumb through the multivolume picture book encyclopedia. The most popular volumes were S (for snakes) and A (for atom bomb). When I read about the bomb's awesome power, I could not understand why we would be any safer in the hall.

These memories flood me because my son Shane is now the same age. Some things have changed after a generation. He has no air raid drills; they are out of fashion. Civil defense is apparently considered futile. In case of war, he will just die at his desk.

The bomb is no longer confined to encyclopedias. It is part of our culture. I was playing with Shane at his school playground when I

73

found a candy wrapper from a package of Atomic Fire Balls. The front of the wrapper showed a red mushroom cloud. (The candy will "explode" in your mouth — get it?)

Fortunately, Shane had run ahead to the swings, so I hid the wrapper quickly in my pocket. It was my first instinct: to hide it from him, to protect his innocence. I did not want to expose him to nuclear pornography.

"What did you find back there, Dad?"

"Nothing."

"But I saw you put something in your pocket."

"Oh, *that*. It was just a candy wrapper."

"With candy in it?" He walked over and felt my pocket.

"Nope. It's empty."

"But then why'd you pick it up?"

"Just trying to keep the playground clean."

Shane returned to the swings and presumably forgot the incident, but I did not. I kept wondering whether hiding my feelings from him was right.

I confronted the issue again after the accident at the Three Mile Island nuclear plant. Shane often plays in the living room with his little brother Ari while I watch the news. But one day the news caught his attention because a woman was crying. Between her sobs, this pregnant resident of Harrisburg, Pennsylvania, was explaining to a reporter that she was afraid her baby might be deformed by low-level radiation.

"Why's she crying, Dad?" Shane asked.

"She's afraid of the radiation."

"What's radiation?"

"Quiet. I'm trying to listen. I'll explain it later." But I didn't.

And it happened again soon after a nuclear-tipped Titan missile exploded in Damascus, Arkansas. A woman was screaming furiously at an air force spokesman who said that they "had the situation under control."

"Why's she so angry, Dad?" Shane asked.

"There was an accident with a nuclear missile."

"What's that?"

"A rocket with a bomb on its tip."

"Who do we shoot them at?"

"Nobody."

"Then why do we have them?"

My impulse to be honest was overcome by my instinct to protect. Once again, I changed the subject.

My evasiveness is quite common among parents, I think. After all, none of the child-rearing books discuss this question. I wish the psychologists who write them could meet Shane and hear his questions. I would like to ask them: *at what age should I begin to tell my son about nuclear war?*

A magazine editor asked me to do a profile of a new organization, International Physicians for the Prevention of Nuclear War (IPPNW). Its members are physicians who feel that the Hippocratic oath requires that they speak out about the medical consequences of nuclear war. During the days I spent interviewing these doctors and writing about their work, I kept thinking about my aborted conversations with my son. The more I heard, the more I understood why I did not know what to say to Shane.

Dr. Yevgeni Chazov, Leonid Brezhnev's personal physician and a heart specialist in the forefront of Soviet medicine, and Dr. Bernard Lown, a professor of cardiology at the Harvard School of Public Health and an expert in the treatment of severe heart attack victims, met at a medical conference in 1964 and again in 1968, when Lown had lectured in Moscow. In 1972, as part of the Nixon-Brezhnev accords, they again worked together during a series of exchange programs. But it was not until a trip to the Soviet Union two years ago that Lown sat down with his Soviet colleague and shared his deepest concern.

"I know that you are a very important man here in Moscow," he told Chazov. "I know that you are the chief physician for the Kremlin and have personally attended to your country's highest officials. But I must tell you frankly that I do not think you are making as great a contribution to medicine as you could be."

"What do you mean?" Chazov replied, puzzled as to why his old friend would suddenly challenge him. "I work sixteen hours a day. I not only attend to patients but am involved in countless national and international health policy matters. How can you say that I am not doing enough?"

"I believe that doctors today must work to prevent nuclear war," said Lown bluntly. "We both know that our two nations are leading the race in nuclear arms. I have been asking myself, if nuclear war is threatening, what is the role of the physician? Historically, physicians played the patriotic role of repairing soldiers' injured bodies. But in a nuclear war, we would be useless. The pain and suffering would be of such magnitude that the medical profession would be unable to respond. I need your help in communicating how disastrous the medical consequences would be. Since we will be unable to treat the 'disease' that would result from nuclear war, we are obligated as physicians to try to prevent it."

"Dr. Chazov later told me what happened after our conversation," Lown recalled as we sat in his office recently. "He went home and said to his daughter, 'This crazy American was in my office today, telling me that I was not doing enough for medicine. He was telling me that it was my responsibility as a physician to try to prevent nuclear war.'

" 'Dad,' his daughter replied, 'I think that crazy American is right.' " Soon after, Chazov joined Lown.

Bernard Lown does not look like a man with a mission. At first glance, he seems just like all the other white-coated doctors who walk through the halls of Boston's renowned medical institutions. He dresses conservatively and appears quite reserved. But his commitment to his cause is not only professional, but personal.

"I was born a Jew in Lithuania, which is now part of the Soviet Union," he told me. "In 1946, after graduating from the Johns Hopkins University School of Medicine, I returned to Europe and visited the concentration camps in Germany where many of my relatives died. As a boy, the country we had admired most was Germany. That was the country of Goethe, Schiller, and Heine. Of Mendelssohn and Beethoven. We looked to the Germans for cultural leadership. To realize that they were capable of such barbarism raised questions, not simply about Germans, but about the human condition." As he paused, he silently recalled the horrors of long ago.

"The Holocaust became a parable for me," he continued, "a parable of what was in store for the rest of the world. If we do not prevent nuclear war, we will all be burned alive."

I am a generation younger than Lown. I never knew the dead, and the dead did not know me. But nevertheless I take personally the holocaust of European Jewry and the holocaust of Hiroshima and Nagasaki. I take them personally out of loyalty, not to the dead, but to the living.

A few weeks later, it was July Fourth. Shane was fascinated by the fireworks and by the tiny "fireballs" that some of his older friends were exploding on the streets.

"What's the biggest kind of bomb?" he asked me.

"What do you mean, 'biggest'?"

"I mean, that makes the biggest explosion."

"An H-bomb."

"Is it as big as our house?"

"I don't think so. I think it's about the size of a car. The bomb isn't very big, but it still makes the biggest explosion."

"How big?"

And I told him.

THERE IS a land where a man, to live, must be a man," began *When a Man's a Man,* a western novel published in 1916. A man must be as strong as "the primeval hills." His soul must be as pure as "the unstained skies, the unburdened wind, and the untainted atmosphere." Accustomed to this "land of wide mesas, of wild rolling pastures," the man of the West wants a freedom "which is not bounded by the fences of a too weak and timid conventionalism."

The prologue concluded: "In this land every man is — by divine right — his own kind. And in this land where a man, to live, must be a man, and a woman, if she be not a woman, must surely perish."

Half a century later, far beneath these "wild rolling pastures," two men enter the silo of an inter-continental ballistic missile (ICBM). They enter the launch control center through an entrapment area, a coffin-like hall ten feet long, five feet wide, and eight feet high. Steel doors clamp shut behind them. They walk through a fifty-foot tunnel into the silo itself. There, encircled in a web of steel, is the missile. It is taller than ten men on horseback. It can kill a great many more people in a split second than all the gunslingers of the Wild West killed in a century.

One of the men, a journalist, looks up at the nuclear warhead. He thinks about the birch trees and dairy herds grazing on the fields above. He feels a nervous chill.

"Relax," says his military escort. "There's nothing to do down here but wait and hope for nothing to happen."

How did the cowboy of the wide open spaces become the mole of subterranean steel tunnels? How was the man of action reduced to a man in waiting, hoping for nothing to happen? It is a paradox. Men of the nuclear age have at their fingertips weapons far more powerful than men of previous eras could even imagine. Yet we experience an unnatural inactivity that would have driven the cowboy mad. It is an age, wrote the French philosopher Raymond Aron, of "virile weapons and impotent men."

What happened to the soldier? In our fantasies, he still lives. In reality, he died at Hiroshima. Hiroshima has changed war and peace, life and death. It has changed sexuality too. After Hiroshima, man and woman alike inhabited a battlefield without borders. Faced with the threat that any major war will quickly escalate from conventional to nuclear weapons, the old sexual rules of war have become obsolete. As the battlefield grew to encompass the skies above and lands halfway around the world, the soldier's identity diffused. He became everyman — and everywoman. Every kind of being — old and young, weak and strong, male and female — now resides in the combat zone once reserved for able-bodied men in uniform. The male soldier in the ICBM silo is safer than a woman pushing a baby carriage in the park.

The emasculation of war was completed at Hiroshima. In World War II, combat between armed adversaries who could see and touch each other was no longer the primary cause of death. Most men died from wounds inflicted by mines and bombs. The victim rarely saw his executioner. Nevertheless, pre-nuclear war was still considered a war fought primarily by men. Although thousands of women and children were killed in the bombings of London and Dresden, most battles were still fought by armies of men.

But in World War III, as at Hiroshima, sex will be irrelevant. Women will not cheer the men who return from battle; the battle will be everywhere the wind blows. There will be no victory. The victor will not rape and plunder, as winning armies have always done. The rape now will be universal, not sexual but biological. We will all, men and women and children together, be raped by our weaponry.

The image is brutalizing. It is painful to write and painful to read, but it is true. None of the standard words — chivalry, courage, battlefield, civilians, victors, losers — retain their original meaning. The heroic soldier has vanished. He has become, as Karl Bednarik pointed out in *The Male in Crisis,* "an anonymous functionary, the lackey of mass destruction." And so the old heroine has vanished too. No longer will women wait passively at home while their brave men go off to war. War has come home to stay.

The nuclear age is now middle-aged. The first post-nuclear generation has matured and had children of its own. More than half of America's citizens now were born after Hiroshima. The only reality we have ever known has been nuclear. Chronologically, the bomb is our technological brother — or our stepbrother. The bomb, after all, had no mother.

The "father of the atom bomb" was an all-male collective called the Manhattan Project. After the first successful test, its director, General Leslie Groves, proudly cabled President Harry Truman: BABY IS BORN. It was an immaculate (male) conception. Although the scientists, politicians, and military personnel who conceived it were male, they announced the birth of the nuclear age with the most feminine metaphor.

Sexual imagery pervaded the entire enterprise. The B-29 that dropped the baby on Hiroshima bore the name *Enola Gay* across its belly. The pilot had named the plane after his mother. And of course the baby was a boy. In later atomic tests, the bomb's fathers would call it Little Feller, Fat Boy, or simply Harry. Later, the steel shell in which an ICBM sat in its silo would, naturally, be called its "crib."

Like any new father, the bomb's creators were elated, at least at first. They expected their son's extraordinary powers to enhance their own. They thought they would control him. "I'll certainly have a hammer on those boys," boasted President Truman at the Potsdam Conference only weeks before the bomb was dropped. After receiving General Groves's cable, Truman was exhilarated. According to Winston Churchill, Truman was suddenly a "changed man." He "told the Russians . . . just where they got on and off and generally bossed the whole meeting."

Such was the quick thrill of the new weapon. It revitalized our sense of mastery. Every word America's leaders uttered carried new weight. They were dominant again. They were in charge. With the bomb they could, in Secretary of State James F. Byrnes's words, "dictate our own terms." This was what manhood was all about: power. The bomb proved that. American manhood was the most potent force in the world.

The bomb's inventors would use their newly acquired omnipotence, they promised, only for good, not evil. They would use the bomb to save lives. They would drop it, wrote Truman in his diary on July 25, 1945, "so that military objectives and soldiers and sailors are the target and not women and children." A week later, he was proved wrong. We had to use the bomb, reflected James Bryant Conant idealistically, in order to "awaken the world to the necessity of abolishing war altogether." But a generation later, his prophecy has still not come true. In the intervening years, we have not abolished war; we have made it more terrible. We have created a potential holocaust in which not a city, not a region, but the world itself will be cremated.

Where else would the eternal male quest for the ultimate weapon have led? The inventor of dynamite, Alfred Nobel, had set out "to invent a substance or a machine with such terrible power of mass destruction that war would thereby be made impossible forever." The quest therefore could not end with Hiroshima; it had to continue.

"Further tests," dreamed Dr. Edward Teller, another of the bomb's illustrious fathers, "will put us in the position to fight our opponents' war machines while sparing the innocent bystanders. Weapons of this kind will reduce unnecessary casualties in a future war." Teller led the male chorus that, as Albert Schweitzer later described it, "sang a hymn of praise to the idyllic nuclear war to be waged with completely clean hydrogen bombs."

After fathering their diabolical child, whose growth they measured not in inches but in megatons, the bomb's inventors soon lost their feeling of unparalleled power. The Russians had also given birth to a nuclear son. The nuclear arms race was under way.

"The combination of Nazi genocide and the American bombings of Hiroshima and Nagasaki terminated man's sense of limits concerning his self-destructive potential," wrote Dr. Robert Jay Lifton, whose works have traced the impact of the nuclear age on our inner life. These twin holocausts "inaugurated an era in which [man] is devoid of assurance of living on eternally as a species." It took "almost twenty-five years for beginning formulations of the significance of these events to emerge," wrote Lifton in the late sixties.

It was then that the first post-nuclear generation was coming of age. Perhaps it was only coincidence, but it was then that the stream of books about men's liberation began to flow. As the next chapter documents, it was then that sexual politics came to the forefront of our culture's consciousness. And it was then that the ultimate irony of our unusable weaponry became clear: it was killing *us,* not the enemy.

Except for the victims of Hiroshima and Nagasaki, the largest number of known victims of nuclear explosions have been Americans. American men and women have been killed by a force as invisible as it is lethal: radiation. A few of the victims were exposed as part of the cleanup crews that entered Hiroshima and Nagasaki after the war. Others were soldiers ordered to watch the A-bomb test at close range. But the largest number lived in the American Southwest near the sites where the A-bomb was first tested during the late forties and early fifties. They live amid the breathtaking landscape described so rapturously in *When a Man's a Man.* But their skies were no longer "unstained," the wind no longer "unburdened."

Usually, ten to thirty years elapse between any low-level exposure to a carcinogen and the onset of cancerous tumors. This is why, beginning in the sixties and accelerating during the seventies, cancer began appearing with frightening frequency in towns such as Parowan, St. George, and Cedar City in Utah and in scores of other towns in bordering regions of Nevada and Arizona. At first, each family struck by this mysterious malignancy viewed it as a personal tragedy. But their views changed when, to cite one example, four Utah farmers, whose land intersected at a crossroad precisely downwind from an atomic bomb site, were all stricken by cancer. Then the tragedy is no longer personal. It is political.

"Well," says elderly Irma Thomas of St. George, Utah, "just within a block of my home there's Wilford, he had cancer, and his wife Helen died of stomach cancer. Carl across the street died of throat cancer, and Ernie died of it, and his wife has it now. The boy next to them died of leukemia, and my sister across the way there, she had breast cancer. She died. And her husband has it now."

Each of her neighbors in this sad little town has a list. Says Elmer Pickett: "My sister, my niece, my aunt, four uncles, my sister-in-law, my mother-in-law, my grandmother, and my wife . . ." Echoes Dave Timothy: "Two of my aunts. Three of my uncles. And two of my doctors."

When an eerie pinkish-red cloud drifted over the area roughly thirty years ago, the spokesman from the Atomic Energy Commission assured them: "There is no danger . . ." In an Atomic Energy Commission film that must make government officials cringe, an army chaplain tells a nervous soldier not to worry about the blast that they are about to witness a few miles away. The chaplain declares that "the army has taken all the necessary precautions to see that we are perfectly safe here." Even though the bomb was, as Truman put it in his diary, "the most terrible thing ever discovered," its fathers thought they could detonate it with impunity. Their arrogance was rooted in ignorance, or machismo, or perhaps a self-destructive mixture of both.

A young soldier, Patrick Stout, was General Groves's driver when he escorted a group of inquisitive reporters to the site where, two months earlier, the first A-bomb (code name, Trinity) had been successfully detonated. To demonstrate how safe the site was, Groves ordered Stout to stand in the bomb crater for half an hour. Patrick Stout later died of leukemia.

"They told us we would be the closest human beings outside of Hiroshima to a nuclear blast," said one of the marines who was ordered to watch an A-bomb test in Nevada only one mile from ground zero. He is dying of cancer.

"Nobody told us anything about radiation," complained a sixty-year-old ex-serviceman who was sent to clean up Hiroshima. He is dying of cancer.

Time magazine called it "A Fallout of Nuclear Fear." The *New York Times* labeled it the "Grim Legacy of Nuclear Testing." But for the men and women whose bone marrow is rotting and whose neighbors are being decimated, it is far more personal than such headlines suggest. It is seven children dying of leukemia within a hundred yards of one's house. And it is women, angry at being betrayed by the government — the men — they trusted. They had left such matters to men before, but they never would again.

"It's a hard thing," said Frankie Lou Bentley of Parowan, Utah. "We're raised all our life to be nice, be nice, be nice, and this happens and we don't know what to do." Frankie Lou Bentley was confused because she did not know whom to blame. When the technology of murder is perfected, no one is responsible.

The experts who created the bomb do not hold themselves accountable. The government admits no wrongdoing. None of the victims can prove which radiation from which bomb triggered his cancer. The assassin is invisible. He is unconscious. He is the Soldier gone mad. His battlefield has no borders. His battle has no end. And his victims are of both sexes, all ages, and even the unborn.

We cannot call such violence war. It can only be called holocaust. The hero has been replaced by the robot, John Wayne by Dr. Strangelove. In the first week of June 1980, several nuclear alerts were called. They were not called by the chairman of the Joint Chiefs of Staff or by the President of the United States. They were called by a faulty computer microcircuit the size of a quarter and worth about $100.

Trapped in such a world, human beings react instinctively. We are afraid. Since we may be killed without warning and without purpose, we are forced to live in fear. But chronic fear is debilitating. Most of us numb ourselves to it. We try to pretend the threat does not exist. A few turn their fear into anger and try to fight the war machine. But no one is unaffected.

Perhaps most deeply affected is the generation that, as Dorothy Dinnerstein described it in *The Mermaid and the Minotaur,* "had grown up in a world silently and intangibly permeated with the possibility that civilization may not, after all, extend into the indefinite future, and for whom a kind of bone marrow detachment from the past became possible." Out of this detachment, Dinnerstein said, came "the beginning of a redefinition, by young men themselves, of the traditional male role."

This is why the perennial male challenge — to be always stronger and more aggressive than one's adversary — reached a historical dead end. The Soldier no longer protected his loved ones from threats to their survival; on the contrary, his weapons are the threat. Another set of virtues — so-called feminine qualities — are now required of him: limits, restraints, control, patience. The "masculine" traits that formerly assured survival will now, if not balanced by the "feminine," assure destruction. The manliness that women once revered because it protected them is now increasingly condemned because it endangers them.

The Soldier's virtues, when taken to an extreme, are worse than the coward's vices. Blindly seek to be more courageous than all other men and you risk foolhardy self-destruction. Respond to all challenges with aggression and you will squander lives in conflicts that could have been avoided. Idolize your strength and you become insensitive to the strengths of others that you may lack. Persevere thoughtlessly and you will fail to respond to changing circumstances.

Be loyal too rigidly and you deny the very freedom of thought and expression to which you allegedly pledge allegiance. The virile virtues have always been in need of limits, but never so desperately as in the nuclear age.

Faced with this dilemma, the Soldier becomes schizophrenic. He amasses weapons with his right hand while his left devises ways to avoid ever using them. The Soldier has not been undermined by an antiwar movement. He has been rendered obsolete by war itself. His heroism has become suicidal. The anachronism of the old archetype is epitomized by the image of a soldier with a sword in one arm fighting, not with his enemy, but with his other arm.

No wonder a new generation of men has rebelled against the military man. No wonder these men have rejected this befuddled man in uniform, at war with himself. In remembering Auschwitz, they depicted the military man as an uptight, stiff-necked mannequin of machismo, as mindless as a wind-up toy soldier. Remembering Hiroshima, they have portrayed him as an absurd anachronism, doing pushups as if his biceps would make a difference in a megaton world.

But our derision has now reached its own dead end. After mocking the square-jawed, tight-lipped, authoritarian model of military manhood, we face our own challenge. We have to find alternatives.

⑥ Antiwar

The Politics of Masculinity

> "Son," an elderly woman addressed a young man
> at a Vietnam Veterans Against the War demon-
> stration in Washington, "I don't think what
> you're doing is good for the troops."
> "Lady," he replied, "we are the troops."
> — Gloria Emerson, *Winners and Losers,*
> 1977

NIGHT FELL at the Pentagon. We were gathered in the parking lot, without blankets and food, and we intended to spend the night. To call it a siege, as some did, is ridiculous. We had no weapons, no strategy, no leader. We were a raggle-taggle non-army. "I could have been a hell of a lot more effective leader of that march," ex–Defense Secretary Robert S. McNamara would tell me a decade later. "If only the demonstrators had been more disciplined and better organized, they could have brought the Pentagon to a halt with only a fraction as many people."

Most newspapers reported the event as a battle, a clash of forces. But it was more personal than that. We were demonstrating at the Pentagon to disassociate ourselves from a certain kind of manhood. We were opposed, not merely to a foreign policy, but to a masculine identity that breeds such policies. We were confronting the five-sided symbol of the soldiering sex.

Even as we opposed it, however, we embodied it. The contradiction was evident. Among us were groups who mouthed the slogan "Fight for peace." (Wasn't that the logic that brought us to Vietnam?) Some of the protesters seemed determined to taunt the national guardsmen into violence. (If they were against violence in

85

Vietnam, why would they want to trigger it at home?) Some of us brought helmets — "just for protection." Many of us were antiwar soldiers, as imbued with machismo as the war machine itself.

In military terms, the U.S. marshals and national guardsmen obviously had a decisive advantage. They were organized; we were not. They carried weapons; we did not. But we had a psychological advantage. We had women on our side. From the White House to Saigon, America's war machine was exclusively male. The antiwar movement was decidedly not.

Among us were hundreds of young women of the guardsmen's generation. As at Kent State, where four students were murdered in 1970, the men in uniform felt undermined by the presence of women who were opposed to everything the military represented. The soldiers felt insulted. Soldiers were supposed to be respected by women, yet the only women present were hostile.

Predictably, some of the women used the only weapons they had: their bodies. These are the ones McNamara remembered when I asked him later about the event. "Females," he said, refusing to call them women, "would rub their breasts against the soldiers who were ordered to stand at attention." He was appalled at the vulgarity of these young women. He did not mention fifty thousand dead Americans; hundreds of thousands more who suffered from war-related injuries and mental illness; an impoverished nation devastated by defoliants and laced by mines; or the billions of dollars needed to build the Great Society that had been squandered on war.

Women's blood ran heavy on the asphalt of the Pentagon parking lot that night. After the TV cameramen went home, the troops were ordered to advance. The number of women beaten by the wedge of the soldiers was overwhelming. "Eyewitness account after eyewitness account," wrote Norman Mailer, "gives brutal, deadening news of the ferocity with which marshals and soldiers went to work on women."

The beating of women proved to be a brilliant tactic. It utterly demoralized the remaining demonstrators. Not only did it terrorize the women; it efficiently undermined the men. We watched helplessly as "our" women were driven off in vans. The hawks, in Mailer's words, "plucked all stolen balls back. With rifles and clubs they had plucked them back."

But the strategy ultimately backfired. Women aligned themselves even more solidly against the war makers. The polls proved it with statistics; women proved it with their eyes. The women of my generation who were active against the war had a look of militance in their eyes that, I suspect, their mothers' had never had. They were not spectators, but participants.

It is ironic that the man who dared to report what happened at the Pentagon that night was a man of many wives and many lovers, a veteran of war and many brawls, an articulate and witty chauvinist scorned by feminists, and a macho writer who used his pen to eulogize Marilyn Monroe. Indeed, Norman Mailer was so flamboyantly male in the old, predictable ways that he could challenge the hawks' monopoly on manhood with impunity. He did not need to fear being dismissed as something less than a man. As the author of *The Naked and the Dead,* one of the most celebrated portraits of soldiers in World War II, Mailer had come full circle. In *Armies of the Night,* the blood belonged not to American soldiers but to their victims:

> At least four times that soldier hit her with all his force, then as she lay covering her head with her arms, thrust his club up like a sword between her hands into her face . . . We could see her face. But there was no face there, all we saw were some raw skin and blood. We couldn't even see if she was crying — her eyes had filled with the blood pouring down her head. She vomited and that too was blood. Then they rushed her away.

I remembered that night whenever I had the opportunity to meet the government officials who defended the war. These encounters usually took place in ivy-covered university buildings, ornate conference centers, or book-lined libraries, rich with polished oak. In such genteel, cerebral settings I listened to McNamara defend the war to a room full of seething students and to McGeorge Bundy respond impassively to our passionate questions.

By 1970, when I was invited to participate in a small gathering that would include Henry Kissinger, I felt numb. At that time, Kissinger was masterminding the air war in Indochina. With Nixon's blessing, he was withdrawing U.S. troops while saturating the countryside with bombs. What could one say?

But one member of the audience, Daniel Ellsberg, who was about to release what would come to be called the Pentagon Papers, knew precisely what he wanted to say to his colleague:

"How can you tell the American people, Henry, that the Nixon administration is 'winding down' the war? You are expanding and intensifying aerial strikes against innocent civilians. You are even sending planes to bomb in countries with which we are not at war. How can you pretend that you are moving toward peace when you are escalating the war? Where is your morality?"

"Dan, it is a sad day when we must discuss such difficult matters by challenging each other's morality," Kissinger replied. "How can I reply to a question which is not about policy at all, but is rather a challenge to my personal integrity?" Although Kissinger's face did not betray it, it was clear that he had been wounded, but he refused to respond to what he considered an illegitimate line of questioning. He acted as if he were the defender of civility, and he portrayed Ellsberg as an overly emotional moralist.

So I did not ask Kissinger about the war. I did not ask about the domino theory, or pacification programs, or the latest negotiations. I asked Kissinger about himself.

"Last year I listened to McNamara, the year before to Bundy, and now I listen to you. You all speak with the conviction that you know more about what is going on in Southeast Asia than any one of us. But there is one thing I know more about than you do — and that is the feelings of young Americans like myself. We consider this war a tragic mistake. I am reduced to wondering about why you and I think so differently. Why do you feel the war is just while tens of millions of young Americans do not? How did *you* see the world when you were our age? What were you brought up to believe was moral and immoral?"

Kissinger deflected my question as he had Ellsberg's. "You do not expect me to psychoanalyze myself up here in front of all of you," he said with the greatest charm. This gathering was not the proper setting for him to explore his own background, he said, but he would be glad to discuss it with me in Washington sometime.

Since then a decade has passed. It is now all history. We have "put Vietnam behind us." Kissinger has written his memoirs, *The White House Years*. He has been a commentator for NBC News, and he has charged enormous fees for the well-publicized lectures that he has delivered throughout the nation. But my question remains unanswered.

Ellsberg, in contrast, was clear and open about the evolution of his morality. He remembered his high school physics teacher telling the class that a terrible bomb was being developed. The teacher did not know whether the Germans or the Americans would make it first, but he believed that no one would use it because of its awesome power. Fourteen-year-old Dan did not think about it until that sum- mer. Walking home one day, he saw the newspaper headlines that told the world that America had dropped the first A-bomb on Hiro- shima.

Good God, he thought to himself. My country got the bomb — and we used it!

He went home and showed the paper to his father. "Dad, you've got to read this. It's the worst thing I've ever read." But his father de- fended the President's decision. Like most Americans, he believed that it was justified because it hastened the end of the war and saved the lives of American soldiers.

Dan's father was an engineer. He designed bomb factories, some of the biggest in the country, so it was not unusual that a few years later he was asked to help construct the Hanford nuclear reactor. It was being built in the state of Washington to produce plutonium for a new, more powerful generation of bombs called H-bombs. His com- pany was excited to have such a major contract. For everyone in- volved, it would mean more money and prestige. But Dan's father re- fused to work on the project.

"These guys are crazy," Ellsberg recalled his father saying at the dinner table. "They've got the A-bomb. Now they want the H-bomb. When is it ever going to stop?"

Dan was nevertheless attracted to the military. That's where the power was, and he wanted to be involved in deciding how it was to be used. He wanted, like so many other men, to prove his manhood. "I volunteered for the marines because they embody the image of the soldier," said Ellsberg in retrospect. "What drew me to the marines was very much the answer to the dare: are you man enough?"

Young Dan was captivated, too, by John Wayne's *The Sands of Iwo Jima.* Later, on liberty with the Sixth Fleet, Lieutenant Ellsberg was in a restaurant in Rome when he saw the Duke sitting at another table.

"That's the guy who recruited me," Dan told his dinner com- panion, and he sent a bottle of champagne over to Wayne's table.

"My heroes have changed," he told me. "When I saw for myself what we were doing in Vietnam, I felt sick. We were destroying a people, but back home all the presidents talked about was toughness. When antiwar students at Harvard tried to block McNamara's car, didn't he shout at them something like: 'I was tougher than you when I was a student, and I'm tougher than you now'? That's all that type of man could think about — 'toughing it out,' 'hanging tough.' I was appalled."

After he released the Pentagon Papers, many of Ellsberg's former colleagues at the RAND Corporation and the Pentagon turned against him. In their eyes, he was no longer a man. They assumed he had gone crazy because they had no other way to understand his transformation. One of his closest colleagues at RAND called him a "classic fanatic." Another old colleague from his Pentagon days once came to hear Ellsberg speak against the war. Afterward, the defense analyst said to him, "The Dan Ellsberg I used to know was analytical, factual, sober, informative. The man I heard today was emotional, irrational, with no relation to reason or argument."

"Of course it bothered me," Ellsberg told me. "No one likes to be the object of character assassination. But I saw myself differently than they did. No one was superficially more 'analytical, sober, factual,' than the officials of the Third Reich. Men like Albert Speer blinded themselves to what was happening by shutting off their emotions. You know what Speer did? He wrote that an old friend came to tell him not to go to Auschwitz, not to go because something was happening there that was so awful that he should remain ignorant of it."

Grabbing a copy of his paper "The Responsibility of Officials in a Criminal War," Ellsberg continued, "Speer wrote — and I quote — 'I did not investigate — for I did not want to know what was happening there . . . From that moment on, I was inescapably contaminated morally . . . I had closed my eyes.' And a few paragraphs later, he puts it this way: 'It is surprisingly easy to blind your moral eyes. I was like a man following a trail of bloodstained footprints through the snow without realizing that someone had been injured.' "

Ellsberg put the paper down. "I am not a particularly caring or compassionate man. I simply did not want to end up like that. That's why I released the Pentagon Papers. I am glad that I woke up in time to do something about it."

Listening to this middle-aged man with gray-flecked hair, sitting in his office filled with books on war and peace, I had difficulty be-

lieving that he was only one man. Could the person who sent John Wayne a bottle of champagne be the same one who was called a traitor and a fanatic for leaking classified military documents?

"I'm not interested in macho bravery anymore," he said. "I'm interested in an entirely different mode of being courageous. I have been reading a lot about the power of nonviolence. Before, the hero was the one who inflicted violence on others. In nonviolence, the hero takes all the risk of violence to himself and endangers no one."

Later, when I was leaving, I noticed a picture of Ellsberg's parents. It reminded me that, as unique as his act of opposition to the war had been, it had been foreshadowed twenty years earlier by a very similar decision made by his father. Had he somehow inherited his moral sensitivities from his father?

"Dad and I were just talking about that," said Ellsberg, smiling. "He told me something I never knew before. I asked him why he had refused to get involved with the H-bomb and he said to me, 'Dan, don't you know? It was because of you. I remembered what you said when you brought the paper home in August 1945.' "

IT IS 1961. Arthur Schlesinger, Jr., a slightly built, soft-spoken professor with no government experience, is arguing against the tough-talking, aggressive secretaries of State and Defense, the director of the Central Intelligence Agency, and the Joint Chiefs of Staff. They want the United States to launch an invasion in the Bay of Pigs on the coast of Cuba. Schlesinger disagrees. They think it will lead to a rebellion that will overthrow Castro. He does not. They believe it will strengthen America in its dealings with the Soviet Union. He does not.

President John F. Kennedy is undecided. The invasion plan is not his idea. He has inherited it from Eisenhower. Moreover, Kennedy is critical of American policy toward Cuba. While campaigning in Cincinnati only a month before he was elected, he had said: "We refused to help Cuba meet its desperate need for economic progress . . . We used the influence of our government to advance the interests and increase the profits of the private American companies which dominated the island's economy . . . Administration spokesmen publicly hailed Batista . . . as a staunch ally and a good friend at a time when Batista was murdering thousands, destroying the last vestiges of freedom and stealing hundreds of millions of dollars from the Cuban people."

Considering the President's own views, Schlesinger might have prevailed and the Bay of Pigs invasion could have been canceled. But it was not. Schlesinger was fighting, not only against the military brass and the most powerful Cabinet members, but against the politics of masculinity.

In words uncannily similar to Walter Lippmann's a half-century earlier, Schlesinger recalled that "the advocates of the [Bay of Pigs] adventure had a rhetorical advantage. They could strike virile poses and talk of tangible things — fire power, air strikes, landing craft, and so on. To oppose the plan, one had to invoke intangibles — the moral position of the United States, the reputation of the President, the response of the United Nations, 'world public opinion,' and other such odious concepts."

The representatives of the State Department were not keen on the idea of an invasion. But they were muzzled, according to Schlesinger, by their "desire to prove to the CIA and the Joint Chiefs of Staff that they were not soft-headed idealists, but were really tough guys, too."

Until the moment the decision was made, Schlesinger did everything he could to make the key actors change their minds. Faced with these reservations, Secretary of State Rusk admitted: "Maybe we've been oversold on the fact that we can't say no." But he didn't say no. The invasion occurred, failed, and became a case study of a foreign policy mistake.

The similarities with Vietnam are striking. It too was a small country with what Kennedy described as "a desperate need for economic progress." Once again, bellicose men of action advocated tough military intervention. Once again, dissenters were afraid of looking soft. It is a drama we have witnessed many times before.

The men who led America into the Vietnam quagmire were noted, by both their admirers and their critics, for their apparent toughness. No one would ever call them soft. The "Awesome Foursome" is what one reverent scholar called Lyndon Johnson, Robert McNamara, McGeorge Bundy, and Dean Rusk. In "How Johnson Makes Foreign Policy," in the *New York Times Magazine* of July 4, 1965, the four were portrayed as if they were front linemen on a winning football team. Robert McNamara said Johnson "had a bias for action rather than inaction." Bundy believed that "the United States is the engine of mankind and the rest of the world is the train." Rusk, though more cautious, always instinctively followed the military line. And Johnson promised never to back down in Vietnam because he refused to be seen "tucking tail and coming home."

"Manhood was very much in the minds of the architects of [Vietnam]," said David Halberstam when interviewed almost a decade after the first sections of *The Best and the Brightest* appeared in print. "They wanted to show who had bigger balls."

Thanks to Doris Kearns's extraordinary portrait of Johnson, we know him more intimately than any other President. We know him as a man who wanted the Great Society "to grow into a beautiful woman," a woman "so big and beautiful that the American people couldn't help but fall in love with her." We know he was afraid that "if I left the woman I really loved — the Great Society — in order to get involved in that bitch of a war on the other side of the world, then I would lose everything at home." But although he feared losing the woman he loved, he feared not being a man more. He was chronically anxious that "if I left the war and let the Communists take over South Vietnam, than I would be seen as a coward and my nation would be seen as an appeaser."

Johnson confided such feelings to Kearns as he lay in bed at five-thirty in the morning. "Pulling the sheets up to his neck, looking like a cold and frightened child," Johnson confided in her. Kearns, who "reminded him of his dead mother," sat beside the bed taking notes.

Johnson (in Halberstam's words) was "more than a little insecure." He was desperately trying "to be seen as a man . . . he wanted the respect of men who were tough, real men, and they would turn out to be hawks." Johnson had two categories: men and boys. Men were "activists, doers, who conquered business empires, who acted instead of talked." Boys were "the talkers and the writers and the intellectuals who sat around thinking and criticizing and doubting instead of doing."

If someone was not a real man, then he ran the risk of being sexually insulted. When told that a member of his administration was "going soft" on the war, Johnson dismissed him: "Hell, he has to squat to piss." He derided influential dissenters, such as Adlai Stevenson, George Ball, and Chester Bowles, as spineless, lacking in will power, "eggheads." When his own vice president began to voice doubts, Johnson lost faith in him. According to Halberstam, Johnson considered Hubert Humphrey "still a boy, better than most liberals, but too prone to talk instead of act, not a person that other men would respect." When, finally, Secretary of Defense McNamara began to question their policies, Johnson dismissed him too, saying, McNamara's "gone dovish on me." That women (including at times his own wife) would question the war did not surprise him; it was only natural, he said, that a woman would be uncertain. But when a man turned soft, Johnson could not forgive him.

One high-level State Department aide who witnessed many planning sessions recalled how Johnson's decision-makers reenacted this predictable masculine drama. "I watched the doves trying to phrase their arguments so as not to look soft," said James C. Thomson, who now directs the Nieman Foundation at Harvard. "But the doves were cowed by the brass and the hard-liners. Particularly those who hadn't served in the armed forces, such as Humphrey, were vulnerable to the uniforms. They never could rebut the techno-military we've-got-to-be-tough language that the generals and the hawks used."

Once the war became a test of masculinity, foreign policy and macho psychology became fused. One of the Awesome Foursome boiled it all down to locker room lingo. "Do we have the will to do it?" he would say. "Do we have the guts?" The implication was that real men had the will and the guts, but boys, eggheads, and women did not.

At the same time, critics of the war were indicting the hawks' character. Halberstam called one of the Awesome Foursome a fool ("There is no kinder or gentler word for it," he added apologetically). The Marxists called them imperialists. Some of the more venomous antiwar protesters called them murderers and fascists. But the truth is far more frightening. They were simply men who were trying to embody an image of manhood that had become anachronistic and self-destructive. The Soldier's solution was to overpower the enemy. But Vietnam was a war in which the ultimate power could not be unleashed. It was a limited war because no one wanted to risk an unlimited one.

In December 1973, Thomson was given an unusual assignment.

He was asked by a group of psychoanalysts and historians concerned with "psychohistorical" issues what he believed were the most vital questions to ask in order to understand America's policy in Vietnam. In a confidential letter, he raised four issues. Has Asia, he asked, "been perceived as 'female' or even as 'the mother' by many American policy-makers over the past two centuries [including] many of those who ran the Vietnam war from Washington and Saigon?" Second, why was Asia "an object, never an equal, usually an inferior ... usually something (someone) we *did things to* ... What unconscious role did what we now call 'racism' and also 'male chauvinism' play in our Indochina involvement?" Third, why did no one in Washington, hawk or dove, dare to say that he favored "withdrawal" from Indochina? "Why is 'withdrawal' (in a territorial sense) such a fearful concept for policy-makers — to this very day?" And finally he asked: "Does the 'manhood' of American policy-makers — and its constant testing and protection — rank notably higher as a factor in their decision-making than in that of other nations' leaders? If so, why?"

They were unusual questions for a former administration official to raise about a war. Before the sixties, such issues were rarely raised; after the sixties, they could not be ignored.

As young Americans were sent to their deaths, every group that did not fit the image of the white, able-bodied, successful male was rebelling against that image. Blacks, Indians, feminists, gays, hippies, and the handicapped shared with white, middle-class antiwar activists a revulsion for the old archetypes of masculinity. They no longer apologized for failing to fit the mold. They were proud of it. They did not want to be like "the best and the brightest." They wanted to measure themselves against a different model of manhood.

A few observers saw that dissidents were rejecting more than foreign policy. In Leslie Fiedler's mid-sixties portrait of the postwar generation, "The New Mutants," for instance, he recognized signs of "a radical metamorphosis of the Western male." In their desire to become "not only more Black than White but more female than male," the men in the cultural and political protest movements seemed to be trying not only "to establish a new relationship with women but with their own masculinity." In their attraction to nonviolent resistance, Fiedler felt young men exploring "the possibility of heroism without violence," something that pre-nuclear generations of men would have found contradictory. This amounted to nothing less than an "abdication from traditional maleness."

Beneath the psychedelic slogans and radical rhetoric, Fiedler sensed a shifting definition of sexuality. A generation of men and women were infusing political dialogue with personal issues. They were not only against the war, as previous generations of dissenters had been. They seemed to believe that, as Susan Sontag put it, "it's the whole character structure of modern American man, and his imitators, that needs overhauling ... That rehauling includes Western 'masculinity,' too."

Initially, women in the antiwar movement followed male leadership just as women Republicans followed their party bosses. No one talked about sexism. The problems were the war, or the military-industrial complex, or capitalism. Men who declared themselves opposed to these evils were therefore good men, and women activists dutifully worked with them. But an awareness slowly grew among women that sexuality cut much deeper than politics. By the mid-sixties, the apparent unity of men and women activists had begun to crack.

In 1964, women challenged the leadership of the Student Nonviolent Coordinating Committee (SNCC). The leaders of SNCC, charged the dissident women, ran the organization under the "assumption of male superiority [which is] as widespread and deep rooted and every bit as crippling to the woman as the assumptions of white supremacy are to the Negro." Their male colleagues in the civil rights movement did not want to listen. To talk about sex, they replied, only deflected energy from the "deeper" issue of race.

In the antiwar movement, the situation was similar. Antiwar men seemed to have the same ideas about women as the men who supported the war. The Port Huron Statement, for example, was in one respect just like the Democratic party platform: it was written by men. Though Tom and Casey Hayden worked side by side with equal determination, it was Tom Hayden who became well known while Casey remained anonymous (until later, as a feminist, she began speaking for herself).

The draft resistance, one of the more heroic forms of protest, was directly involved with sexuality. Before, only men could go to war; now, only men could go to jail. Women who said "yes to men who said no" found themselves caught in a male-dominated world. If abandoning the draft card was "the first act of freedom," as one 1967 resistance statement put it, then women had no way to free themselves.

Feminists recognized with dismay that antiwar men could be just as sexist as any other men. While the men of the New Left were proud that they had turned against "the John Wayne thing" of the Green Berets, the women were struck by how much of it they had retained. Encircled by national guardsmen at an antiwar demonstration, Jane Lazarre recalled feeling different, not only from the soldiers, but from her father, husband, and son, who all stood beside her. "In some small and strange way they were closer to those soldiers than I was. They were a part of the game ... My father and James [her husband] were there to march for peace. Yet I sensed an acceptance of the violence they abhorred, a comfort at least with its existence. I wondered if I would be able to protect my son from a fascination with that masculine reality."

In every major poll relating to the war during the late sixties and seventies, the results were the same. Women were more strongly opposed to war than men. With rare exceptions (such as the wives of men missing in action), the feminine force in the Vietnam debate was overwhelmingly on the side of peace. Joan Baez, Jane Fonda, Shirley MacLaine — behind these publicized stars were thousands of women who violated the sexual etiquette of war and entered the antiwar battlefield. Whether at a rally or a march, a sit-in or a teach-in, these women did not consider war simply men's business. They knew it was their business, too. Born after Hiroshima, they knew they had been living on the "battlefield" every day of their lives. When the next war came, men were not going to protect them. In their bones, they knew war had changed.

For these young men and women alike, the link between masculinity and militarism was broken. Nuclear weapons had made the link brittle, and the Vietnam war had made it come apart. Although trained through girlhood to revere the soldier and despise the deserter, many women suddenly reversed their affections. Their instinct for survival adapted to the nuclear age. As always, they wanted men who would protect them, not endanger them. And so the subterranean sexual meaning of war slowly shifted. Women searched for a different kind of husband and planned to raise a different kind of son.

Black Americans, meanwhile, were waging a similar struggle with traditional images of masculinity. Perceptive black men had been diagnosing the ills of white masculinity for generations. Along with the Indians, they were its primary victims.

Black men had been deprived of all the cultural, political, and economic supports that white men took for granted. Throughout our history, we white Americans had provided ourselves with a subordinate and (according to us) inferior species. In vast numbers we imported from Africa men with black skins whom we placed in our fields, even in our homes. They were accepted as long as they did not act like free men. Although muddled by the usual historical squabbles, one fact is incontestable: white men forced black men to act like children in order to survive.

"It was the pursuit of manhood," wrote Michelle Wallace in her essay on black macho, "that stirred the collective imagination of the masses of blacks in this country and led them to almost turn America upside down." They wanted to be men — on their own terms. They did not want to become men by becoming "white" but by becoming themselves.

Along with women and blacks, the poor were also restless. They no longer were willing to feel like second-class citizens simply because they had less money. Just as sex and race were affected by the revolt against the old masculine images, so was class. The old archetypes had been based on the white man's power, not only over women and other races, but over other white men as well. A lawyer or doctor or executive could feel superior to a factory worker because he was a better Breadwinner, a more educated Expert. Money validated this masculine one-upsmanship. The professional might earn five or even twenty-five times more money than the worker for the same hours of labor. Despite democratic rhetoric to the contrary, men tended to look up to those who earned the most for their labor and down on those who earned the least. The men at the top were models of manhood. According to the Horatio Alger myth of money and manhood, any man in the working class was somehow lacking in manly virtues. If he had had those virtues, he would have climbed the ladder to success.

In the sixties, this too was challenged. Both culturally and politically, many of the sons and daughters of the elite identified with the disenfranchised. They wanted to overcome the distance they had been trained to maintain between themselves and the working class.

In one of the most revealing documents of that era, "The Negro Family: The Case for National Action," Daniel Patrick Moynihan described the "special quality about military service for Negro men." The military is "an utterly masculine world, a world away from women, a world run by strong men of unquestioned authority." Every man needed the army, according to Moynihan. But black men especially needed it because their masculine self-image was so impaired. Moynihan slid across his own rhetoric. Whenever any group of men, black or white, failed to fit the patriarchal model, it was assumed that something was wrong with them. The model itself was not questioned. The military symbolized the great masculinizing force. For men who deviated from the masculine norm, the white establishment prescribed a quick cure: military service.

Now, as then, the military is a focal point of sexual politics. The power to make men soldiers is the government's single most powerful tool for shaping young men's masculinity. Neither the draft nor its successor, the volunteer army, can be understood strictly as a military matter. Like the tax issue of who will pay, the military question of who will fight evokes the sexual, racial, and class contradictions of our society.

The movement against the draft still comes to life whenever the idea of the draft is resurrected. When President Jimmy Carter called for draft registration in 1980, demonstrations began immediately. "One, two three, four," chanted the demonstrators of the eighties, "we don't want your macho war!" In July, one young draft resister sent the President an open letter. "I hereby inform you, Mr. President," wrote twenty-year-old James Douglas Peters,

> that I will not register ... We have tried militarism, and it has failed the human race in every way imaginable. Only by reversing the process of militarism can we hope to preserve our planet and our species. If we do not, if we continue behaving like barbaric violent cavemen of our prehistoric past, rather than relying on our evolved ability to reason, then sooner or later ... someone will push the button and terminate life on this planet.

This shift in masculine consciousness posed a problem for the American government. White, middle-class, educated men like Jim Peters did not want to become soldiers. So the "All-Volunteer Force" was invented. Instead of drafting a cross section of American men, the military would rely exclusively on volunteers. Translated into socio-economic reality, this meant a military force largely composed of the poor, the less educated, and racial minorities. Using increased pay and benefits, military planners tried to compete with civilian jobs. Since they could not inspire service from the privileged, they intended to buy it from the underprivileged. They abandoned the principle that it was every man's duty to serve his nation. Instead, military service became a job like any other. If a man could get better pay and benefits in uniform than out, he considered volunteering.

An ideal was replaced by a commercial. Although some ad campaigns still depict adventure and excitement, the military's public relations men became more practical. The modern army ads spell out salary, educational opportunities, vacations, and other down-to-earth data. So they say less about manhood, more about fringe benefits.

But the attempt to purchase armed forces with dollars alone has not worked. Whether liberal or conservative, observers concur that the volunteer force is a failure. Money has not breathed new life into the anachronistic image of the Soldier.

"We've got to find the motivator," said the navy's deputy personnel director, Rear Admiral Carl J. Siberlich. Faced with the highest desertion rate the navy had ever seen, Siberlich asked, "Who are the guys out there who want to go to sea?"

The army faces the same dilemma, even among its officers. At West Point, a visiting journalist asked a group of Vietnam-generation cadets, "What do you think you will be doing in the army in ten years?" The cadets laughed uncomfortably. "Look," one of them said, "there isn't a single member of the junior class who is going to stick with the army after a five-year commitment . . . Who needs it?" Said another, "There aren't any heroes anymore."

Even established officers are losing morale. One out of every six army colonels selected to command troops turned down the opportunity because it would have interrupted their lives too much. It is further evidence that the armed services are confronting, as the *Washington Post*'s George C. Wilson observed, "the radically changed value system among the young who fight the wars." When Wilson asked the nation's top-ranked soldier, army chief of staff General E. C. Meyer, why so many carefully screened officers were now turning down command posts, Meyer replied, "The biggest change in the value system is the working wives; I really don't see the near-term solution to that." Army wives, it seems, are no longer willing to be shipped around the world at the Pentagon's whim. Their officer-husbands chose loyalty to their wives over loyalty to the Soldier.

But the influence of changing images of masculinity has been even more directly felt by the military. When President Carter inaugurated the eighties by reinstituting the draft, his action had an unprecedented twist: women were included. Debate exploded because a raw nerve had been exposed. The cover of every news magazine portrayed women soldiers. *Parade* magazine splashed the headline "Should U.S. Women Kill?"

Confusion ran so deep that feminists themselves were divided. Some thought that women's military service would help to overcome women's second-class status. "There is simply no way to move ahead without taking the risks of equality," argued columnist Ellen Goodman. "If we refuse this strange 'opportunity,' we step backward." But others disagreed. "If equal rights is all about insisting that women should be as warmongering as men, we've blown it," said Congresswoman Patricia Schroeder.

Whatever position they had taken on the political spectrum, men and women were enveloped in confusion. The question of who should make war perplexed us all. The Supreme Court finally decided in 1981 that the male-only draft was constitutional. But this opinion, too, was an exercise in anachronism. The (then) all-male justices wrote as if Hiroshima had never happened, as if combat happened only to a few people on some faraway battlefield. They continued to pay homage to the Soldier because nothing has effectively replaced him.

Like other masculine archetypes, the Soldier could not be dislodged by weekend consciousness-raising workshops, dissolved by psychedelic rituals, exorcised by exotic mantras, or banished by New Age idealism. Soon the most Pollyanna-like prophets of the New Age were lamenting its demise. The world, said *Greening of America* author Charles Reich, was "silently changing . . . people who had looked so beautiful were gone . . . The world was becoming savage."

In fact, what happened was not a regression. It was merely the recognition that no new image of man had been constructed. A new culture cannot be built only on negation and dissent. It requires affirmation and leadership.

7 **Politics**

Beyond Hard and Soft

The world has a need to develop more thoughtful
and wise leaders; that is more pressing than the
need to develop impressive and extensive weapons.
— Lloyd S. Etheredge, *A World of Men,*
1978

IN LATE 1979, Secretary of State Cyrus Vance had much on his mind.
The shah of Iran was homeless. The SALT talks needed attention.
Relations with the Soviets were deteriorating. Concerns about nu-
clear proliferation were growing. Trouble was brewing in Central
America and the Middle East.

Despite these weighty problems, Secretary Vance took the time
to send out a directive to all the U.S. embassies and consulates
around the world concerning homosexuality.

TO ALL DIPLOMATIC AND CONSULAR POSTS: PRIORITY

INFORM CONSULS: VISAS

SUBJECT Section 212(a) (4) of INA: Homosexuals

The legislative history of the term "sexual deviation" clearly and un-
equivocally contemplates the inclusion of homosexuals. The Congres-
sional mandate to exclude remains effective.

Secretary Vance felt compelled to reaffirm this section of the Immi-
gration and Naturalization Act (INA) because the U.S. Public
Health Service had recently decided that homosexuality is not a medical condition. Gays, according to the Public Health Service, are not
"sick." Confusion reigned, but with his directive, the secretary of state
put the matter straight. The Carter administration upheld the tradi-

tional interpretation of the law. Foreigners who are gay were forbidden to enter the United States of America.

I hardly noticed the news story about Vance's action. But to a gay man named Barry Capron it mattered a lot. Born and raised in America, Capron moved to Holland several years ago where he developed a successful acting career. In order to continue working there, he became a Dutch citizen. But his family, and his heart, remained in America. When Capron read about Vance's ruling, he was outraged. It meant that he could not go home.

I would not have known about him except for a coincidence. His parents, who live nearby, held a press conference to protest the government's action. After listening to Barry's mother, I wanted to know why "the greatest country on earth," to use every President's favorite phrase, was so afraid of men who made love with men.

A few weeks later, I visited Capron at his home in Amsterdam. A tall, thin, good-looking man with a crown of blond curls, he lived by himself in a simply furnished apartment. Posters on the walls highlighted his acting career.

"When I grew up in America, I always heard about 'the melting pot.' But I grew up with the clear feeling that I had to choose," he said. "Either I was a heterosexual, red-blooded American, or I was a faggot. There was a fork in the road, and every man had to choose one road or the other."

Did he find the atmosphere different in Holland?

"Absolutely. I'll give you an example," he said. "I was at the butcher's the other day. He's a typical Dutchman, quite conservative. 'I saw you in the papers,' he said to me. He had seen an article about how I was fighting the Vance thing. 'Well,' he said, 'I just want you to know that my wife and I are one hundred percent behind you.' Now that just doesn't happen in America. Back home, either you're a real man or you're not. Here, you can just be yourself."

Instead of hiding his sexual preference, Capron had gone to the American consulate and informed them that he was a homosexual. "Just act normal and don't make an issue out of it," the consular official told him. But Capron refused to lie about himself. On January 16, 1980, his visa to enter the United States was canceled.

"The Carter administration preaches human rights to others," Barry wrote to his family, but it "does nothing to eliminate such glaring injustices in American law."

I sympathized with Capron and told him so. But I said I was not surprised that American politicians had refused to change the statute. The world faces crises far more pressing than whether or not a few homosexuals can enter the United States. Capron and his parents could not expect Speaker of the House Thomas P. (Tip) O'Neill or Senator Edward M. Kennedy to respond to their pleas for help. Politicians, I thought, were too busy.

"Let me show you a letter that the Dutch Parliament sent to the American Congress," Capron answered, handing me a letter addressed to the House of Representatives, dated January 1980, and signed by 132 out of 150 members of the Dutch Parliament:

> Information has reached us that your country's State Department has ordered that visas should not be issued to non-Americans who consider themselves to be homosexuals . . . We find this deeply disturbing. We had thought that such regulations could not arise in our times . . . A country which claims to value so dearly a respect for human rights all over the world, by acting in this way, is acting directly contradictory to the same necessary respect for human rights.
>
> We consider the right of each individual to experience his or her own sexuality in his or her own way as a matter which belongs to a person's private domain, and as such is an undeniable right of every person.

The letter was never answered.

When America excludes any group, even communists, some congressman will always step forward and defend the cause of freedom. But around the issue of homosexuality there is an almost unbroken silence. Only a few political leaders seem willing to stand up for this sexual minority.*

This is hardly a mystery. Congressmen do not need sophisticated polls to tell them that standing up for gays does not win votes. The New Right would call any politician who did so soft on homosexuality and would target him for defeat in the next election. A con-

---

* Senator Alan Cranston and Congressman Anthony Beilenson have introduced bills to repeal the statutes excluding homosexuals. Senator Edward M. Kennedy has called for its repeal also. Anne Wexler and Patricia Derian, officials in the Carter administration, favored repeal as part of Carter's human rights policy. The Reagan administration, however, has been silent.

gressman or a senator cannot afford to lose so many votes over such a "peripheral" issue. After all, some voters might come to believe that he himself is deviant. Why should he lose votes just to defend the rights of Barry Capron? Why should "real men" speak out for "queers"?

This is how unfree even free men are. Privately, many congressmen may tell you that the INA statute is abominable. But publicly they are silent. And so it is with many public issues. In theory, this nation's leaders are free to choose their positions on any issue. But in practice, they feel compelled to take the tough or hard position and to shun the soft.

"Makes you wonder about America, doesn't it?" Capron asked.

On the flight home from Amsterdam, I wondered about America's fear of homosexuality. When I was younger, I shared it. Face to face with a man of another race, a man of different political views, a man who had served time in jail, a man who was an alcoholic, I remained sure of myself. But face to face with a man who was gay, I felt uncomfortable. I became conscious of myself and of my own assumptions. I felt threatened.

I no longer felt that way. I had been afraid of homosexuals, I decided, because I had been afraid of a part of myself I did not know. I had been trying to deny a softer, more feminine part of myself. Having recognized and accepted that part of me, I had no reason to be afraid of gays. I knew myself. So I could let them be themselves.

The men who despise homosexuals are the hard-driving, tough-talking, red-blooded Americans who presume that conservative male heterosexuals occupy the moral center of the universe. But the closer I come to such men, the more *their* manhood seems to be the problem. Their desire to dominate is so desperate that the desire dominates them.

In 1972, I wanted to challenge and change American foreign policy. Tired of marching in the streets and writing critical articles, I wanted to enter the government and change our policies. I wanted to stop being a powerless protester and start being effective.

A friend high in the government suggested I apply to the White House Fellow program. Each year a dozen fellows are selected from hundreds of applicants from around the country. These men (and, predictably, a woman or two) serve as special assistants to members of the Cabinet and even to the President himself. I applied, and after rigorous screening and interviews by a regional panel in the Midwest, I was selected as a finalist.

In the spring of 1972, twenty-five of us arrived at Airlie House, an estate in the Virginia countryside frequently used for government retreats, where we would spend a few days in seclusion with the selection committee. On the basis of these final interviews, one out of two would join the inner circle of power.

At my interview, I stared nervously into the impassive faces of several men, including two of President Nixon's most trusted aides. Each of them had before him my dossier, which included an FBI security check into my antiwar activities. After wide-ranging questions, the committee chairman, who served as Nixon's chief head-hunter, put his folder down.

"Let me ask you a question pointblank," he said. "If you were given an order by your superior, would you obey it?"

He was aware, of course, of my resistance to the draft, and he wanted to find out if I had outgrown my rebelliousness. As the stern, squinting man waited for my answer, my mind raced. I knew that if I assured him of my obedience, I might well become a White House Fellow. If I did not so assure him, I certainly would not.

"Yes, sir, I would obey an order," I said. But the words tasted so bitter that I quickly added, "As long as I didn't believe it was morally wrong."

"What you mean," he said, "is that you would *not* obey an order unless *you* happened to agree with it — is that right?"

"That's right, sir. If the order had moral implica——"

"Thank you, Mr. Gerzon," the chairman cut in. "That will be all."

When the envelope embossed with the blue words *The White House* was slipped under my door before dawn the next morning, I knew what it would say. Although in good conscience I could not have acted otherwise, I was bitterly disappointed that I had been rejected. After we returned to Washington, John Ehrlichman held a reception for us at the White House. Within its walls, I sorely wished that I had been a winner instead of a loser.

Like many young men, I had a weakness. I wanted so badly to be initiated into the world of power that I was willing — almost — to forfeit my conscience. To win my manhood, I was prepared to sell myself.

But I chose otherwise. If I had any regrets, they were short-lived. Soon the intrigues of Watergate filled the papers. Those well-scrubbed, clean-shaven white American men with names like Magruder, Kalmbach, Krogh, and Dean began telling us their shabby tales. Before long, Stans, Mitchell, Haldeman, and Ehrlichman added theirs. By then I was far from Washington, a member of a liberal think tank funded by the Carnegie Foundation at Yale University. My colleagues in academe, like most Americans, felt superior to the President's yes men. I did not. I listened to their televised testimony knowing that I was a potential accomplice. Had I answered just one question differently, I might have been among them.

B Y THE BEGINNING of the 1980s, America was engaged in a sexual civil war — not between men and women, but among men themselves. A new word had entered the debate over foreign policy: *macho*. While the Reagan administration called its opponents soft, the administration's critics called it macho.

In early 1979, Richard Reeves had observed the rise of a "macho coalition," a national reassertion of toughness that would settle for nothing less than full-scale preparation for war. Evoking this country's frustration following the Soviet invasion of Afghanistan and the hostage-taking in Iran, Reeves wrote: "When America was America, it wasn't pushed around . . . Are we going to take that *or are we going to act like men?* Fight! That's where the new macho talk may be leading us."

The resurgent need to prove our national virility was impatient with the spirit of détente. We wanted action. Predictably, the 1980 election, like so many that preceded it, was a barrage of tougher-than-thou rhetoric. Jerome Wiesner, a former science adviser to Presidents Kennedy and Johnson, called it "the old arms scare again," and asked for a "reasoned debate about the facts and the options open to us." But the politics of masculinity prevented it. The 1980 election was yet another exercise in bullying. Ronald Reagan rode the macho mood all the way to the Oval Office.

Fearing that we were losing control over the world, Americans rejected the soft peanut farmer and elected the hard cowboy.* As Daniel Yankelovich wrote, the voters "were more than ready to exorcise the ghost of Vietnam and replace it with a new posture of American assertiveness." Reagan played his role to perfection. His hideaway was not a farm (like Carter's) or a beach house (like Nixon's) but a ranch. Every conflict became a test of our national resolve. Vietnam was not a tragic mistake, much less a failure, but a war that the American soldier "was denied permission to win." When he met with Mexico's President López Portillo, he gave a rifle as a gift. The Reagan administration represented an energetic attempt to return to the "John Wayne thing." It hoped that young men would once again idolize the Soldier. As Lieutenant Colonel James Hunt, coordinator of army ROTC programs, put it during Reagan's first year in office: "A lot of these kids don't remember Vietnam — that helps us a lot."

The Soviets, meanwhile, turned our macho rhetoric against us. Calling America's bellicose behavior intellectual and political cowardice, the Soviet scholar and Politburo member Georgy Arbatov scolded the Reagan administration. He told them that it takes "much more political courage to face realities [than to find] refuge in machismo."

Even America's European allies were concerned. The British, the French, and the West Germans were all alarmed at Washington's enormous reliance on military threats as the foundation of American diplomacy. The Europeans told the Reagan administration that mili-

---

* When a reporter once asked Carter if he had rejected the macho tradition of previous presidents, he replied by contrasting himself to his predecessors. Unlike Gerald Ford, whose use of military force during the *Mayaguez* incident resulted in the unnecessary loss of American lives, Carter claimed he "would not feel the need to demonstrate strength through warlike gestures." At the end of his one and only term, Carter would highlight his achievement: no American had died in combat.

But peace did not appease the macho coalition. Carter was swamped by this tidal wave of toughness. His triumphs — forging an agreement between Israel's Begin and Egypt's Sadat at Camp David and relinquishing control over the Panama Canal — were both peaceful victories. They did not answer the need for conquest. One retired army officer, pleading for ratification of the Panama Canal Treaty, lamented, "What do those opposed to the treaties want? Do they want to reject the treaties to keep the canal labeled American to display our national virility?" Unfortunately for Mr. Carter, the answer was yes.

tary approaches, while important, should be kept in balance with political and economic solutions. They felt called upon to forewarn the new American President that geopolitical diplomacy, unlike grade-B Westerns, requires more than a six-shooter in one's hand.*

European protesters, horrified that Reagan's bellicose attitude toward the Soviet Union would lead to nuclear war, called him "the neutron cowboy." Suddenly, the word *cowboy* was everywhere. Reagan was the new "cowboy hero," said one political scientist. He was experimenting with "cowboy economics," said another. "In the age of space travel," wrote the economist Kenneth Boulding bitterly, ". . . we have landed in what future historians may well call the first cowboy administration." In Reagan's world view, observed former Undersecretary of State George Ball, "Diplomacy is for sissies." Columnist Mary McGrory echoed, "Peace is sissy stuff at the White House." Reagan saw himself as "the last warrior," editorialized the *New York Times*, "rooted in the romanticized America of Western movies." Reagan was fashioning, complained a *New Republic* writer, a "John Wayne foreign policy."

Even though the Reagan administration publicly denied these charges, it privately acknowledged them. "Everybody got his rocks off on Poland and demonstrated their masculinity in their recommendations to the President," said Secretary of State Alexander Haig, in remarks later leaked to the press.

The old archetypes reasserted themselves because no new ones had taken root. Men reverted to the familiar, if anachronistic, images of masculinity because they did not know where else to turn. Faced with an apparent choice between being soft or hard, the safest course in a troubled world seemed obvious.

---

* Like father, like son. As the grownups grew more bellicose, the sale of war toys boomed. The market for kids' weapons had been depressed for several years following the Vietnam war. Sears, Roebuck stopped advertising them, and parents stopped buying them. But by the end of the seventies, the sale of war toys began to rise almost as fast as the Pentagon's budget. According to the Toy Manufacturers Association, the revival followed the hostage-taking in Iran and the Soviet invasion of Afghanistan. Overall, sales skyrocketed. By decade's end, one company in the $25 million-a-year war toys business was pleased to report the return of a "growing subculture for war games." And Sears, Roebuck's Christmas catalogue resumed advertising war toys as fitting presents to give on the birthday of the Prince of Peace. For young and old, macho revival had begun.

The choice itself was false, for once a policy decision is cast in such terms, each decision-maker's masculinity becomes involved. In his study *A World of Men,* MIT political scientist Lloyd S. Etheredge examined what he called "the private sources of American foreign policy." He conducted lengthy interviews with more than a hundred male State Department officials as well as with a comparison group at the Pentagon and at the Office of Management and Budget (OMB). As anyone aware of twentieth-century history would agree, Etheredge concluded that there is a "darker side to heroic ambition." In particular, he found that the more active and powerful a man considers himself, the more likely he is to perceive Soviet foreign policy as aggressive and expansionist. Etheredge found that many of the men wanted to ensure America's world role "of being protector, a leader ... a provider," in order to bolster their own self-image. His conclusions are chilling:

> Major beliefs about the Soviet Union arise partly from the imagination of the decision maker himself and may often tell more about the decision maker than about the Russians ... the personality makeup of presidents and foreign policy elites contains those ingredients — and in significant measure — that make war more likely.

Those most enamored of being hard were, not surprisingly, to be found at the Pentagon. It was there that Etheredge found the greatest portion of men who had what he called "a Walter Mitty view of themselves — striving, heroic, grandiose." For example, when he asked his interviewees whether they would have favored the Bay of Pigs invasion, four out of five at the Pentagon said yes, far more than at the State Department or at OMB.

Etheredge's study is certainly not the final word on the policies of masculinity. It is only a modest beginning. But he established beyond doubt one basic fact: men bring their own personal doubts and insecurities into policy-making. The more unconscious those personal factors are, the more dangerous they are. If we reflexively choose the hard option, not because it is the best one but because it matches our masculine imagery, we are no longer making decisions freely. We are merely acting out an ancient, now lethally dangerous, drama.

It is not only foreign policy decisions that have been influenced by masculinity. Policy alternatives in many areas tend to be described as hard or soft, tough or weak. Although most policy-makers are not aware of it, these terms trigger predictable, less than rational responses. Even complex, technical subjects such as energy or economics have been cast in these pseudo-sexual molds.

Debate about American energy policy, for example, has polarized into hard versus soft. As described by Amory Lovins, the hard path would lead to increased consumption of coal, oil, gas, and uranium converted into premium energy forms (liquid fuels and electricity) by large, complex, and centralized plants. The soft path would lead to reliance on renewable resources (sun, wind, and farm and forestry wastes) converted into usable energy by smaller-scale, simpler technologies. Even before Lovins christened the two divergent approaches, the two sides had already formed opposing armies. Pro-nuclear advocates of hard energy sources derided those who believed in alternative technologies as fuzzy-headed and emotional. Anti-nuclear proponents of the soft path mocked their adversaries' blind faith in nuclear technology and pleaded with them to respect rather than to dominate the earth. The lines were drawn. Margaret Mead, for one, warned that the terms "hard" and "soft" were sexually loaded and might polarize the debate still further by arousing "anxieties in the middle-aged men that run the world." But her warning went unheeded. Sexual politics soon clouded the energy debate as much as it had foreign policy.

Even economic debates had sexual overtones that crept into discussions about unemployment. It was soft to provide jobs or job training, hard to tackle the problem by trying to strengthen the economy and in turn create more jobs. Regarding affirmative action, it was soft to spend time and energy to find outstanding women candidates for job openings; it was hard to speak of preserving standards and to warn against reverse discrimination. Similarly, regarding welfare, it was soft to be concerned about how the poor would survive on so few benefits, hard to suggest that food stamps and nutrition programs could be cut back.

Not surprisingly in a decision-making system populated almost entirely by men, advocates of the hard position — on foreign policy, energy, economics, or whatever the issue — had the upper hand. But the number of women with a feminist perspective as well as the number of sympathetic men had increased to the point where the hard position no longer won by default. It now had opposition. In the skirmishes that broke out in virtually every institution — from the armed services to the universities, from churches to banks, from state houses to news rooms — sexual politics emerged into the glare of public debate.

To grasp fully the level of real resistance to women as leaders, there is no better exercise than to imagine a woman as President of the United States.

In America, we take the idea of a woman President as little more than a joke. We are not as crass as the Nazis, who blatantly defined their regime as a "masculine movement." We are more civilized. We consider the possibility of a woman President in the same light as we might imagine a woman playing center on a football team: not impossible, but self-defeating.

We wouldn't even know what to call her. Mrs. President? Every time someone referred to her spouse as the First Husband, the laughter would be deafening. And how could she be commander in chief, having had no military experience? Lacking the aura of John F. Kennedy's PT boat or Carter's nuclear subs, she would be, quite literally, defenseless.

Chronically worried about whether our nation is strong, Americans would find the prospect of a woman President troubling. Picture her behind the lectern of a televised presidential debate. The closest she has come to a battlefield was on a family outing to visit Gettysburg. The only uniform she has ever worn was while playing clarinet in her high school band. Should she outflank her male opponent by becoming a hawk? Should she parry his innuendoes that she cannot grasp the stark realities of war by invoking her experience in domestic affairs? Or should she attempt the unprecedented, arguing that she can deal with military issues more objectively? Should she claim that she, unlike most men, is not consumed by the need to prove her aggressiveness and toughness? ("Stress your military experience," her opponent's advisers would no doubt tell him. "Make the American people feel scared about the idea of a woman as commander in chief. You can really screw her on the defense issue.")

The first woman presidential candidate would be trapped in a maze of anti-female double binds. If she were single, she would have to break two barriers at once: one against a woman President, the other against an unmarried one. She might attract some free publicity by dating a dashing young senator or an eligible Hollywood superstar, but the price would be exorbitant: gossip. Given the security and publicity issues involved, a courtship by any presidential candidate is almost impossible, and a courtship by a female one absolutely impossible. Hard-working celibacy would not be an option, either. Americans want their nuns in convents, not in the White House. Meanwhile, the cartoonists would depict her as dowdy if she dressed plainly, as a sex kitten if she dressed well. Heaven help her if she sunbathed.

If a woman presidential aspirant were married, her problems would be just as great. Would her husband play only a ceremonial, supportive role, like the typical First Lady? If so, he would be pitied. Would he be given substantive policy roles? If so, the President and her husband would almost certainly find themselves having to deny the charge that it was he, not his elected wife, who decided certain policies.

Single or married, the first woman President would endure criticism that would cut more deeply precisely because it would be double-edged. In addition to the usual attacks by the party out of power, she would be challenged by the sex out of power. Her leadership would be analyzed in terms of sexual as well as partisan politics. If she encountered dissent within her predominantly male Cabinet (as most presidents do), some of her critics would say that women do not have leadership qualities. If she vacillated on complex issues (as most presidents do), they would say that women are indecisive. If she engaged unsuccessfully in arms control negotiations with the Soviet Union (as most presidents do), they would say that women aren't tough. If she relied heavily on her male Cabinet or staff, they would say she was dominated by her advisers. And so on.

Even though the Senate, the House, and even the White House would still be overwhelmingly in male hands, men would fear that they had been displaced. They would decry the dawning of an era of matriarchy. The unrelenting probing of her behavior, both publicly and privately, would reach a level so intense that it might prove intolerable. But if male resistance prevented her administration from working effectively and she decided not to run for reelection (or even resigned), it would not prove that the first woman President had failed. It would prove that we had failed her.

Confusion in America about leadership runs deep. Simply putting women behind more desks, while necessary, will not solve the problem. "The Leadership Crisis in America: Are Women the Answer?" asked a *Ms.* magazine cover story on the eve of the 1980 election. "Concern about the lack of competent, high-principled leadership seems to crop up in every discussion and public opinion poll," observed the editors. "Obviously, women could provide the largest pool of untapped talent."

Unfortunately, women are just as confused about leadership as men. The women's movement claimed to want to have more women in power, and yet at the same time it was often anti-leadership. In another article in the same issue of *Ms.*, Charlotte Bunch wrote that this anti-leadership bias "often hampered the growth of women by burying female talents within group anonymity, and reinforcing stereotypes of women's weakness." Once a woman became a star, she was often charged with selling out.

The leadership crisis cannot be reduced to sexuality. A woman who is judged (and therefore compelled to perform) according to traditional masculine standards will make little difference. Only when the numbers of women in leadership positions become great enough will they begin to make an impact on the way society works. In the short run, observed Susan Sontag, women will gain access to power individually. But in the long run, as their numbers grow, women will be "contributing to a transformation of power itself."

But what about men? If some feminist writings are to be believed, the only question that matters is how quickly women gain access to power. In fact, how men act as leaders will continue for the foreseeable future to have the most powerful impact on public life. The "transformation of power itself," as Sontag called it, will not be a result simply of women rising to the top. It will come about only if men change too. Now our leaders are stuck in the semiconscious swamp of hard versus soft, strong versus weak. Waist deep in sexual politics, they have lost sight of the real choices: fair versus biased, humane versus callous, effective versus wasteful, and so on. They care more about appearing manly than about actively leading.

It is unlikely, despite the boasts of our leaders, that they will develop long-term solutions to any of the domestic and international problems our nation faces. They will try so hard to look tough and hard-nosed that they will not perceive policy issues accurately. In his memoirs of the Nixon years, former Secretary of State Henry Kissinger called this macho element "the paranoid cult of the tough guy." Until our government is free from this cult, we are not free. As James Fallows said, "The cause of rational discourse . . . is served when these extrarational pressures are admitted and explored, rather than left concealed. The effect they can have when concealed is stupendous."

If we are to prosper, much less have peace, we cannot allow these "extrarational" factors to continue to cloud decision-making. Our survival depends on the emergence of a new kind of leader, who has worked not only for power, but for self-awareness. These leaders would not automatically adopt the hard position; nor would they automatically assume that being soft would work. On the contrary, they would transcend these pseudo-sexual alternatives. They would move beyond hard and soft and bring *all* their sensitivities to bear on the tasks of leadership. They would not reenact an anachronistic masculine role. They would be free, at last, to act.

PART II

In Private

WE HAVE MET the Frontiersman and the Soldier; next we encounter the Breadwinner, the Expert, and the Lord. But all these images overlap and reinforce each other. Within our psyches they are virtually interchangeable. The five archetypes are meditations, five paths by which to explore ourselves more deeply.

For good reason this book focuses on masculine archetypes, not feminine. Shelves of books in most bookshops are devoted to exploring women's consciousness, while only a handful comment on men's. But now, as we turn to the private lives of men, we must be careful that our focus on masculinity does not mislead us. Men are not to blame for all human anguish, just as they are not to be credited with all human achievement. They share responsibility with women. Sons have mothers, brothers have sisters, boy friends have girl friends, husbands have wives. Whatever occurs between the sexes ultimately requires the collusion of both.

For men to be Frontiersmen, women have to follow in their footsteps. Women must match the Soldier's exaggerated toughness with their own exaggerated fragility. And, as we shall see, women need to complement the Breadwinner's arrogance with their dependence, the Expert's authority with their docility, and the Lord's self-righteousness with their devotion.

No purpose is served by blaming one sex for the other's pain. The point should not be to assign blame but to alleviate pain. Any person whose senses are not dominated by ideology knows that both sexes can be victims and both can victimize. Men can hurt women; women can hurt men. It is our shared responsibility to break the pattern.

⑧ The Breadwinner

Images of Family

> Only if we perpetuate the habit of speaking
> about "the position of women" in a vacuum will
> we fail to recognize that where one sex suffers,
> the other sex suffers also.
> —Margaret Mead, *Male and Female,*
> 1949

IN MARY LAVIN'S short story "Lilacs," an old man, Phelim Malloy, provides for his wife and two daughters by selling manure. The dunghill, located in the corner of their small yard, produces such a foul odor that his wife and his daughters complain constantly.

"But if it could be put somewhere else," suggests his wife, Ros, "and not right under the window of the room where we eat our bit of food."

"What I don't see," interjects his daughter Kate, "is the need for us dealing in dung at all."

His daughter Stacy says nothing; she is in bed with a headache, which afflicts her every Wednesday, when a fresh load of manure is dumped. She wants to have lilacs in the yard and get rid of the smelly muck altogether.

But when Malloy suddenly dies, Ros takes over the manure trade. To her daughters' amazement, she argues that they must keep the dunghill where it is. It is their only livelihood.

Soon afterward, unaccustomed to the heavy work, Ros passes away. It is then that Kate, who is concerned about her dowry, leaps to the dung's defense. Then Kate marries, and Stacy becomes the sole mistress of the house. The first thing she plans to do, she tells the family lawyer enthusiastically, is to plant a few lilac trees and get rid of the dunghill.

"But what will you live on, Miss Stacy?" asks the lawyer. And there the story ends.

Poor Phelim Malloy! For decades he made a living that permitted his wife to live comfortably and his daughters to go to boarding school. And he worked knee-deep in manure for most of his adult life. Neither I nor my friends have such malodorous occupations. Our wives and children live with lilacs, not dung. What we have in common with Phelim Malloy, however, is that our families are becoming aware of how our occupations detract from their lives. They want us to work, of course, but they want us to be husbands and fathers too.

Perhaps if I had lived a generation earlier, I could have seen the commuter train that I rode every weekday for more than three years as a symbol of my worldly success. But times have changed. My wife expected to see her husband and expected me to see my children. And I expected it too. Therein was the dilemma. No matter how I stretched myself, I could not be a father *and* a breadwinner.

So the commuter train became, instead, a symbol of my dilemma. In the morning, I would catch the 7:44 or the 8:12. The first would bring me to the office before most of my colleagues; the second, only after everyone else was hard at work. Whenever I could, I took the 8:12. That way I could at least say good-morning to my children.

I would leave the office between five and six, while many of my colleagues were still at work. An hour would pass before I was home. My sons, then both under five, would already have eaten dinner by the time I arrived.

I wanted to be with them, and they wanted to be with me. But it was the end of their day and time for bed. "They're tired," my wife would say to me. "Better let them sleep." Of course, she was right. And yet my day with them, and theirs with me, was just beginning.

I was also tired, quick to lose my temper, and hungry. After several years of this shuttlecock schedule, I was confused too. I was making a living, my wife was taking care of the kids (and teaching part-time), and the children were growing up. We were all doing what we were supposed to do, but it was not working — not for me, not for my wife, and not for our children.

We are among the lucky ones. My income is higher and my schedule more flexible than most. I miss fewer events in my children's lives than, for example, my friend George, a foreman at a nearby factory. George wants to see his son play football after school "more than anything else in the world," he tells me. His son plays quarterback on his junior high school team, but George has yet to see a game. When the traffic is good, he catches part of the last quarter (by which time the coach has put in the second-string quarterback). When the traffic is bad, his son is already showering in the locker room.

"Paul set a school passing record, but I never saw him complete a single pass," says George. "Again and again I apologized: 'Gee, Paul, sorry I missed the game.' He used to say, 'That's okay, Dad,' but now he just grunts."

George has stopped trying. Paul has stopped caring.

The problem is not limited to clock-punchers. Richard earns twice as much as George but sees his son even less. A sought-after lawyer, Richard reached the top, and stays at the top, by "doing what needs to be done." This means that he may be in Europe or Japan for several weeks or preparing briefs under intense pressure. His job is flexible (at least in theory), so he squeezes out time now and then to watch a baseball game or to reserve a weekend for skiing. But in a competitive world, any time "lost" to family puts his firm at a disadvantage. He may forfeit a client, miss an opportunity, lose the "inside track."

Several years my senior, Richard met me over lunch one day shortly after I had been promoted. I told him how much I regretted missing out on my children's lives. "Welcome to the club!" he replied heartily. Was he sardonically commiserating with me? Or was he genuinely welcoming me to that relatively exclusive professional club whose members' time has such a high market value that they cannot refuse to sell it? I now think he was doing both: congratulating me on my success and forewarning me about its ultimate price. (He is now divorced. His wife has custody of their children.)

I used to think that Carl, a professor of history, had this problem solved. When my wife and I both worked, he and his wife once advised us on how to organize a two-career family. Their method was to take turns. When he was under pressure, she would cut back, and when she had to switch into high gear, he would slow down. It all sounded so simple. Most afternoons, Carl could be seen picking up his daughter at school.

What I did not realize was that this freedom from external encumbrances did not resolve his masculine dilemma. When I talked with him a few months later, he was fuming. He resented other faculty members' subtle but unmistakable jokes. "They have no right to question my allocation of time," he argued. "They prefer leisurely lunches or gossiping in the faculty club to spending time with their own children. But why do they try to impose their priorities on me?"

Beneath his irritation, Carl had his own doubts. Although he had tenure, he still felt the spur of academic competition in his flank. "I'm working at a competitive disadvantage," he said. "How can I convince myself, much less them, that my work is to be taken seriously — that I am producing? Maybe I *am* drifting. If I really cared about this book, if I really thought that it was any good, I wouldn't be leading my life like this."

George, Richard, Carl, myself — we were all struggling with a predicament we could not even name. Once we have families, we cannot afford to take our shoulders from the wheel without being inundated with unpaid bills. There is no time left in our lives to think about it. And even if we thought about it, what good would it do? We have to make a living. We have to support our families. Our only way out, it often seems, is to become so successful that at last we can stop. But then it is too late.

LATE ONE NIGHT, holding high a blazing torch, Daniel Boone went hunting for deer. After waiting for the gleaming light to reflect in the eyes of his prey, he saw a pair of firelit eyes through the underbrush. He raised his rifle but did not fire. Something about the eyes seemed odd. Moving toward them slowly, he finally realized that they were a woman's. She ran away, but according to legend, Daniel soon came courting and made her his wife.

In reality, she was much more than Boone's wife. Nearly as tall as her husband, Rebecca Bryan Boone was a remarkable woman. Single-handedly, and often under harsh frontier conditions, she cared and provided for their children while Daniel was gone for months on various expeditions. When Daniel was kidnapped by the Shawnee, she moved her children hundreds of miles on horseback through hostile Indian territory. When her aging husband was racked by rheumatism, she went hunting and brought back enough game to feed them all. Yet she is depicted in the popular nineteenth-century biographies of the legendary "Col. Daniel Boone" as merely an "amiable Spouse" without any personality of her own. Why, in the legend of

Daniel Boone, was the courage and competence of Rebecca Bryan Boone omitted? One suspects that his early biographers, if given the opportunity, would have erased her from the legend altogether. After all, this is precisely what the writers of frontier fiction did. Their heroes avoided all intimate relationships with women. James Fenimore Cooper's Natty Bumppo, whose life was chronicled in a series of five novels published between 1823 and 1841, *The Leatherstocking Tales,* was perhaps the first American literary figure to become famous abroad as well as at home. He became the symbol of the frontier man for more than one generation of readers. Yet he never once loved a woman. Wedded to the wilderness, accompanied by his loyal friend, Chingachgook, he speaks of heterosexual love as if it were alien to him. When he refers to marriage, it is clear that he considers it a form of captivity. It symbolized "a kind of *emasculation,*" suggested Leslie Fiedler in *Love and Death in the American Novel,* "since the virility of Natty is not genital but heroic and cannot survive in the marriage bed any more than beside the hearth."

To be a hero, then, a man either should avoid becoming entangled with women altogether or should marry a woman who remains obediently in the background. It is as if man becomes heroic by virtue of the distance he places between himself and the feminine.

Whether on the frontier of yesteryear or in the inflationary, urban economy of today, a competent and enterprising woman would be an extraordinary asset. Just as Rebecca's hunting abilities made the Boone family more secure, so today do wives' professional skills enable a family to derive greater rewards from the marketplace and to live more comfortably than would be possible with only a single wage earner.

Yet such a woman has not been highly prized by American men. A woman able to earn enough to support herself and her family did not appeal to us, she threatened us. In a poll conducted in 1946 by *Fortune* magazine, men were asked whether they would prefer to marry a girl who had never worked, one who had been moderately successful in her work, or one who had been very successful. By a wide margin, men preferred the woman of *moderate* success.

Men do not mind a woman who "helps out" or who may "supplement" the family's income. But the notion that one's wife can function just as capably in the marketplace as oneself breeds anxiety. It deprives us of another dimension of heroism — the heroism of The Breadwinner.

The Breadwinner's virtue is equal to his productivity. To his wife and children, he is a hero because he provides for them. To his country, he is a hero because he makes the economy work and grow. The Breadwinner prides himself on his family's material well-being: the more they have, the better a man he is. Even if the Breadwinner's wife works as long and hard as he does, he is nevertheless the provider. If she is employed, he earns more money. If she works as a homemaker, the economy puts money in his pockets and nothing in hers. He can make money; she can only spend it.

In an economy that assumes men are the providers and sets wages accordingly, many women need the Breadwinner. Without him, their lives are strained. Consider the plight of women whose husbands are laid off, or who turn to drink, or who are incapacitated by illness or injury, or who abandon their families and evade child support. The wives of such men consider the Breadwinner to be a model of masculinity without equal. They revere the Breadwinner, the man who brings home a paycheck every week and who works year after year without complaint.

This ideal image of the Breadwinner, however, has been politicized. Instead of inspiring reverence, it triggers debate. Narrow-minded advocates of women's rights declare that the Breadwinner oppresses his wife. According to them, he does not serve his family; he rules over them. He does not take care of his wife; he exploits her. He does not work to provide for his loved ones; he works to achieve success for himself. He is driven by ambition, not love.

Equally narrow-minded men's rights advocates avow precisely the opposite. The Breadwinner is not the oppressor; he is the victim. "My first wife was completely dependent on me," complained one man. "I was always playing a role of some sort. She wanted me to take on three jobs so she could have the kinds of things she wanted."

By placing both arguments side by side, it is clear that they are rationales for rage at the other sex. Fortunately for all of us, the truth is both more complex and more human. As Studs Terkel's *Working* poignantly revealed, most men today do not see themselves as powerful, dominating figures. On the contrary, they portray themselves as struggling to find ways to survive and, if possible, to grow, despite the mounting pressures of making enough money to support themselves and their families.

Our bodies often speak more eloquently than our words. When

the twentieth century began, men could expect to live nearly as long as women. A woman's life expectancy was 48 years, a man's 46. But by the mid-1970s, according to the U.S. Department of Health, Education and Welfare, the average woman could expect to live 76.5 years, while the life expectancy of the average man was only 68.7 years. According to some estimates, by the year 2000, men may die a full decade sooner than women.

"It is time that men . . . comprehend," advised James Harrison of the Albert Einstein College of Medicine, "that the price paid for belief in the male role is shorter life expectancy. The male sex role will become less hazardous to our health only insofar as it ceases to be defined as opposite to the female role . . ."

Of the many lethal aspects of masculinity, none is more so than the pressure of work. What is debilitating is not work itself (the chronically unemployed die earlier than other men), but the anxiety and helplessness of bureaucratic employment. Those who are self-employed or who can run their own shop outlive those who are trapped between superior and subordinate. "Longevity depends less upon fitness or genetic inheritance," observed John Stickney in *Self-Made,* a study of entrepreneurship, "than upon work satisfaction, a quality linked to autonomy."

Some men reject the role altogether. Others defend it as the wisdom of tradition. Both responses are oversimplified. All human societies and all human families face the question of how work is to be divided among its members. Every society and every family must find its own answer. In America, our response has varied enormously over our two-hundred-year history.

In colonial America, women had relatively greater occupational freedom than in some later periods. Colonial women were butchers and gunsmiths. They ran mills and shipyards. They worked as midwives and sextons, journalists and printers. They learned a trade, as did men, through apprenticeship. But in the 1800s, a woman's role narrowed. By midcentury, fewer female shopkeepers and business women were at work than before the Revolutionary War. They might be allowed to indulge in such careers before marriage, but once appropriated by a man in marriage, they were, as Alexis de Tocqueville pointed out, "subjected to stricter obligations" than were women in Europe.

Between these two periods came industrialization, a process in which the "home become *divorced* from the workplace," with femininity identified with the former, masculinity with the latter. Before the Industrial Revolution, both sexes usually worked at home. Indeed, home *meant* work. Although women's tasks were different, they were interdependent with men's. They focused on household care: spinning wool and flax, cooking, preserving and curing, animal care, gardening, and countless other productive tasks. But after the Industrial Revolution, concludes historian Amaury de Riencourt, "the wife as the husband's productive partner and fellow worker disappeared."

Before industrialization, men frequently took responsibility for training boys as young as six years of age. If a boy did not work with his father, he was apprenticed to another man to learn a trade. Accordingly, most child-rearing manuals in colonial America were written for mothers *and* fathers. Because fathers were nearby, working in a family farm or shop, they played a large role in the rearing of their children, particularly their sons. After industrialization, when men went away to a job, their sons could not follow, and child-rearing advice more often was directed to women only. Boys were still expected to be men, of course, but they spent the first decade of their lives in a world in which they rarely saw grown men at work.

This transition to an industrial society was neither immediate nor simple. Not all men left the farms and family-run shops; not all women lost their productive functions. But the shift was nevertheless profound. The home came to be seen, in Christopher Lasch's phrase, as a "haven in a heartless world."

In marriage, the role of the Breadwinner became paramount. The husband-wife relationship was a union of opposites.

SHE WAS:	HE WAS:
family oriented	success oriented
pure	worldly
gentle	aggressive
moral	pragmatic
emotional	rational
delicate	tough
weak	strong

By splitting the national character in half, one feminine and the other masculine, the nineteenth-century family engaged in a holding action against the tumult of history. Women would embody tradition; men would embody change.

Feminist historians have every reason to question this unwritten patriarchal contract that governed the American family. One does not need a lawyer to realize that some of its clauses make it a dangerous document for women to sign. Dare a woman renounce a career so her husband will provide for her? Once a career is foregone, what will assure the quality of his care? Who will guarantee that the contract will be honored? What will happen should the marriage end? Do women want to spend their lives being taken care of by the Breadwinner?

These questions were first raised by early feminists, such as Angelina Grimké, Amelia Bloomer, and Charlotte Perkins Gilman. They are now being posed again by today's feminist historians, economists, and sociologists. But one issue rarely raised is: If women were being discriminated against, what was happening to men? Were they ruthlessly forcing the second sex out of the professions and back into the home? Were they reducing women to economic dependence and domestic isolation in order to ensure their own supremacy? Or were they themselves oppressed, struggling workers caught in the grinding gear of industrialization? Were they merely downtrodden and disillusioned men who sought in women a nurturant refuge from a heartless world?

Some contemporary feminists who have blamed the Breadwinner for relegating women to domesticity do not feel obliged to try to understand men's experience. "What is a man, anyway?" asks the narrator of *The Women's Room*. "Everything I see around me in life tells me a man is he who makes money." She dismisses the question of why men act as they do with ignorance and arrogance: "I don't claim to know, and I don't even care much. I figure that's their problem." Of course, women are entitled to be as indifferent and bitter as they want to be; after all, they have much about which to be angry. But it will not serve their cause. To pretend that men's pain is irrelevant to women is understandable, but unwise. It will not result in equality, much less in intimacy.

Consider, in contrast, the portrait a male historian draws of nineteenth-century American men. "How was a man to be manly?" asked contemporary historian Peter Gabriel Filene, summarizing the insecurity and confusion of men in the closing decades of the century.

"Feminism aroused such furious debate less because of what men thought about women than because of *what men were thinking about themselves.* They dreaded a change in sex roles because . . . they were finding it acutely difficult to be a man. The concept of manliness was suffering strain in all its dimensions — in work and success, in family patriarchy, and in . . . sexuality. The masculine role was uncertain."

Unaccustomed to such expressions of concern for men, some feminists have criticized Filene. In a review of his work, Cynthia Russet wrote, "Many men were antagonized by the very first stirrings of women's rights around 1848, and many of them continued to be hostile thereafter. Are we to assume an uncertainty in the masculine role that extended over half a century? Might the reason be less subtle? Might Victorian males, early and late, perceiving the advantages that accrued to them as 'Lords of Creation,' have simply opposed rocking the boat?"

It is odd that a woman historian would find prolonged masculine uncertainty so hard to accept. After all, for both women *and* men, the economic world was being transformed. To provide for a family, then considered to be a masculine responsibility, was a far different task at the end of the century than at the beginning.

As historian Mary P. Ryan observed, men now labored in "a world gone mad with change, acquisitiveness, and individualism." From countryside to city, from farm to factory, from self-employment to company employee, workers were entering an unfamiliar and often threatening world. The foundations of the marketplace were shifting. While promoting the cult of the true woman, men were becoming enmeshed in its masculine counterpart: the cult of the self-made man. As early as the 1830s, men began to feel the pressure of a new, frustrating, and contradictory definition of success. While fantasizing about the heroic exploits of Daniel Boone or the mythical world of Natty Bumppo, the Breadwinner found himself faced with jobs that were anything but heroic. He was not a solitary figure on the landscape. He was part of an organization that was becoming increasingly complex and bureaucratic. He was not his own boss, but an employee whose livelihood depended on pleasing the man who was.

How, then, was a man to become a success? The hero of Horatio Alger's novels emphasized the importance of dressing neatly and modestly, of being punctual and reliable, of eliminating slang and colloquialism from one's speech. In short, he symbolized "the qualities of character and intellect which make the hero a good employee."

Hero and employee: the words themselves jar when juxtaposed. They seem antithetical, and in Horatio Alger's own life they were. Although we associate his name with virile success, Horatio Alger never married, and he spent his life in boarding houses. The only woman he ever lived with was his sister. He attended Harvard Divinity School and briefly served as minister to a small congregation in Brewster, Massachusetts. He left the ministry for reasons that were, until recently, obscure. In fact, he was accused by a parish committee of "unnatural familiarity with boys." Alger did not deny the charge; he acknowledged that he had been "imprudent" and left.

No wonder men felt insecure. They were caught between the too-good-to-be-true heroes of Horatio Alger and an increasingly bureaucratic reality where only aggressive, often ruthless men could become Carnegies and Rockefellers. "The inner conflict in young Americans between the will for righteousness and the will for success," observed historian Bernard Wishy, "must have been extraordinary." The conflict had a direct impact on masculinity, for it was men who were supposed to climb the ladder of success. They placed on women the burden of being righteous because the burden of success was heavy enough.

As Daniel Boone and Davy Crockett etched their virile exploits in the national consciousness, the workingman in Boston, New York, and Philadelphia was caught in the web of industrial civilization. Coping with rent, work, children, and urban life, he had little reason to feel secure, much less heroic. To have a wife at home who took care of him, and who was grateful for his hard-earned wages, was the least he could expect. Regardless of what his work might be, he could feel manly because only men performed his particular function.

The most reliable method of ensuring the manliness of the Breadwinner's role was to construct an economy in which only men could be providers, which is precisely what we did. From the Civil War to World War II, women were excluded from the work force to a greater degree than either before or since. "The isolation of women from work was a significant phenomenon," concluded the economist Eli Ginzburg, "for only about eighty years" — roughly from 1860 to 1940.

Although Rosie the Riveter led postwar women back into the

economy, women are still unable to be the Breadwinner. Even if they are allowed and sometimes even encouraged to bring a second income into the family's bank account, the economy is structured to ensure their continued dependency on the *real* provider. Compared to men, women earn less money today than they did a quarter-century ago. In 1955, they earned 64 percent of what men earned. Today they earn less than 59 percent. Two thirds of full-time working women earn less than $10,000 a year, and less than 7 percent of all working women are managers. In other words, whether working or not, all but a few women still depend on the Breadwinner.*

This sexual division of labor, however, takes its toll on both men and women. The syndromes are so common that they now have names: women suffer from the "Cinderella complex," men from the "Breadwinner complex." "Women are brought up to depend on a man and to feel naked and frightened without one," wrote Cynthia Dowling. "We have been taught to believe that as females we cannot stand alone, that we are too fragile, too delicate, too needful of protection." To avoid being responsible for themselves (and their offspring) and to avoid the hardships and indignities of working for a living, such women cling to men. Even if the relationship is not emotionally fulfilling, at least these wives have a security blanket to protect them from economic woes.

Except for their unhappiness, men who suffer from the Breadwinner complex have precisely the opposite symptoms. They are addicted to their work. Although it causes physical and emotional strain, they climb the ladder of success as quickly as they can. They feel completely responsible for their families' economic well-being. They are determined to stand alone and to admit to no feelings of weakness or vulnerability. They expect themselves to stand up under the strain. Unable to spend much time or energy on their children, they numb themselves to their fathering role and focus increasingly on their career.

The Cinderella/Breadwinner marriage obviously does not work very well anymore. The husband sees his wife as free from the stress of a job, and envies her; she sees him as having a paying job and social

---

* In 1979, 5.5 million wives earned more than their husbands. This is twice the figure in 1970. All indications are that the number of "Mrs. Breadwinners" will continue to increase.

recognition, and envies him. Both of them, observed Margaret Mead in *Male and Female,* are "dissatisfied and inclined to be impatient with the other's discontent."

Even though men are still considered to be the Breadwinner, the two-career family is now common. Old expectations clash with new realities. The Breadwinner still expects to be greeted by the housewife; the working woman expects her husband to share her domestic duties. The Breadwinner expects his wife to be an old-fashioned mother who bakes bread, while she expects him to be a modern father who shares household chores. With work and home no longer divided neatly between the sexes, problems proliferate. When workers in the late sixties were asked about job-related problems, only 1 percent of the conflicts cited related to the family. By the late seventies, the percentage had risen to 25 percent, and it is still rising.

A typical conflict is that if the Breadwinner is to compete successfully, his wife and children must move when the company wants to relocate him. His wife's career (if any) and friends must be forfeited. The children's school life must be disrupted. The family, like excess baggage, must be crated and shipped to accompany the Breadwinner on his quest for success.

In addition to practical matters are the interpersonal ones. Unrivaled by any nation on earth, America extols competitiveness. The Breadwinner is willing to compete for success against other men, but not against women. For women, competition has been deemed unfeminine. Nineteenth-century child-rearing manuals enjoined parents to have their daughters avoid the "ruder and more daring gymnastics of boys." Never was she to try to swing higher than her friends, to outdo, to excel. Her virtues rested in solidarity, unity, attachment.

As the sexes split, so do the philosophies of work and family. The capitalist marketplace must be competitive, or waste and corruption ensue. The loving family must be cooperative, or animosity and envy take root.

It is a bizarre division of life. Unwieldy and unworkable, the arrangement is bound to produce tension. Competition cannot be worshiped outside the home and banished within it. A world in which men compete and women cooperate is nothing more than a prescription for inequality.

As long as men cast themselves (or are cast by their wives) as Breadwinners, the pressure on them to achieve will be intense. If a man expects to spend the prime of his life single-handedly supporting his wife, his children, and his home, he has locked himself into a role that cannot help but produce physical and psychological stress. In addition to this stress, he may now bear the resentment of his wife, who is trapped in the home, and the alienation of his children, who complain that he is distant. In such a family, the Breadwinner will neither live long nor live happily. Indeed, the family itself may come apart.

Instead of resenting feminists for attempting to rewrite the masculine-feminine contract, we should be grateful. They are challenging a contract that serves us no better than it does them.

⑨ The Expert

Images of Knowledge

Let it not be said, wherever there is energy or
creative genius, "she has a masculine mind."
> — Margaret Fuller, *Women in the
> Nineteenth Century*, 1845

Why is thinking something women never do?
Why is logic never even tried?
> — Professor Henry Higgins in *My Fair Lady*

SEVERAL YEARS AGO, when I first started writing about masculinity, I
considered it simply a subject that I intended to study. I began by
reading American history and assumed that, with enough research,
the pieces would fall into place. It was simply a question of supporting my argument with the relevant facts. If I had written such a book,
I might indeed have known something about masculinity. But I
would have learned nothing about myself.

Life intervened. I was asked to help create, and later to edit, a
global newspaper called *WorldPaper*. It was a challenge that required
all my energy and enthusiasm and took me from Cairo to Colombo,
Bogotá to Beijing. Foolishly, I tried for a few months to work on this
book during nights and weekends. It quickly became clear that I was
losing touch with my children and my wife. That I was trying to write
a book about the meaning of manhood only made it worse. How
could I write about men's changing values at the price of betraying
my own?

It hurt to abandon the book, but I had no choice. For three years,
I thought the only work I was doing on it was to read an occasional
book and to clip relevant articles. But I now realize that I was doing

the most important work of all. I was learning that the subject was part of me. If I merely gathered information, reviewed the literature, organized my facts, and wrote down my findings, I would have been only another specialist who knew everything about his subject except his own stake in it.

Even after I realized the intimate connection between myself and my subject, I still tried to avoid exploring myself. I had illusions about my own masculinity that I did not want to give up, questions about my own behavior that I did not want to ask, and episodes in my own childhood I did not want to remember. The early drafts of this book are a study in self-evasion.

My difficulties, I think, reveal a common masculine dilemma. I was so eager to do my job — that is, to write this book — that I tried to avoid self-exploration. My subject was something "out there," an intellectual wilderness I had to master. It was too frightening to see that the uncharted terrain was inside me.

Why did I put the subject so far from my self? When did I begin to treat my emotions as if they were a liability rather than an asset to my intellect? What led me to divide myself into a part that knows and another part that feels? How had I learned to approach learning this way?

I was trying to answer these questions without success when my wife, Shelley, and I were asked to lead a workshop for high school teachers. Our job was to tell the teachers, who taught courses in family living and child development, about current research and teaching methods concerning sex roles. After spending several evenings planning the workshop, Shelley and I thought we were well prepared.

As soon as we walked into the university seminar room, we realized that we had overlooked one obvious fact: of more than two dozen teachers, not one was male. And we learned, after taking a quick poll, that many of them did not have a single male student in their courses.

It dawned on me that older women were teaching younger women about changes in sex roles. The situation was so extreme that one teacher, whose course included an exercise in making a marriage contract, asked girls to play the role of husbands. She had no choice: the potential husbands were not there to play themselves. They were across the hall in their calculus or economics classes.

"If you can't get young men in your classes, you'll only reach half of the people who need to learn about this," I commented. "Why don't they take the courses you offer?"

"The problem is guidance counselors and parents," one teacher from a big urban high school replied. "They tell the boys not to waste time on these fluff courses. To get into college, they're better off taking math and physics, or even English. Not Family Living."

"At our school," said a teacher from a small private school, "we call the course Personal Survival. We try to teach some of the skills needed to live satisfying adult lives. But we have the same problem: boys won't take it. They want to take courses that will look better on their records."

In high school, I was just like them. I would not have been caught dead in Family Living. It was a mushy course for people with nothing better to do — in other words, girls. When I graduated, my mind was crammed full of facts: grammatical, historical, mathematical. I needed them to get high college board scores. I had never once been asked to study family structures, the pressures on marriage and the reasons for divorce, child rearing and child development, sexuality — or masculinity. These were not considered a necessary part of a young man's education.

College, unfortunately, often only reinforces this one-dimensional education. As a Harvard student in the sixties, I automatically considered myself an independent critical thinker. My classmates and I had no intention of mindlessly accepting tradition. We held that nothing was safe from our scrutiny. Certainly not Harvard. We questioned its relations with the Defense Department, admissions policies, dress codes, financial investments, community relations, racial biases, and everything else. Or so we thought.

As it turned out, I overlooked one issue entirely. I never once wondered why all of my professors were men. I never once considered the implications of being educated at a university that, even a decade later, had a tenured faculty with only 3 percent women.

At the height of the student movement, I wrote a book about the generation gap, published my senior year. I claimed to be writing about youth's dissent, and in some areas I did so thoughtfully. But as the book's opening paragraph revealed, my awareness of women's experience as something different from my own was almost nonexistent. I wrote that I intended to describe the white, middle-class "generation of young people who were born after the Second World War." In the next phrase, however, I unconsciously switched to "young men." The book touches on women's experience only in the sections dealing with sex and marriage — that is, only when it mattered to men.

Today, the masculine mentality of the book is painfully apparent. I assumed that men were at the center of social change, women at the periphery. In retrospect, it is remarkable that no one criticized this shortcoming. The book won recognition from the American Library Association and was praised in newspapers throughout the country; I appeared on the *Today Show* and scores of other talk shows. And no one ever asked me what happened to the half of my generation that was not born male.

I suppose that I was no worse — and no better — than other men. That is why I remained so unaware of my intellectual prejudice against women. It fit. Like so many of my classmates, I arrived in Cambridge with the inbred notion that women were less intellectually motivated, if not less gifted, than we were. I was welcomed by an institution of higher learning that did not permit more than a handful of women to teach. I studied subjects in which men were always the professors and women, at best, section leaders or subordinate instructors. I assumed that women were less high-powered intellectually; certainly they seemed less ambitious and perhaps less capable. This assumption was never challenged during four years of Harvard's expensive tutelage.

When I recently returned to what paradoxically is called my alma mater, I was struck by the difference a decade can make. For the young men who study in those ivy-covered halls, such obtuseness is no longer possible. The Harvard man — and the intellectual style he represents — is being scrutinized. It made me think anew about the old one-liner: "You can always tell a Harvard man, but you can't tell him much." The humor seemed hollow.

"Harvard makes me so damn angry," a member of the interdepartmental Women Students' Coalition told me. "Harvard has an image of intellectual excellence and an image of femininity. The two are incompatible. The intellectual should be confident, aggressive, competitive. The woman should be supportive, helpful, accommodating. If you are a woman intellectual, the contradiction can be excruciating." She felt that men believe the true intellectual is always supposed to have an answer, to be in control. He was never supposed to say in wide-eyed amazement: "Wow, I never thought of that" or "I'm really confused about this." To do so was to admit ignorance and uncertainty. It was to appear vulnerable. For a Harvard man, this was bad form. He was always supposed to appear well informed even when he was not.

If you investigate any particular incident — from a professor's sexual harassment of a female student to the failure of a department to offer tenure to a qualified woman candidate — disputes quickly ensue. The accused professor will say the student acted seductively; the department chairman will say the rejected candidate had a difficult personality.

What is incontestable, however, are the numbers. In October 1980, the Women's Equity Action League (WEAL) filed a complaint against the Kennedy School of Government at Harvard with the Department of Labor's Office of Federal Contract Compliance. The school's dean excused himself with the plea that the school had made every effort at compliance. But he could not deny the numbers. At the time the WEAL brief was filed, the school's faculty consisted of forty-four men and three women.

It is no coincidence that the target was the Kennedy School. Its offices are filled with former and would-be political insiders with far-reaching influence in all the halls of power. The presence of women is inversely related to proximity to power. The number of women declines as one travels up the academic pyramid. Today there are more women than men undergraduates in America's colleges. But men vastly outnumber women among junior faculty. The disproportion is even greater among senior faculty. And at the apex, among the deans of colleges and the heads of departments, women are rarely seen.

A few years ago, Harvard established the Women's Studies Committee. It encouraged faculty members to pay greater attention in their courses to issues pertaining to women. But, as is the custom, the chairman of the committee is a tenured faculty member (that is, male). When I asked the committee's coordinator whether she thought it would make much progress, she sighed. "It's going to be slow. Let's face it," she said. "Most white male faculty members, trained in their disciplines anywhere from fifteen to thirty years ago, are not interested in issues dealing with the study of women. And they are not about to become interested, either."

I wish I could have taken those "white male faculty members" to my tenth reunion last year. They would have been amazed at their former students' discussions. We who had been taught so much about economics and law, who were so well versed in literature and science, who had made names for ourselves in politics and the media, who were now at other schools and universities teaching the next generation — we talked more than anything else about our relations with women. We talked about how unprepared we were to start families, to be fathers as well as workers, to adapt to lovers or wives who were feminists. We talked about how much we had to learn as men, and how much we wished that we had started sooner.

Perhaps the most successful of my classmates is a lawyer in a prestigious New York firm. Everyone marveled at his quick rise in his profession. His brilliance is undisputed. Pitted against lawyers with twice his experience, he came out on top. But when I saw him, his inner sadness was so intense that it could not be concealed by his hearty handshake and greeting. He was in the midst of a divorce. He felt helpless. He had wanted his marriage to work "with all his heart," he told me, but his wife was inexplicably dissatisfied. She complained that he was distant, unresponsive, unreachable.

"She said to me, 'I can't live with a man who lives only in his head,' " he told me bitterly. "Now what the hell does that mean? We make love. We talk. We go out to dinner. What is she after?"

———————

THE ATTEMPT to consign women to intellectual inferiority is nothing new. It is at least as old as Aristotle. "The author of nature," wrote the father of Western logic, "gave man strength of body and intrepidity of mind to enable him to face great hardships, and to woman was given a weak and delicate constitution, accompanied by natural softness and modest timidity, which fit her for a sedentary life."

How did Aristotle know this? He knew it because he was an Expert.

At his best, the Expert pursues the truth — the fabled *veritas*. But at other times the Expert uses his mind to pursue power: power over nature and all its creatures, power over women and other men. Whoever knows more has power. In a technological world, the power of the mind is vital. Knowledge then is a weapon, a political tool. Those who have access to it have power; those who do not are powerless.

Unlike the true seeker of knowledge, the Expert is often more concerned with protecting his power than with establishing the truth. When others disagree, he tends to dismiss them as emotional or irrational. He will say that they do not have the facts or that they are biased. His attitude is condescending. His mind is powerful. It has made him indispensable. He is the Expert; he knows more.

"No person of the feminine sex has ever produced an original scientific work," wrote Auguste de Candolle, one of the first historians of science, in 1885. Woman's poor performance did not result from lack of opportunity. It was caused by the peculiarities of her mind, which "takes pleasure in ideas that are readily seized by a kind of intuition" and to which "the slow method of observation and calculation by which truth is surely arrived at are not pleasing." Woman's mind is also flawed by its "feeble independence of opinion" and its "horror of doubt." She is endowed with a "reasoning faculty less intense than in man." And so Candolle concluded: "These reasons are more than sufficient to explain the position of woman in scientific pursuits."

For centuries the Expert proceeded to defend his biases as objective fact. For decades scientists (that is, white middle-class men) measured the cranium, that exquisite casement of the human brain. After establishing that modern man had a larger brain than primitive man, they began to test other hypotheses. They struggled to establish scientifically that the white race had larger brains than the black, that men had larger brains than women. They assumed that bigger meant better.

They were impressed by the size of the zoologist Cuvier's brain (1830 grams), the novelist Turgenev's (2012 grams), and those of other intellectual giants. But they were shocked when more weighty brains (2269 and 2800 grams, respectively) were discovered that belonged to a retarded London newsboy and to an epileptic idiot.

The Expert revised the hypothesis. If women are not inferior because they have smaller brains, then they are inferior because they have *different* brains. Armed with their cranium counters, the men of science discovered that the frontal lobe — the region of the brain that performs higher intellectual processes — was more pronounced in men. This "proof" of male intellectual superiority was eventually discredited.

The search for differences in the brain continues today. Neurobiologists are now fairly certain that sex differences are caused by the action of hormones during embryonic development. It has long been known that an adult female rat, given male sex hormones soon after birth, will not exhibit typical mating behavior, nor will she ovulate. Similarly, an adult male rat that is castrated early in life will not act like a male even if it is later injected with testosterone, the male sex hormone. With photographs showing the differences between male and female rat brains, specialists now debate whether the differences are parallel in humans.

Assume that the differences exist. Assume, for example, that there are indeed sex differences in the distribution of synaptic connections of nerve cells in the preoptic area of the brain. Or assume, as does Julian Jaynes, that "mental abilities in women are spread over both the left and right hemispheres" and that "psychological functions in women are not localized into one or the other hemisphere of the brain to the same degree as men." Does that make women less or more intelligent than men? Does it render women more or less capable of making a scientific discovery or of running an organization?

The Expert's brilliance, and his blindness, is the paradox of our time. He has created a technological society, a society that has used technical knowledge to create wealth and power of unprecedented proportion. The Expert's technology has transformed every aspect of life: farming, medicine, business, communication, education, even the family. The Expert's domain is the growing knowledge industry, or what the economist John Kenneth Galbraith has called the "technostructure." It is the Expert's intellect, not his physical strength or courage, that makes him a hero. His frontier is knowledge; his weapon is data. His goal is to possess information and skills that are invaluable and that he can use to benefit himself, his employer, and, if possible, his society. His knowledge is essential to creating a livable future.

If the Expert used his talents to offer a unique part of himself to the world, it should not matter whether a woman does also. But if a man also uses his intellectual talents in order to make himself feel manly, then he will feel threatened if a woman has similar pursuits. Whether it is the scientist in his laboratory or the novelist at his typewriter (or, as we shall see, the minister in his pulpit), it should not matter if a woman is entitled to perform the same task. It should not matter, but it does.

From Aristotle onward, the Expert has considered the second sex to have a second-class intellect. In the past, the Expert often blamed the inferior performance of women's minds on their mysterious bodies. No one spoke with more authority about the ramifications of women's "weak and delicate" bodies than American doctors. In the nineteenth century, they seemed obsessed by a woman's body. The more they learned about the unique anatomical features in its hidden hollows, the more power they attributed to them.

According to a learned professor addressing an American medical society in 1870, it seemed that "the Almighty, in creating the female sex, had taken the uterus and built up woman around it." To cure women of their ailments — from backaches to nervous exhaustion to unruliness — physicians would probe the sexual interior. While denigrating midwives for their superstitious and folkloric methods, medical doctors would leech the uterus, inject it, cauterize it. It was a new frontier.

By 1906, one knowledgeable gynecological surgeon estimated that one hundred fifty thousand women in America had been separated from their ovaries by the surgeon's knife. The ovariotomy, boasted one of its staunch advocates, made the patient more "tractable, orderly, industrious and cleanly." In the Expert's informed judgment, this was how woman should behave.

Dr. J. Marion Sims was praised by his male peers as "the architect of the vagina." He was cited as one of "the three men who in the history of all times had done most for their fellow men." His disciples called him the father of gynecology. He invented the speculum and, he says, "saw everything as no man had ever seen it before ... I felt like an explorer in medicine who first views a new and important territory." Although he admitted that he "hated ... investigating the organs of the female pelvis," Dr. Sims nevertheless chose to specialize in them.

According to the Expert, the uterus was the mind's worst enemy. Shortly after the Civil War, Dr. Edward H. Clark of Harvard argued that higher education in "masculine" subjects (including science) would cause women's uteruses to atrophy. Such scholars were convinced that if women tried to use their brains as men did, they would destroy their femininity.

Even in the twentieth century, studies were conducted that "confirmed" the incompatibility of women and higher education. One such study showed that less than a third of female college graduates married compared to 80 percent of women in general. The renowned psychologist G. Stanley Hall found the educated woman to be the "very apotheosis of selfishness." By developing her brain rather than her uterus, she has "taken up and utilized in her own life all that was meant for her descendants."

"Beware!" warned one of these self-appointed Experts. "Science pronounces that the woman who studies is lost!" When the gifted writer Charlotte Perkins Gilman collapsed with a nervous disorder, she sought out the greatest nerve specialist in the country. His prescription: "Live as domestic a life as possible . . . And never touch pen, brush, or pencil as long as you live." Leave creativity to men, implied his patriarchal prescription, and be a housewife.

Had the Expert been more self-confident, and therefore more modest, he could have developed medical science quite differently. Instead of displacing midwives, for example, the Expert could have trained them to deliver babies. But doctors, proud of their new skills and new status, were not interested in sharing them with the women who traditionally assisted in childbirth. Instead, they emphasized that they, as professional men, were alone qualified to bring new children into the world. And they succeeded. In New York City, shortly after the turn of the century, three thousand midwives were still at work. By 1914, half of them were gone. By World War II, there were just over two hundred; by 1957, only two; and in 1963, the last midwife retired. The Expert had won: he alone was in charge of a woman's body. Unable to bear children himself, the Expert achieved the next best thing: power over those who could.

The antipathy toward women of these early medical scientists is still shared by much of the male scientific community, although it is expressed more subtly now. In James Watson's extraordinary account of the discovery of DNA, *The Double Helix*, only one woman is prominent among the scores of British and American scientists portrayed in its pages. Although Rosalind Franklin played a central role in this exciting scientific drama, Watson could speak of her only with derision. Listening to her lecture on her X-ray analysis of DNA, he talked of her "nervous style" and her lack of "warmth and frivolity." He wondered "how she would look if she took off her glasses and did something novel with her hair." It is the classic double bind: if she is not pretty, she is dismissed as unfeminine; if she is pretty, she is treated as a sex object. She could not be both feminine and a scholar.

Only after Franklin's early death did Watson recognize how unfair he had been. He realized "years too late the struggles that the intelligent woman faces to be accepted by a scientific world which often regards women as mere diversions from serious thinking. Rosalind's exemplary courage and integrity were apparent to all when, knowing she was mortally ill, she did not complain but continued working on a high level until a few weeks before her death." With this posthumous praise, the Expert belatedly acknowledged that a woman, too, contributed to discovering the genetic code.

Now women scientists work in every area of research. But their distribution is peculiar: the highest percentage are in biological research; the next highest in chemical; and the lowest, in the physical sciences. As one biochemist put it: "The closer the work is to living organic process, the more women there seem to be."

Nowhere in the hard sciences is the confrontation between Expert and woman more volatile than in the nuclear power controversy. The Expert cannot understand why women are so vehemently opposed to nuclear power. By a factor of two to one, women are more critical of nukes than men. Similarly, a survey of local anti-nuclear movements found twice as many women activists as men in leadership positions. Instead of being grateful to the Expert, women are turning their backs on this, his ultimate invention.

Stung by this rejection, the Expert has begun to woo women. The Atomic Industrial Forum, representing companies with a vested interest in nuclear power, has tried in vain to represent itself as the housewife's savior. It has organized thousands of pro-nuke coffee hours designed to convince women that their liberation depends on atomic energy. ("Frankly, I'd rather face a meltdown," said one pro-nuke ad campaign for women, "than a morning of housework without my home appliances.") The group has hired speakers who complained that, although women composed more than half of the electorate, they "had less than half the knowledge."

Unfortunately, this is how the Expert thinks. If women disagree with him, it is because they have no expertise. It is not because women's reproductive organs and responsibility for children may make them acutely sensitive to the long-term hazards of radiation. It is because women are uninformed or, to put it bluntly, dumb.

Cut off from his own femininity and belittling the views of women, the Expert seals himself in a world of technological half-truths. Instead of taking the overwhelming resistance of women to nuclear power as a sign that he should proceed with caution, he only becomes more condescending toward them. He keeps them out of positions of power and does not listen when they criticize his use of power. The Expert — who is variously called the boss, the manager, or the decision-maker — shuts out the chorus of critical voices and surrounds himself with his own data. Only there does he feel at home.

If the hard sciences are dominated by men, one might guess that the softest sciences would be women's domain. Indeed, social sciences such as anthropology, psychology, and sociology — which involve the study of real human beings, their emotions and social bonds — are now studied and taught by many women. It is in these disciplines, not surprisingly, that so many feminists have found their professional homes. But the roots of social science, like science itself, are deeply rooted in sexual bias. Many of the seminal works of Western philosophy and social science are burdened with the Expert's distorted view of masculinity and femininity.

"What is truth to woman?" asked Friedrich Nietzsche. "From the beginning nothing has been more alien, repugnant and hostile to woman than truth — her great art is the lie." Woman's striving for equality, according to the author of *Beyond Good and Evil* and other landmarks of Western philosophy, is a sign of decadence, not progress. She should not become man's equal; she should fear man. For the woman who "unlearns fear surrenders her most womanly instincts."

Woman is fearful; man intrepid.

"The fundamental fault of the female character," wrote Arthur Schopenhauer, "is that it has no sense of justice . . . women are defective in the powers of reasoning and deliberation."

Woman is inferior; man, superior.

"Woman's sensibility is rudimentary rather than highly developed," explained Émile Durkheim, whose works are respectfully studied in introductory sociology courses. "Society is less necessary to her because she is less impregnated with sociability . . . very simple social forms satisfy all her needs. Man, on the contrary, needs others . . . he is a more complex social being."

Woman is simple; man, complex.

"If there was nothing else to do but love . . . woman would be supreme," concluded Auguste Comte, sometimes called the father of sociology. "But we have above everything else to think and to act . . . therefore man takes the command . . . woman's life is essentially domestic, public life being confined to men."

Woman is emotional; man, decisive.

Yes, according to the Expert, the intellect is clearly a masculine gift. Women are creatures of myth and superstition. When the Expert finally turned to the study of the human mind itself, he brought these deeply entrenched biases with him.

Failing to substantiate men's supremacy through biology, the Expert turned to psychology. Women tend toward hysteria (from the Greek *hystera*, womb). By contrast, men are gifted with the creative intellectual force of life, our capacity for seminal thought, our *logos spermatikos*. It was with such logic that the premier and predominantly male science of the mind, psychoanalysis, began to study the predominantly female problem of hysteria.

The founder of psychoanalysis, Sigmund Freud, believed that "human beings consist of men and women and that this distinction is the most significant one that exists." He was careful not to let his profession seem biased, saying merely that "women are different beings — we will not say lesser, rather the opposite — from men." But in his revelations of his personal life, he threw self-restraint to the winds. Writing of his own courtship, he admitted, "If, for instance, I imagined my gentle girl as a competitior, it would end in my telling her, as I did seventeen months ago, that I am fond of her and implore her to withdraw from the strife into the calm uncompetitive activity of my home."

Some of his followers excuse Freud for his views on women by pointing out that he was only reflecting his time. But they underestimate their mentor's critical faculties. In fact, Freud was specifically opposed to women's equality and made a point of expressing this view. For instance, although he praised John Stuart Mill, the author of *On the Subjugation of Women,* as "perhaps the man of the century who best managed to free himself from the domination of customary prejudices," he took particular exception to Mill's views on women. The founder of psychoanalysis did not merely reflect his era's prejudices against women. He forthrightly endorsed them.

Feminists are now unsparing in their criticism of Freud. "Psychoanalysis," said one, "is a child of the hysterical woman." At least in one sense she was right. Modern psychiatry is a tool primarily in the hands of men and is used primarily on women. Almost nine out of ten of the American Psychiatric Association's twenty-five thousand members are men; two thirds of their patients are women. It all fits perfectly the traditional paradigm: men are Experts; women are not.

But the era of complacency is being challenged. "Is it possible that the issues raised around women cut deeper into American psychiatry than even racism and homosexuality?" asked Dr. Alan Stone, then president of the APA, in an address to its 1980 convention. "That the questions raised in connection with women touch our personal as well as our professional identity?" Later, speaking privately with a reporter, Stone said the answer to both questions was yes. "I believe psychiatrists, the majority of them, are still deeply convinced that a lot of the problems they see are the results of bad mothering," he continued. "A lot are deeply concerned that the women's movement attacks the traditional role of women that is central to mothering. That set of convictions runs deeper than many are willing to admit."

The arrogance of the Expert is not limited to science, whether soft or hard. If men had tried to bar women from science alone, they might have succeeded. They could have fooled women into believing that the study of man's universe was men's work, and that women should deal with the finer, more feminine pursuits of art, literature, and theater. But the Expert was not so gracious. He wanted to be in charge of those fields, too. When the French Academy, founded in 1635, recently voted on whether or not to accept a distinguished writer as its first woman member, one man who voted nay explained: "A woman as a woman has simply no place in the academy. Of course, I have a great deal of admiration for her work. But it is like putting a dove in a rabbit hutch. Adding one inhabitant like that makes the place overpopulated." This illustrious French scholar willingly resorted to barnyard logic in order to keep a woman from sharing his honors. The Expert wants to keep women not only out of science, but out of any creative expression that leads to fame — or power.

Consider, for instance, art. Surely in the world of color and form we can expect to find creative women at work. Surely there we should find these fair creatures, so aesthetically aware, so attuned to color, so patient with detail, so habituated to confinement in the home, so endowed with leisure. Nothing seems more natural than the delicate hand of a woman, poised with brush in hand before an easel. Yet where in the museums of the world, where in the grand illustrated volumes of art history, are the women? Did they not exist, or have they been lost? They were caught, in Germaine Greer's phrase, in an "obstacle race." Until the nineteenth century, almost all women painters were related to men painters. It is their male relation whose paintings hang in the museums, whose names are indexed in the expensive art books.

Instead of compassion for the special obstacles faced by women artists and writers, the Expert tends to question their fitness. When Norman Mailer describes the novel as the "Great Bitch" and proceeds to list three dozen male writers who have "had a piece of her," his insecurity is obvious. His need to place himself above women becomes transparent when he gratuitously adds: "One cannot speak of a woman as having a piece of the Bitch." By reducing the writing of novels to screwing bitches, Mailer claims the creative act for men only. It is as if he feels compelled to eliminate half his competition in order to enhance his own claim to fame.

So the Expert claimed the arts as well as the sciences for himself. As far as the Expert was concerned, the true woman was one who was content to express her creativity as mother and wife. Perhaps more women would have followed this advice if only the Expert himself had let them. But his arrogance was so great that he proclaimed himself the Expert even about "women's work." It was he who knew about matters nutritional, pedagogical, and spiritual.

As the science of nutrition developed, one looks in vain for any sign that the Expert recognized that those aproned figures who did all the cooking might know something about it. But, by turning cooking into science, the Expert once again disenfranchised women. Eventually, the housewife was given her second-class field of home economics. But nutrition remained a science, the province of those with advanced degrees. They rarely entered the kitchen to cook, but they nevertheless knew more than those who did. (If a man cooked, he was called a chef and became the Expert of gastronomy.) Perhaps this is why the gap is still so great between what we know about nutrition and what we ourselves eat.

Even more striking, however, is how the Expert appointed himself the supreme authority on raising children. In the age of expertise, men assiduously avoided caring for children. That was women's work. Only men who were somehow unfit to do real work would allow themselves to be engaged in child care. In generation after generation, men left the care of young children to women while they went off to be Frontiersmen, Breadwinners, and Soldiers. Yet it was men who took the lead in the study of child development.

We must give the Expert credit. He is bold. Regardless of his ignorance, he is always ready to claim omniscience. "If a man wishes to raise the best grain or vegetables . . . all admit that he must study the conditions under which alone such things are possible," observed one turn-of-the-century male expert on child rearing. "But instinct and maternal love are too often assumed to be a sufficient guide for a mother."

What is needed, concluded the Expert, is a rational, systematic, scientific approach — devised, naturally, by men. It must be foolproof, because children will still be raised by women, not laboratories. "The home we have with us — inevitably and inexorably with us," lamented John B. Watson, one of the early behaviorists, in his 1920s opus *The Psychological Care of the Infant and Child.* "Even though it is proven unsuccessful, we shall always have it. The behaviorist has to accept the home and make the best of it."

The slur is unmistakable. If only the (male) scientist rather than the mother could shape the family environment, children would develop into happier and finer human beings. No brilliant scientist stepped forward, however, to provide that care. While claiming superiority even in this, the most maternal sphere, men did not venture into it themselves. The Expert wants only to provide the theory; he will leave its practice to women.

In one of history's finer ironies, many men now find themselves with equal, if not sole, responsibility for their children's upbringing. Many of us are suddenly being thrust into the mother's role. On the sidelines, we were such experts. Thrown into the fray, our bravura disappears. The hero in Robert Miner's novel *Mother's Day,* for example, develops ulcers as soon as he takes over the responsibility for his two children. "Labor pains, perhaps, for mothers of my gender," he muses. Even the most mundane tasks, like carting kids with lunchboxes off to school, drives him crazy. For all our vaunted intelligence, we find ourselves incompetent to care for children. Like the father played by Dustin Hoffman in *Kramer vs. Kramer,* suddenly we are incapable of even making scrambled eggs.

That is one reason why the Expert wants to keep his distance from children: they do not reinforce his illusions about himself. He wants everyone to be enchanted by the power of his mind, the breadth of his knowledge. But children are unimpressed by lofty mental acrobatics. They want to be with people who care for them, who will enter their world. The Expert cannot. He is too busy being smarter, older, stronger, or more important. He cannot be with children because he has lost touch with the child in himself.

The Expert's knowledge about children has reached almost godlike proportions in the current abortion debate. No man in Washington has ever had an abortion or been pregnant. No man has experienced a baby growing within him that he did not want or could not care for. Yet when bills deciding who can or cannot have abortions are written, debated, and passed in Congress, the actors are virtually all men. Calling themselves pro-life, they are, once again, playing the Expert. They will decide at what moment life begins. They will discover the instant of the soul's inception. They will decide which women should give birth and which should not. They will be masters of the womb.

When the Expert leaps to the defense of the unborn, he tells himself that his motives are rooted in fatherly love. Indeed, he portrays himself as the savior of the helpless child-to-be, nobly pitting himself against the irresponsible mother and the amoral abortionist. But if the Expert's concern were truly for the child's welfare, why would his concern end so abruptly as soon as the child is born? Why would he cut welfare payments to poverty-stricken families, thus jeopardizing a child's health? Why would he allow infant formula to be promoted aggressively in the Third World, causing widespread disease and death? Why would he slash school lunch programs, which are the only hot meal of the day for many poor children? And why, finally, would he undercut young women's access to birth control, without which unwanted pregnancies are inevitable?

Just as children and cooking were dominated by male Experts, so was church. The religious roots of the Protestant West were profoundly misogynist. Luther, Calvin, Knox — the fathers of Protestantism adopted the most patriarchal attitude imaginable. According to them, we were not all God's children. We were his sons and daughters, as different as good and evil. For all the claims of the Reformation, Luther's derision of women equaled, if not surpassed, those of his predecessors. He denounced those who advocated equal education for both sexes, claiming that "if one takes women from their house-wifery . . . they are good for nothing." Not to be outdone, Calvin's Scottish disciple John Knox issued his *First Blast of the Trumpet Against the Monstrous Regiment of Women* (1558), which maintained that giving women any authority whatsoever was "repugnant to Nature . . . For who can deny but it is repugnant to Nature that the blind shall be appointed to lead and conduct such as do see? That the weak, sick, and impotent persons shall nourish and keep the whole strong? And finally that the foolish, mad and phrenetic shall govern the discreet and give counsel to such as be of sober mind? *And such be all women, compared unto men.*"

Such irrational prejudice, even if camouflaged behind the Expert's authority, was bound to produce contradictions. And it did.

To nineteenth-century American men, the true woman was a symbol of purity and moral righteousness. Yet we did not dare allow women in the pulpit. It was a stark contradiction. Women embodied spiritual virtues, yet were deemed unfit for the ministry.

A curious hybrid emerged: the womanly minister. The image of nineteenth-century male ministers became increasingly feminine. Respected ministers such as William Ellery Channing were praised by their colleagues for being "almost feminine" in character. The highest accolade was to be considered of "womanly temperament." The minister who had "an almost feminine sensibility" or "feminine gentleness of demeanor" was highly regarded. It meant that one was devoted to God with the same purity and self-sacrifice that women epitomized.

The minister's virtues — sweetness, meekness, gentleness, sensitivity — were precisely those that American men ascribed to women. "This was a comparison," observed the historian Ann Douglas, "which could function in two directions: if the minister was like a woman, why shouldn't the woman be like a minister?" Why, in other words, shouldn't the woman *be* a minister? If ministerial traits were feminine ones — not competitiveness, aggressiveness, toughness, and self-centeredness, but cooperation, sensitivity, gentleness, and self-sacrifice — why not turn to women? If they possessed the desired traits in such abundance, why search so hard for men who were like women when God, in his infinite wisdom, made woman herself?

The implications were not lost on the 1908 Convention of the National American Woman Suffrage Association. "As man accords to woman moral superiority," read one of the convention's resolutions, "it is his pre-eminent duty to encourage her to speak and teach in religious assemblies."

Feminist thinkers believed that, if women had not been held down by a patriarchal church, religion might have taken a very different form. "Had the religions of the world developed through her mind," Charlotte Perkins Gilman suggested provocatively in *His Religion and Hers*, "they would have shown one deep essential difference, the difference between birth and death. The man was interested in one end of life, she in the other. He was moved to faith, fear, and hope for the future; she to love and labor in the present." It was a challenge, a spiritual critique of a male-dominated religion. But men did not want to listen.

The self-made men of business and politics often viewed the ministry with disdain. As Harriet Martineau, an astute British traveler, noted, successful men in the marketplace considered clergymen to be "halfway between men and women." Similarly, Frances Trollope, who visited this country in the 1830s, observed that she "never saw or read of any country where religion had so strong a hold upon the women or a slighter hold upon the men."

During the nineteenth century, congregations became increasingly feminine, and Protestant clergymen grew anxious. By 1890, a Congregationalist minister could devote a sermon to the troubling question: "Have we a religion for men?" While women flocked to the sensitive, woman-like men of God, the men who were building America — the Frontiersmen, Breadwinners, Soldiers, and Experts — were lamenting the decline of religion. They found it tragic that the militant, heroic, and aggressive qualities of Protestantism were waning, only to be replaced by effeminacy. They feared that "religion in the old virile sense" (in the words of Henry James, Sr.) might disappear altogether. They were worried that God was becoming soft.

By the beginning of the twentieth century, ministers were announcing with Rooseveltian fervor that the image of Christ should be remasculinized. "The masculine military side of the Bible is too often overlooked," said one. "Christian art and Christian preaching need a strong tonic of virility," echoed another. They advocated portraying Jesus as heroic and domineering, not gentle and loving. They did not want a humble carpenter. They wanted an Expert.

10 Boyhood
Father's Heir, Mother's Son

The boys on the ice with their skates.
There is a stone on the ice.
One boy did not see it, and has had a fall.
But he is a brave boy and will not cry.
    — *McGuffey's Primer,* 1831

All boys love baseball. If they don't, they're not
real boys.
    — Zane Grey

BEHIND THE CHRYSLER FACTORY were the baseball diamonds. Inside the factory, men shaped auto bodies. On the diamonds, men
shaped us.
    Baseball was not a sport, but a ritual. I started playing when I
was nine years old. The boys on the team (girls remained in the
bleachers) ranged in age from nine to twelve. When I went to my first
practice, I didn't even know which way to run around the bases. My
teammates, born with baseball in their blood, made sure I learned
quickly. Three years later, I was third baseman on the Chrysler Little
League All-Stars.
    It was on those diamonds that I first learned to be a winner.
Shaped like the hardest of all precious stones, the diamond was a
gymnasium of American virtues. Although a strict system of rules had
to be observed, the true athlete could still rise to heroism. Bases could
be stolen and home runs hit. Line drives could be snagged and no-
hitters pitched. Moments of glory were possible on those dusty fields
behind the car factory.

For girls on the edge of adolescence, no similar ritual was available. They would spend hours at each other's homes, talking. I overheard tales of clothes, cosmetics, and fumbling courtships, but I was not very interested. I was busy mastering skills, competing, and proving myself. I am grateful to baseball for the opportunity to build what coaches through the years invariably called a "good self-image." But that image of myself, I realize now, was built in part on prejudice.

My good self-image rested on the assumption that I was somehow intrinsically more masculine than boys who did not wear the All-Stars cap. I was prejudiced, not only against boys who were less agile, but against a part of myself. I believed that if I did not compete and succeed, I was not as masculine as I should be. Too few hits, too many bobbled grounders, meant something was wrong with *me*. If I was not proficient at baseball, it meant I was not proficient at being a *man*.

What made matters worse was that, no matter how well I did, it was seldom good enough. When I made the freshman basketball team, the boys who had been cut envied me. But what obsessed me was that I was only on the second string. Even when I won a letter sweater, high school's coveted emblem of manly achievement, my self-doubts were not stilled. My letter was for tennis, after all, which was not a contact sport.

To acquire my good self-image, then, I sacrificed an inner freedom that would take years even to begin to recover. I forfeited the freedom *not* to compete. I absorbed the insidious notion that to compete is manly, and that to win is more manly still. I learned to measure other boys, and myself, against a standard of masculinity that omitted many of the most vital qualities a man can possess. I became obsessed with developing the parts of myself that were included in this standard. And I neglected, or actively suppressed, other sides of my personality because they were not part of this arbitrary sexual accounting.

Like all but a handful of men, I did not become a professional sportsman. The day came when the bats were put away, when the tennis tournaments were over, when the buzzer no longer sounded. The sports mania of adolescence was behind me. I had become a man with a job and a family. My letter sweater and my trophies were in the attic. Competitiveness did not solve marital tensions. Home runs did not impress a crying child. Cleats would only scratch the oak floors in the office. I would say (as members of my sex tend to) that it was a "new ball game." Except that it was no longer a game, but life itself. I was no longer a boy trying to be like Mickey Mantle. I was a man trying to raise my sons to be like . . . like whom?

"He's his father's boy," women would say as they watched our two-year-old son run into my arms after a fall. I knew what they meant. For the first two and a half years of his life, I had been with him as much as his mother had. For nine months Shelley nursed him. But after he was weaned, he seemed to find special comfort in my arms and would turn to me as often as to his mother.

Wherever we lived during those years — on a quiet street near Yale University, on a farm in central Maine, and on Capitol Hill in Washington, D.C. — I was part of his daily world. I fed him, diapered him, played with him, loved him. Those years were a wonderful gift, a gift of time.

But I am grateful only in hindsight. I did not know how lucky I was. I learned only after our second son was born.

"He's his mommy's boy," women said of our younger son. Again, I knew what they meant. Instinctively, he reached out for his mother when he was hurt or anxious. For the first years of his life, I was unavailable to him. I had a job that required long work hours and a twenty-mile commute, and I traveled abroad frequently. Even when I was home, I was often only half there. I did what I could, but my energy was divided. And he knew it. Now that I am, at least temporarily, working out of my home again, I feel him starting to count on me.

In the long run, the early differences in how I fathered my two boys may not matter much to them, but the experience has taught me a great deal. If I had worked away from home full-time-plus — not just for three years but until my boys were in their teens — there would have been a gulf between us. They would never have known what it meant to rely, every day, on a man. I would have seen them on weekends, holidays, birthdays. I would have felt more like their uncle than their father. For them, comfort and care would have been primarily, if not solely, feminine gifts.

As they grow older, they will move out into the community more and develop strong ties outside our family. But during these years, the family is their essential world. How I care for them will leave indelible marks, perhaps not on their memories, but on their unconscious minds. I want them to know in their hearts that both men and women can nurture and that both sexes have other things to do. I want them to be open to finding sensitivity and intimacy in their relationships with men as well as women.

I am not worried that they will be "effeminate." I am more concerned that they, like most boys, will feel compelled to deny their feminine qualities. Because I have cared for them as well as worked (and my wife has worked as well as cared for them), perhaps no such denial will be necessary for them. Perhaps they will learn to integrate the masculine and feminine more fully than their parents ever will.

AS CHILDREN GROW, they learn what they can expect from their mothers and fathers, and from women and men.

In most white, middle-class, postwar American families, boys learned their lessons in sexuality well. As infants, when we were wet or hungry, women took care of us. Women were the care givers, the baby sitters, the nursery school teachers. They were the ones to whom we turned when we were hurt, who were there when we needed them, who attended to our feelings.

But men? They were too busy and important. They left for a grownup male world where work was done and children were not admitted. They provided but did not nurture. They embodied power but not love. They were important but distant. We admired them, but we didn't count on them.

Families teach such lessons well. A boy's daily experience instructs him to be his father's heir, but his mother's son. It reinforces him to bond to men for power, to women for love. It teaches him to equate the first sex with the world outside the home, the second sex with the world within. It leads him to believe that women's purpose is children and men's purpose is work. It imparts a world view that he may never unlearn.

We begin to learn these lessons in sexuality long before we learn to read or write or even talk. In the first years of life, as Laurens van der Post's symbolic tale "The Sword and the Doll" illustrated, boys and girls are asked to play their respective roles in an archetypal drama. Looking into their children's room before retiring, a couple observes their sleeping son and daughter:

> ... the little girl had been overcome by her fatigue in the act of trying to lift the Dutch doll her grandmother had given her from its miniature play-pen. Her fine black hair hung over the side of the little bed ... Her outstretched arm held the doll firmly in hand and her face was buried deep in the white pillow.
>
> The boy had been overcome in a more orderly moment. He still lay more or less in the position wherein his mother had settled him but he too had a hand out of the covers. It was clasping the sword drawn from its sheath. His long yellow hair was disordered on the pillow and the lead soldiers were scattered over the bed where he had once more fought an enemy right up to the gateway of his sleep.

The scene elicits as deep a reaction in their parents as it does in the reader, reactions that are only partly conscious. Says the archetypal female voice: "You should not give your son a sword. That is the root of violence, of war." Replies the archetypal male: "It is natural. Girls gravitate to dolls, boys to swords. Take the doll from her, she will still grow up and make babies. Take the sword from him, he will still grow up and make war."

A boy who has been raised, consciously or not, to survive the combat of the battlefield (or the marketplace) cannot avoid the soldier's traits. He inevitably considers his mind and body as weapons, tools for survival that will permit him to dominate rather than be dominated. Boys who care — who express softness, tenderness, sensitivity, suppleness, gentleness — are considered feminine. Similarly, girls who conquer — who take initiative, seek competition, demonstrate toughness or a desire to lead — are considered masculine. As puberty approaches, the line is drawn.

Most parents consider the time their daughters spend playing house and the time their sons spend with bats and balls as play. But it is more than that. It is the way the young prove that they are growing up to be the kind of men and women their culture expects. When boys gather at the neighborhood basketball court or baseball diamond on Saturday morning, they are counting more than points.

Still much too young to recognize the other meanings of the phrase, boys call it a "pick-up" game. Sides are chosen by two boys, who take turns picking their teammates. If an odd number are present, one person does not play. Everyone knows what the order of selection signifies. Those chosen first are best; those chosen last, worst. And the one who sits out is the worst of all.

At the football field and the hockey pond, the ritual is boys ranking boys. In school, they are ranked academically as individuals — not by themselves, but by their teachers. But among themselves, in what sociologists call peer culture, their true measure is taken. No one asks a boy what his grades are, or what his father does, or whether he's been to Europe. That comes later. What his friends care about, to put it bluntly, is whether he is a winner or a loser. They care about whether having him on their team makes victory more likely or less.

Boys who don't like this standard for measuring manhood don't show up. They search for their masculinity somewhere else — on the street corner, in the library, at the piano, on the stage. But among American boys, there is no question which test is basic. It is the test of boy-against-boy competition.

"The most dreadful aspect of sports in school," recalled Joseph Pleck, author of *The Myth of Masculinity*, "was the daily choosing up of sides for whatever the game was during the lunch period. Whatever it was, I was always picked last." In high school, Joe's class held a father-son picnic and softball game. "I was the only person ... not to get a hit; I struck out every time," he said. "I don't think I have ever felt so ashamed of myself as I felt then, or felt that anyone was so ashamed of me as my father was then. In the picnic which followed, my father and I avoided each other completely."

Other dimensions of their father-son relationship also mattered, of course. His father, for example, enjoyed working in the backyard and hearing the sound of Joe's piano-playing through the back porch windows. Unfortunately, however, any other dimensions were secondary. None of them mattered as much as what Pleck calls the "archetypal Testing of the Sons' Strength before the Fathers of the Tribe." Father and son "had to go through a male sex role ordeal that would leave us feeling horrible about each other and ourselves." The ordeal was excruciating because both father and son had learned their culture's lesson that masculinity equals competitiveness.

Even social scientists agreed that this is what fathers were for. The reigning theory for decades was Talcott Parsons's formulation of the expressive mother and the instrumental father. According to Parsons, successful social groups always separate the expressive functions (emotions, nurturance, intimacy) from the instrumental (intellect, skill-building, work). The father is the link to the world, the adult who embodies the larger society within the family. The mother keeps the internal affairs of the family intact, smoothing over tensions and maintaining that "family feeling." In other words, men compete; women cooperate. Revered as the sociological gospel, Parsons's grand theory should sound familiar, for it ruled the nineteenth century. It implied that if the situation were reversed — if women worked and men loved — the earth would spin off its axis. It suggested that women who sought greater instrumental satisfactions had deviated from some sacred norm, and that men who tried to be more expressive were in similar danger.

Parsons's bias was reflected throughout the social sciences. Time and time again, studies appeared with imposing titles such as "The Changing American Parent" or "Patterns of Child Rearing," which were based entirely on interviews with mothers. Fathers were considered nonexistent or at best marginal. When a study entitled "Father Participation in Infancy" appeared at last in 1969, it only confirmed the gravity of the problem. "It causes [us] great embarrassment to report," admitted its two male authors with unusual candor, "that the actual data on father participation were secured by interviewing mothers. Perhaps we did not have the courage of our own convictions to . . . reorient our work schedules to coincide with the work schedules of fathers." Only in the seventies did the first serious examinations of interactions between fathers and young children emerge from academe. Said the author of one of the first of such studies: "It took me a half-hour to review all the literature. And I read the full articles, not the abstracts."

Just as revealing as the academic writing are the traditional how-to books for fathers. Most suggested that fathers should spend time with their children. But the reasons they offered were uniformly narrow. Men were not to nurture their children, but to ensure that the "child achieves a firm and solid gender identity during the pre-school years." Boys, the experts argued, "cannot do a very good job of imitation if the model is not around much of the time." Apparently, the purpose of fathers is to imprint sex roles. We are the experts of quality control, hired to ensure that boys become men. Our presence is required, like a notary public's. We embed the seal of manhood on every generation.

The old refrain "like father, like son" is usually invoked to suggest that it is fathers, not mothers, who mold sons. But the truth is more subtle. What both father and son share is that they both spent the most formative years of their lives in women's hands.

If we are honest, we must look at ourselves not as heirs of the patriarchy, but as our mother's sons. We must see ourselves in a way that no one except our mothers has ever seen us. As John Irving put it, "We are obliged to remember everything." Until we hear in our own voices the screaming of a hungry child; until we recognize in our own eyes the frightened look of an infant seeking his mother; until we can look at our hands and remember when our fingers clasped an open nightgown as we nursed; until we recognize in ourselves a baby totally dependent on his mother's care — until then, we do not know ourselves.

Masculinity that cannot do this, no matter how it swaggers, is weak. It depends on forgetting. We forget the earliest years of our lives. We minimize or deny their importance. We do not dare to recall these years and their well-kept secrets out of fear that our manhood will unravel. We are afraid to remember, in Dorothy Dinnerstein's words, that a woman is the

> will's first adversary ... In our first real contests of will, we find our-selves, more often than not defeated ... and the victor is always female ... The child's bodily tie to the mother is the vehicle through which the most fundamental feelings of a highly complex creature are formed and expressed. At her breast, it is not just a small furnace being stoked: it is a human being discovering its first great joy, handling its first major social encounter, facing its first meeting with a separate creature enormously more powerful than itself, living out its first awareness of wanting something for which it must depend on someone else ... This tie is the prototype of the tie to life.

This bond is forged in those years, hidden beyond the mists of memory, in which women were all-powerful, all-knowing, all-controlling.

This is one of the origins of men's need to control women and keep them in "their proper place." Those formative years affect us throughout our lifetime. No aspect of society is immune to their influences. As self-proclaimed guardians of the intellect, we know so much about so many things. But about our human beginnings, we are as ignorant as babes. It is the short-sightedness of our sex, our masculine myopia, our patriarchal amnesia.

The most basic image we have of a woman who is ours is of our mother. As boys, we turned to our mother for care and support. We were her pride and joy, if only because her role permitted few other forms of pride or joy. It is these memories that are triggered when we express our expectations of our wives. We expect them to support us emotionally more than we expect ourselves to support them. It is only natural, after all: we learned it as boys.

When a woman is expected to sacrifice more than half her lifetime to caring for others, she will expect something in return. With extended life spans and fewer children, parents have to let their children go and face the second half of their adult lives without them. A father who has been relatively uninvolved in child care and has always given first priority to his work may do so with little pain. But a mother who has been permitted no other avenue of self-expression of equal importance to the mother-housewife role may be heartbroken. As Margaret Mead observed, "She is working herself out of a job."

We came into the world, as Betty Friedan wrote, to "mothers who had to keep their children babies or they themselves would have no lives at all." Their husbands were gone. The home had been depleted of all its productive functions. The family had become isolated. More educated than any preceding generation, they naturally found full-time motherhood constricting.

In a 1947 article pointedly titled "Why Women Fail," Della Cyrus, a mother and social worker, wrote:

> No one can estimate what the shock which getting married and having a child gives to this American educated woman . . . From the exhilarating threshold of the world with all its problems and possibilities, from the daily companionship of men and other women, she is catapulted into a house — a house, furthermore, from which she has no escape . . . And so her first experience of what it means to be a mother, however much she may love her baby, is an experience full to overflowing with confusion, disappointment, humiliation, and above

all, loneliness ... We should find a satisfactory way to care for children away from their mothers part of the time so that mothers can be a fully developed, responsible part of the world their children will inherit.

Men did not want to hear this argument. They claimed that children need their mothers' devoted attention every hour of every day. Some women disagreed. Simone de Beauvoir, for example, considered the notion that child rearing was woman's supreme goal in life as "having precisely the value of an advertising slogan."

As we fathers portrayed ourselves, we were concerned for our children's welfare. We would work hard and strive for success so our wives could afford to stay home to nurture. In fact, the arrangement is not necessarily good for the children. The notion that one woman, the mother, should have virtually total responsibility for her children's daily care is contradicted by the facts. Margaret Mead concluded that "anthropological evidence gives no support at present to the value of such an accentuated tie between mother and child ... On the contrary, cross-cultural studies suggest that adjustment is most facilitated if the child is cared for by many warm, friendly people." Yet it was the needs of the child that men (and women) invoked in order to keep women at home.

After creating a society in which women were the all-powerful nurturers, men began to worry about their creation. Having compelled women to devote themselves exclusively to child rearing, we then blamed them for being overprotective. Since midcentury, men who worried about masculinity often considered the overprotective mother to be one of the greatest threats. She is occasionally made the butt of male humor, as in Philip Roth's *Portnoy's Complaint*. But beneath the caustic humor is often the resentment of boys who feel emasculated, of a nation that fears the loss of its virility. In failure and defeat, men of course fear the power of women. But even in moments of strength and victory, we also fear it.

In 1945, proud of our national victory, American men returned home to face an uncomfortable question. Why had two million men been rejected by American draft boards for being psychologically unfit? According to the army's surgeon general, those rejected lacked "the ability to face life, live with others, think for themselves and stand on their own two feet." The statistics created a storm of self-examination. What was wrong with these men? Why were they unfit to be soldiers? Amazingly, the ensuing debate led neither to a critique of war nor to a critique of masculinity. It led instead to the discovery of a scapegoat — Mom.*

Mom was held responsible for men's failure to measure up to military standards. The (male) experts concluded that men's failure to be warriors was caused by women's failure to be mothers. Dr. David Levy's influential volume in 1943 gave the syndrome a name: *Maternal Overprotection*. As the surgeon general described it, the problem was the perfect mother:

> From dawn until late at night she finds her happiness in doing for her children. The house belongs to them. It must be 'just so'; the meals on the minute, hot and tempting ... Everything is in its proper place, Mom knows where it is. Uncomplainingly, gladly, she puts things where they belong ... Anything the children need or want, Mom will cheerfully get for them. It is the perfect home ... Failing to find a comparable peaceful haven in the outside world, it is quite likely that one or more of the brood will remain or return to the happy home, forever enwombed.

In *Their Mothers' Sons*, Dr. Edward Strecker, consultant to the surgeon general of the army and navy, attributed the unmanliness of those rejected by the military to their mother's overprotectiveness. This intimidating critique left even well-educated, independent-minded women stricken with self-doubt. In her memoirs, Margaret Mead told of a conversation with Levy. "Are you going to be an

---

* Curiously missing in this debate about the failure of motherhood was Dad. Calling Momism "the silent disease of America," sociologist Hans Sebald devotes hundreds of pages to the "Momistically impaired male," a victim of his overpowering mother's "cunning styles" and "gruesome strategies." But he only devotes a handful of pages to exploring Dadism, which he calls "a novel concept that has not yet emerged in the social science literature." He justifies focusing on what he calls the "mother's activity" rather than the "father's inactivity" with the comment: "the mother-child relationship is the *immediate* problem and the father-child relationship ... the solution to the problem." An interesting point. But if the father is the solution, why does he remain unmentioned? In Sebald's *Momism*, published in 1976, there are no discussions of how to enable fathers to spend more — and better — time with their sons. If mothers "Momistically impair" their sons and fathers enhance their growth, the logical conclusion is that Dad should do more parenting. But Sebald skirts the issue. Like most men, he is quick to criticize femininity, but slow to question masculinity.

overprotective mother?" Levy asked her in what Mead called his "marvelous therapeutic voice." She answered sincerely, as if talking to a priest at confession, "I'm going to try hard not to be."

According to this convenient argument, mothers could be blamed for everything. Phillip Wylie's *Generation of Vipers* (which coined the term Momism) and scores of other books pointed their pseudo-scientific fingers at Mom. As Betty Friedan recalls, "In every case history of the troubled child; alcoholic, suicidal, schizophrenic, psychopathic, neurotic adult; impotent, homosexual male; frigid, promiscuous female; ulcerous, asthmatic, and otherwise disturbed American, could be found a mother."

But women who did not overprotect their sons, who sought other avenues of fulfillment besides mothering, were also open to criticism. They could be, and were, attacked for giving their sons *too little* attention. In books such as *Modern Woman: The Lost Sex*, experts manipulated their data to prove that women who wanted something more from their lives than motherhood were destined for unhappiness. It was a double bind. If a mother spent all her time doting on her son, she was overprotective. If she didn't, she risked being neglectful.

The double bind for sons was just as painful. On the one hand, they were supposed to love and respect their mothers. That was what it meant to be a good boy. On the other hand, they were expected to shun housework and child care. They were supposed to exhibit all those traits that women allegedly did not possess and to excel at those endeavors in which women did not engage. Yes, they were to love Mom, but they were not to resemble her in any way. Nothing was worse than to be tied to mother's apron strings. No greater insult was there than to be called a Momma's boy. It meant that you were dependent on your mother. It meant you acted like you needed her, were connected to her. It meant that you spent more time doing things with your mother than with other boys. It meant that you were something less than a man.

As boys grow up, they may retain the ability to say "I love you, Mom" whenever protocol requires, but their inner feelings are quite different. Most sons need to put a great distance between themselves and their mothers in order to prove that they are men. We act as though we were never dependent on our mothers and, therefore, on women. We become men who want women to act as though they are dependent on us. We portray ourselves as strong and independent creatures on whom the fragile and needy second sex can lean. We strive to show that we are real men, which means that anything vaguely feminine about us has been discarded like outgrown clothes.

At every stage of our lives — boyhood, manhood, marriage, fatherhood — we reveal our fear of dependence on women. It underlies all our images of masculinity. It is revealed in the Frontiersman's refusal to acknowledge his dependence on Mother Earth; in the Breadwinner's efforts to turn his wife into a housewife; in the Soldier's need to deny as feminine his cowardice through battle; in the Expert's determination to outdo women in every sphere of life; and in the Lord's conviction that only men are like gods.

In boyhood we are determined to become men by denying what is feminine in us. We are divided against ourselves. As long as this division remains, the certainty of manhood and the intimacy of marriage will elude us.

11 Manhood

The Elusive Goal

There is no steady unretracing progress in this
life ... Once gone through, we trace the round
again; and are infants, boys, and men, and Ifs
eternally.

— Melville, *Moby-Dick*

IT WAS NOT concidence that when love entered my life, so did violence. I fell in love for the first time with a high school classmate, Diana. She was a cheerleader, the most feminine of all roles. Even now, almost twenty years later, I think of her when I see cheerleaders practicing. In one cheer, they would shout each letter of each member of the starting line-up's name as they ran onto the basketball court, heralding them as if they were heroes. They had mastered the art of feminine support: they remained on the sidelines while acclaiming the men who played the game.

In this, Diana was wholehearted. In winter, her face would glow when the ball swished through the hoop; she would look crestfallen when it fell short. In autumn, chanting "Hit 'em again, hit 'em again, harder, harder," her body pulsed to the rhythm of her words. Even if she was not the most beautiful cheerleader, she was certainly the most magnetic. She made us feel like men.

Before she and I started dating, she went with a fellow two years my senior, a leading figure in one of the male clubs known for its toughness. Since he and Diana had broken up (or so she said), I felt no qualms when our study dates became romantic. Soon she and I were together almost constantly. When she invited me to a party sponsored by her club, I accepted. After all, she was "mine."

Midway through the evening, however, her former beau arrived with several of his hefty club brothers behind him. "They want you," a friend warned me, then quickly disappeared. My strategy, which was to pretend that I had not noticed their arrival, became impractical when three of them had me cornered. And I had no club brothers to back me up.

"Let's go outside," said Diana's old beau.

"What for?" I was still playing dumb.

The purpose of our outing was to settle with our fists who Diana belonged to. He obviously felt that he had staked his claim first and that I was trespassing on his territory. I believed that she had the right to choose for herself to whom she wanted to belong. Neither of us, perhaps not even Diana herself, considered it odd that at the age of sixteen she should belong to anyone.

As it turned out, the other boy friend and I didn't fight, at least not that night. "Why'd you let him talk you out of it?" one of his buddies asked him. He was outraged at being deprived of what was to be the high point of his evening.

A few weeks later, after a basketball game, my adversary and I passed each other under the bleachers. Without warning, he punched me hard in my right eye. My fist was raised to return the blow when several arms pressed me back against the wall.

"Whatsa matter?" he shouted at me contemptuously. "Are you gonna cry?"

The impatient crowd pushed us in opposite directions. Stunned, I felt my eye to check if it was bleeding. Only then did I feel the telltale moistness. Although no tears trickled down my cheeks, they were still evidence against my manliness. First, I had weaseled out of a fight. Next, I let him hit me without ever returning the blow. But the most damaging evidence of all were my barely averted tears. To be hit and to cry was the ultimate violation of the code of masculine conduct.

That happened half a lifetime ago. I no longer see my unwillingness to fight as an indictment of my character. Had I been as old and as tough as my adversary, perhaps I would have handled our conflict differently. Perhaps I would have fought. Perhaps I even might have won. Instead, aware of my relative weakness and inexperience, I chose not to. I wanted to protect my eyes, my mouth, my groin. I thought I might need them in the future. But the deeper reason had nothing to do with self-protection but with love. I could not understand what the winner of a fight would gain. Would Diana accept the verdict of our brawl? Like a Kewpie doll at the fairgrounds, would she let herself be claimed by whichever contestant came out on top? If her love could be won by violence, I was not sure I wanted it. I wanted her to love me for who I was, not for how I fought.

My problem, my friends told me then, was that I was too sensitive.

Strange how things change. The image of manhood against which I am measured has changed so much that now, almost twenty years later, I am told I am not sensitive *enough*. When tensions build in our relationship, Shelley will admonish me for being out of touch with my feelings. "You are always so defensive, always trying to protect yourself," she will say. "Why can't you be more open to your feelings?"

How can I explain it to her? How can any man explain it to any woman? Women are not raised to abort all tears. They are not measured by their toughness. They are not expected to bang against each other on hockey rinks and football fields and basketball courts. They do not go out into the woods to play soldiers. They do not settle disagreements by punching each other. For them, tears are a badge of femininity. For us, they are a masculine demerit.

Nothing has made me see this more clearly than talking with Richard Ryan, a former alcoholic. Sitting in the sun one afternoon by a lake near his home, Richard reminded me of a masculine rite of passage I had almost forgotten.

"After I gave this rap about alcoholism at the high school, this kid came up to me and said, 'Can I talk with you privately, Mr. Ryan?' Usually that means that either the kid's parents are alcoholic or he is. But not this kid. He said to me, 'Mr. Ryan, I've never been drunk, never smoked a joint. What's wrong with me?'

"So I said to him, 'Nothing's wrong with you, man. You're doin' fine.'

" 'But why do I feel I have to lie to my friends about it?' he asked. 'If they knew I didn't drink or smoke they'd make fun of me.' "

Richard Ryan rolled over onto his stomach as he finished the story. Either the sun or his emotions made him hide his face.

"I always felt like I had to lie as a kid," Ryan told me. "I liked to bake cookies. I liked to watch my kid brothers and sisters. I liked to write poetry. But my dad made me feel that was wrong somehow. So I started to pretend I *didn't* want to do it."

I had heard the lament so often now that I pushed him for specifics. "But what did your dad do? Did he walk in and say, 'Get out of the kitchen' or 'That's women's work'?"

"No, no. Nothing like that. It was more subtle." He thought for a moment. "For example, when my mother's mother died, I wanted to be her pallbearer. Grandma had been very special to me. I felt like she'd carried me all my life. When she died, I wanted to carry her once. So I asked my dad if I could be a pallbearer. He said, 'Only if you promise not to cry. Pallbearers can't cry!' I knew if I lied and said I wouldn't, he'd let me. But I felt like that'd be betraying her. How could I go to her funeral and not cry? Since I wouldn't promise, my dad refused to let me do it."

Now in his mid-thirties, Ryan runs a project called Creative Drug Education. He visits high schools and talks about alcohol and drug abuse. But he doesn't preach. He tells his own story:

"When I used to go out and get bombed, guys would say, 'He drinks like a man' or 'He holds it like a man.' Being drunk, I really felt like I was something great. The other guys and I, we were like a pack, and drinking was our bond. We'd get together and, because we drank, we'd say stuff and hug each other and do all sorts of things we'd never let ourselves do if we were sober."

Only after reaching the age of thirty did Richard realize he was an alcoholic. "I've only recently felt I can be who I am," he continues. "All those years I felt I had to blot out a whole side of myself. I used alcohol to make myself feel good about myself. After I quit drinking, I thought I was free. But then I realized I was addicted to smoking. And I mean *addicted*. My withdrawal from nicotine was almost as bad as from booze — the shakes, sweating, couldn't sleep. I found it hard to be around people without a cigarette in my hand. It was the whole Marlboro man thing — it made me look cool, made me feel like a man. When a friend told me I should stop, I told him, 'Anybody can quit smoking. It takes a real man to face cancer.' I said it as a joke, but I meant it. That's how sick I was."

Richard no longer looks sick. He is big and muscular. We swam out to the middle of the lake and back and, when we dried off, he wasn't even out of breath. He is respected by the people with whom he works. Teachers tell me he is more effective with young people who use drugs than anyone they've ever met.

As we walked back to the car, I saw a sadness in him, a wound that had not yet healed.

"What you thinking about?" I asked, not knowing a better way to probe.

He laughed. "Oh, I was just thinking about Grandma's funeral. You know what? Every one of those pallbearers cried."

———————

IN WESTERN societies, there are clearly no longer any rites of passage. The very existence of terms such as teenager (the German word is *Halbwüchsiger*, half-grown) shows that the absence of this social institution results in an in-between stage. All too often adult society avoids this whole question by regarding those in their teens in terms of the high school health book definition. Adolescence, it says, is the period when the person is no longer a child, but not yet an adult. This is defining the concept of adolescence by avoiding it altogether. This is why we have a youth culture. It is where adolescents go (and sometimes stay) before they become grownups.

Despite the absence of any established initiation rite, young men need one. By default, other institutions take the place of these missing rites. Some commentators on growing up in America point to sports or fraternities, for example, to demonstrate that our culture does have various kinds of initiation rites. But they are wrong.

Sports, for instance, can hardly serve as the means for gaining manhood. Sports are games. Except for the professionals who make their living from them, these games have little connection with real life. Moreover, only a small minority of males in American high schools and colleges can participate in athletics. As dozens of articles document, sports play a key role in enabling boys and young men to test their physical prowess, but they do not alone make a boy a man.

Fraternities, too, are a painfully inadequate means for gaining manhood. Except for token community service projects once a year, most fraternities are disconnected from society. How can they provide a socially recognized initiation rite when they involve only members of the younger generation? Frat members do not go off into seclusion with the adults of the "tribe." They go off into seclusion with themselves. They are initiated into youth culture, perhaps, but not into the world of adults.

The young man facing adulthood cannot reach across this great divide. He has only rites of impasse. There is no ritual — not sexual, economic, military, or generational — that can confirm his masculinity. Maturity eludes him. Our culture is famous for its male adolescent pain. From James Dean in *Rebel Without a Cause* and Dustin Hoffman in *The Graduate* to the more recent box office hits *Breaking Away, My Bodyguard,* and *Ordinary People,* young men try to prove they are grown men. But to no avail. None of the surrogate initiation rites — car duels, college diplomas, after-work drinking rituals, first paychecks, sports trophies — answers their deepest needs. None has proven to be what William James called the "moral equivalent of war."

The only rituals that confirm manhood now are imitations of war. The military academies, for example, like boot camp itself, involve many of the ingredients of primitive rites of passage. Young men are secluded with older men. They must endure tests of psychological or physical endurance.

Pat Conroy's novel *The Lords of Discipline,* which depicts life in a southern military academy, and Lucian K. Truscott IV's *Dress Gray,* which portrays West Point, showed how boys are turned into men — the kind of men the military needs. But, as we have recognized, the Soldier is no longer the hero. The Vietnam war was "billed on the marquee as a John Wayne shoot-'em-up test of manhood," wrote Mark Baker in *Nam,* but it ended up "a warped version of *Peter Pan* . . . a brutal Never Never Land where little boys didn't have to grow up. They just grew old before their time." Similarly, the heroes of Conroy's and Truscott's tales are not the brave soldier but the dissenter. Nevertheless, because military service is the only rite of passage available, men are drawn to it like moths to light. We need to prove our manhood and will take whatever paths our culture offers.

With the option of going to war foreclosed, young men seek to prove themselves by performing other manly deeds. The most obvious surrogates for war often involve violence too. It is not directed at the enemy, but at each other and ourselves.

Each week, the news media overflow with accounts of young men between the ages of fifteen and twenty-five who have committed acts of violence. Too old to be boys, too young to have proven themselves men, they are finding their own rites of passage. Here are three, culled from the newspapers:

A Boy Scout leader smashes his new car on a country road at 100 miles per hour: he is "showing off" to the four scouts who were riding with him. Now they are all dead.

A 16-year-old who lives in a comfortable suburb throws a large rock from a freeway overpass through the windshield of a car. The victim, a 31-year-old housewife, suffers a concussion but survives. "You do it for the thrill," the boy says. "It's a boring town," says one of his classmates.

A teenage boy is so upset that his girl friend has jilted him that he threatens to kill himself. Talking to her on the phone, he says he will drive over to her house and smash his car into the tree in her front yard if she will not go out with him. She refuses. So he does it, killing himself.

Many movies are made as surrogate rites of passage for young men. They are designed for the guy who, in actor Clint Eastwood's words, "sits alone in the theater. He's young and he's scared. He doesn't know what he's going to do with his life. He wishes he could be self-sufficient, like the man he sees up there on the screen, somebody who can look out for himself, solve his own problems." The heroes of these films are men who are tough and hard, quick to use violence, wary of women. Whether cowboys, cops, or superheroes, they dominate everything — women, nature, and other men. Young men cannot outmaneuver the Nazis as Indiana Jones did in *Raiders of the Lost Ark,* or battle Darth Vader, or outsmart Dr. No with James Bond's derring-do. To feel like heroes they turn to the other sex. They ask young women for more than companionship, or sex, or marriage. They ask women to give them what their culture could not — their manhood.

Half the nation's teenagers have had sex before they graduate from high school. The easiest way to prove oneself a man today is to make it with a girl. First we make out or put the make on her. Then we make it. We are not, like our "primitive" forebears, joining together with a woman as adults. We are coming together in order to become adults, if not in society's eyes, then in our own.

"You in her pants yet?" one of the high school jocks asks his classmate in *Ordinary People,* the Academy Award–winning movie directed by Robert Redford. We prove our manhood on the football field or the basketball court by scoring points against other men. We prove our manhood in sex by scoring with women.

The young man, armed with lines like "Don't you love me?" is always ready for action. He wants to forge ahead, explore new territory. After all, he has nothing to lose. He has no hymen, no uterus. He is free to play the role of bold adventurer, coaxing the reluctant girl to let him sow his wild oats in her still virgin land. "I love you, but I don't feel ready," she may say. She may be afraid that her refusal may jeopardize her relationship with her young explorer, but she is even more afraid to get pregnant. She may feel less mature than her sex-hungry companion. But the emotional reality may be precisely the opposite. Certain of her femininity and of her pregnability, she dares to wait until the time is right. Insecure about his masculinity and obsessed with proving it — to himself and his buddies, if not to her — he needs to score in order to feel that he has made the team.

Sonny Burns, the sexually insecure hero of Dan Wakefield's *Going All the Way*, finds himself engaged in an amorous overture on a double date. But he admits to himself, and to a generation of readers, that he is doing so not because he finds his date exciting. On the contrary, she bores him. He does so because he wants to impress his buddy in the front seat. He must prove he is a man, and a man takes whatever "pussy" he can get. Pretending to be passionate, he thinks about the high school rating system, according to which boys reported their sexual scores: "The next day, when the guys asked you what you got the night before, you could say you got finger action inside the pants. That wasn't as good as really fucking but it rated right along with dry-humping and was much better than just the necking stuff like frenching and getting covered-tit or bare-tit. It was really pretty much of a failure if you parked with a girl and got only covered-tit."

Even if he wins, the victory is private. There are no fans in the bleachers as he crosses home plate and scores. He has not proved himself a man to adult males, as did young men in traditional rites of passage. His sexual conquest is a rite of passage only in his own mind. If adult society were to pass judgment on these back-seat gymnastics, it would probably be negative. The responsible adult would ask him if he was ready for marriage. Could he support her if he had to? And of course the answers are no. He has become an adult sexually, not socially. He has proved his virility in the dark of night. By the light of day, the proof has vanished.

As Margaret Mead pointed out in *Male and Female*, our culture leaves adolescents in a quandary. We give them extraordinary freedom but tell them not to use it. "We permit and encourage situations in which young people can indulge in any sort of sex behavior that they elect," wrote Mead a generation ago. "We actually place our young people in a virtually intolerable situation, giving them the entire setting for behaviour for which we then punish them when it occurs." It is a cultural arrangement for which some young women pay an awful price.

Whether veiled in fiction or revealed in autobiography, women recall the ritual of modern courtship with caustic humor at best, more often with bitterness. So objectified do they feel that they develop a detached attitude toward their bodies. Reports the cheerleader heroine in Lisa Alther's *Kinflicks:* "Joe Bob would dutifully knead my breasts through my uniform jacket and padded bra, as though he were a housewife poking plums to determine their ripeness." Later, she would observe him sucking "at my nipples while I tried to decide what to do with my hands to indicate my continuing involvement in the project."

But Alther's good-natured response is not typical. Other sagas of car-seat courtships and apartment affairs leave their heroines harboring a deep distaste for men. Some declare themselves feminists or lesbians. Some become depressed. Others, as in Judith Rossner's *Looking for Mr. Goodbar,* are killed by their lovers. And a few, after great turmoil, find a man who will treat them gently, with genuine care.

The movie theater, that public living room for a nation of young lovers, reflects this yearning too. For those who have grown weary of the macho hero whose physical prowess is enough, Hollywood has provided a countertype. For those who are not infatuated with the Soldier, there are now movies about the anti-soldier. "In what may be an emerging genre in the movies," wrote Paul Starr in his review of *Coming Home, An Unmarried Woman,* and *Alice Doesn't Live Here Anymore,* "there appears a character who expresses in his personality and in his relations with the heroine a new idea of masculinity. He might be described as the emotionally competent hero . . . He is the man to whom women turn as they try to change their own lives: someone who is strong and affectionate, capable of intimacy . . . masculine without being dominating." The new hero, though perhaps not rugged and tough in the familiar mold, can be intimate. He can feel. "The new softer image of masculinity seems to represent what is distinctive and significant in recent films, and I expect we will see more of the post-feminist hero because the old, strong, silent type no longer seems adequate as lover — or as person."

Who, then, is to be the young man's hero? The gentle, post-feminist figure extolled by the new genre of films and by the roughly five thousand men's consciousness-raising groups across America? Or the self-sufficient, hard-hitting tough that Eastwood tries to embody and that the military breeds? Faced with such polarized and politicized choices, how does a boy become a man? By being hard or by being soft?

From the sensible to the absurd, we have answers. We have so many shifting, contradictory criteria for manhood that they confuse rather than inspire.

American boys coming of age encounter sexual chaos. A chorus of liberation advocates, now with bass as well as soprano voices, encourages them to free themselves from the oppressive male role, to become softer, and to consider themselves women's equals. But another vociferous group beckons them in another direction. For every pro-feminist man, there is his counterpart, who denounces those "fuzzy-headed housemales, purporting to represent 'men's liberation,' but sponsored by NOW." One Minnesota men's rights leader argued, for example, that men who support women's liberation are "eunuchs," motivated by an "urge to slip into a pair of panties." According to him and his followers: "Men's liberation means establishing the right of males to be men, not to liberate them from being men."

The hard-liners and soft-liners both have their respective magazines, organizations, and conferences. Repulsed by the cacophony, most young men try to ignore it. But the questions gnaw at them anyway. Although the pro- and anti-feminist activists irritate them, young men cannot deny their own uncertainty. They are caught between the competing ideals of chauvinism and liberation. The old archetypes do not work; the new ones remain vague and incomplete. If we are not to be John Wayne, then who?

Into the vacuum created by the demise of the old archetypes rush myriad images. Each hopes to inspire a following. Masculinity becomes the target for everyone from toothpaste advertisers to Hollywood superstars. These salesmen of self-help all have their diagnoses for the young man struggling to find his own identity. Some take the pose of proud aging lions, defending the traditional masculine role as Western civilization enters a precipitous, psychosexual decline. In *Sexual Suicide*, George Gilder warned of the imminent feminization of man and masculinization of woman and called on men to reassert their superiority.

Others do not oppose liberation but rather seem to exploit it. Cynically catering to masculine insecurity, they describe the world of white-collar commuters as a stark and brutal asphalt jungle in which men must constantly flex their aggressive personalities in order to survive. According to Michael Korda, author of *Power!* and *Success!,* life is nothing more than a series of encounters in which one dominates or is dominated, intimidates or is intimidated, achieves power over or is oneself overpowered. "Your gain is inevitably someone else's loss," philosophizes this latter-day Nietzsche, "your failure someone else's victory."

There are also the advocates of liberation who seek to free us from the manacles of machismo. Although they are constructive in intent, they too increase the confusion. In their attempt to free us from one-sidedness, they double our load. They now want us to be "assertive *and* yielding, independent *and* dependent, job *and* people oriented, strong *and* gentle, in short, both masculine *and* feminine." The prescriptions are not wrong, just overwhelming. Their lists of do's and don'ts, like Gail Sheehy's *Passages,* seem too neat, too tidy. They write of "masculinity in crisis" with such certainty. They encourage us to cry with such stoicism. They advise us to "be personal, be intimate with men" with such authority. It is all too much.

Whichever model young men choose, they know the traditional expectation of their culture. At least until the seventies, Americans of all ages and of all educational and income levels were in wide agreement about what traits are masculine. According to one study, based on more than a thousand interviews, men are expected to be very aggressive, not at all emotional, very dominant, not excitable, very competitive, rough, and unaware of others' feelings. And women are expected to be more or less the opposite.

If this is what maleness is, then a young man must find ways to demonstrate those traits. Without a rite of passage, he can only prove what he is *not.* Not a faggot, a pussy, a queer. Not a pushover, a loser, or a lightweight. Not a dimwit or a dunce. Not a jerk or a nobody. Not a prick or a pansy. Not, above all, anything that is feminine. Indeed, without clear rites of passage, the only way to be a man is essentially negative: to not be a woman.

If we are to be masculine, then they must be feminine. We convince ourselves that women are yielding, that they are more interested in our careers than in their own, that they are interested in sex whenever we are, that they are fulfilled by raising children. That, we assume, is who they are. Should one of them act differently, then something is wrong, not with our assumptions, but with her.

Having entered physical manhood, we are nevertheless emotionally unsure of ourselves. The more unsure we are, the more we stress that we are not "feminine" and the more we are threatened when women act "masculine." We try to rid ourselves of any soft, effeminate qualities. We gravitate toward all-male cliques in the form of sports teams, social clubs, or professional groups. When we are with a woman, it is virtually always in a sexually charged atmosphere. To be merely friends is nearly impossible because it suggests that we have something in common. We are trying, after all, to prove precisely the opposite, which is why so many marriages fail.

12 Marriage

Where Roads Diverge

divorce, n. A complete or radical separation of things closely connected. Middle English, from Old French, from Latin *divortium*, separate, divorce, fork in the road.

FRIENDS OF OURS are visiting one Saturday evening.

HE: *But why didn't you say something? Why did you wait until it was too late?*

SHE: *I did say something. Many times. But you weren't listening.*

They sit on our couch, still husband and wife, but not for long. I know them — we all know them — in numbers too painful to count. They are our friends, our brothers and sisters, ourselves. One day they are in love, marrying the woman or man of their dreams. Then, another day — one, five, twelve years later — they are "in trouble." The person they loved more than anyone else in the world is now hurting them more than anyone else in the world.

HE: *But if you were so unhappy all those years, why didn't you tell me? Maybe I would have changed. It's not fair to say suddenly: "It's all over."*

SHE: *I told you long ago; time and time again I tried to talk with you, but you wouldn't listen. You were always too busy. Five years ago, remember, I wrote you a letter. I thought that way you would have to hear. I wrote you a memo so you'd pay attention to it like you do at the office. I told you then that our marriage was not working for me. But you still didn't pay attention. You thought I was just going through a "phase."*

When she talks, she doesn't look at him. She is afraid to talk with him alone. She will discuss their relationship only if someone else is there. It is not just because she is afraid he might hit her (which he does only rarely). No, it is because she is afraid he will confuse her.

HE: *But I always encouraged you to do whatever you wanted: to get a job, to go back to school, to get help with the house. I always told you how much confidence I had in you. Why do you blame me for your not feeling fulfilled?*

SHE: *Encouragement? Confidence? It was all condescending. You were the coach; I was the player. You were the professor; I was the student. You wanted me to grow as long as it was in your direction, as long as it did not threaten you.*

Now his face shows pain. Normally immobile and tough, it is lined with remorse. He has invested seventeen years in his marriage. Their children are teenagers. His home is beautiful. He is well known. But the failure of his marriage undermines his manhood. If his woman now wants to leave him, is something wrong with him? Or with her?

HE: *I'm sorry that I was so moody. I know I was working hard, gone too much. But that's already started to change. I had to build my career then, you know that. I had to establish my reputation. I'm more relaxed now — you said so yourself. Be fair now. How can you throw it all away just when it's getting better?*

SHE: *Work. Again the old excuse. I am so tired of your sorrys. I don't hold your career against you. I know I chose my life. I don't even regret cleaning up after you, taking the vacations you wanted, taking care of the children and the house when you were gone. But don't you dare say that I am throwing it away. You* threw *it away, piece by piece, year after year.*

HE: *What do you mean? I loved you more than anyone then, and I still do.*

SHE: *On your trip to England: she was just for fun, right? And that woman at work: she was only a passing thing, right? And the last one. That's what hurts. I could forgive you your failings, and they were many, as long as I trusted you. But when you destroyed that trust, you took away the only thing I had left.*

She cannot continue. She can hold her tears back no longer. But he does not cry. He cannot. He becomes angry.

HE: *One day we're married; the next day we're getting a divorce, just like that. It's not fair. You have closed your heart to me, shut me out. You won't even give me another chance. Why are you so afraid to try again?*

SHE: *You have hurt me so many times. If I opened myself to you again, you would just hurt me again. I know it. When we had just got married, I hated it when you left. But not anymore. I knew it was all over when I finally realized that I was happier when you were away than when you were home. I am not going to give you the power to hurt me again, ever. I have closed my heart. You're*

right. It's like closing the door to keep out the winter wind. It's self-preservation.
They had married soon after college. He had their wedding picture in his office: he, magnificent in his dashing air force officer's uniform; she, exquisite in her white wedding gown. They were walking down the path in front of the church, faces radiant with hope for their future.

HE: *All right, let's get divorced then. If that's what you are determined to do, let's do it.*

SHE: *Right now I just want to live apart. I want to see what I feel like when you are not there dominating me. I just need some time. You can find a place to live for the summer and then we can see . . .*

HE: *Look, let's not mess around. You say it's finished: okay, it's finished! We'll get a divorce and be finished with the whole mess.*

SHE: *You see, you still want to be in control, don't you? You have to be the one in charge. You're terrified even to think of dealing with me as an independent person. No matter what you say, you can't even imagine being married to your equal.*

The last sentence is shouted at him as our front door shuts. Her husband is gone into the night. She sits on our couch, alone, crying. It is the end of another marriage.

The dismal scene on our couch tonight reminds me of another one long ago. I do not remember what actually happened; I have blocked it from my mind. But this is how I can best recall it.

The girl is curled on the living room rug. Her face is hidden. The boy turns on the TV and fiddles with the channels. He wants to see *Superman,* but it's not on yet.

He knows his mother has been crying. She has dried her eyes, but still he knows. She is holding a Kleenex. She doesn't look at them but goes straight upstairs.

"Let's have a little talk together, kids," says their father, motioning them into the den. He has come home to explain. He is trying to be gentle, but his anxiety makes his words sound brittle and abrupt.

They sit on the couch, facing their father. Everything is still except the girl's sniffles. Their father sits at his big oak desk, his Rembrandt print on the wall to his left and his son's swimming trophies on his right. He is trying to appear calm, in control, but his daughter's crying disconcerts him.

The boy knows this. He even knows what his father is going to say now, but he is still curious *how* it will be said.

"You both know how much I love you, don't you?" their father begins hesitantly. "I loved you when I lived here with you, and I loved you when I lived downtown too, didn't I? Well, I want you to know that I always will love you, and take care of you and" — he begins talking faster — "what I am going to tell you now about your mother and me doesn't change this at all, understand?"

His daughter stares into her lap, motionless. His son, staring straight at him, thinks, Come on, out with it. He doesn't like the way every sentence ends by being turned into a question because he has no answer. He just wants it over.

"Your mother and I have decided that we can't live together anymore without fighting so much that we make each other unhappy, and you unhappy, and so we have decided to stop being married. I won't live here anymore, but I'll see you as often as you want, okay? I will stay living in the apartment where you come to swim and — "

His sister, her fists clenched and pressing into the couch, erupts: "You mean you're getting *divorced*, that's what you mean, isn't it? Then why don't you just say it, why don't you just say it?" Her words dissolve into angry sobs.

They all wait silently until the crying stops. If only she wouldn't cry, thinks the boy, we could get through with this.

"All right, *divorced.*" Their father emphasizes the word, resenting its bluntness. "I want you to understand, that's all, because it's hard for me to leave this house, the yard — everything I've worked for since long before you were born. It's hard for me to live away from both of you." For a moment it looks as if he might cry, but he catches the tears before they fall. He always does. "I want you to understand that I still love you because if I lost your love, well, then I would be losing just about everything, wouldn't I?"

If she would simply nod her head, like I'm doing, the boy thinks, it could end right now. But no, she's got to be all emotional. She has to make a scene out of it.

"You know what Mommy says?" the girl blurts out. The question dangles sharp and heavy, like the blade of a guillotine. "She says you told her that you'd love her forever, and that you promised it to her and to God, and now you're breaking your promise." She lets her deadly sentence hover, emboldened by the power it gives her over her father. "Now you tell me that you will always take care of me, that you'll always love me, but why should I believe you? How do I know you aren't lying to me just like you lied to Mommy?"

For crying out loud, the boy thinks. She's going to push him and push him until he gets angry. Why doesn't she just shut up?

His father casts a grateful glance at him, as if thanking him for acting so "maturely." The boy nods, completing this manly pact.

"Come on now, you're still my little princess, aren't you? Just because your mother and I can't get along doesn't mean you and I can't. Tell you what!" His full charm springs to life. "You know those figure skates you wanted for Christmas? Let's buy them this week so we can go to the skating rink this weekend! What do you say?"

She remains silent, staring into her lap, but her posture softens. Her fists unclench. She takes a few deep breaths. She runs her hand through her hair to straighten it.

Thank goodness, the boy thinks. No more tears from her and no anger from him. It's finished.

"All right," their father says, standing up. "I'd better be going now. We can talk more about this when I see you this weekend." He kisses them both on the cheek. Then they go their separate ways: the daughter to her room, the father to the front hall to get his coat, and the son to the kitchen to make a peanut butter sandwich.

Five o'clock on the nose. The boy reads the time with satisfaction, thinking. Despite my sister, it didn't take too long.

He turns on the television. *Superman* is just starting. He pulls his father's big, cushioned chair in front of the TV. Familiar phrases fill his head: "faster than a locomotive," "able to leap tall buildings at a single bound," "fighting for truth, justice, and the American way." Contentedly, he sits down to eat his sandwich.

How self-protective memory is. The boy and the girl were my younger brother and sister. I, the observer, remained untouched. My concern for them has blocked out how *I* reacted. I am left with almost no recollection of my own pain.

I do remember one day, though, looking at my mother's bed. I was accustomed to seeing the white cotton bedspread, neat, even, unwrinkled. My mother tucked it beneath the two pillows at the head of the bed and then pulled it firmly over them, so firmly that I could feel their softness just by looking at their profile. My world then, like that bed, seemed all in order.

But that day only the left pillow remained. The bedspread sagged where the missing one had been. As tight as my mother pulled the bedspread, it still wrinkled. She must have noticed it too, for after a few months, she moved the lone pillow to the center. I liked the new symmetry better, but it didn't change how I felt. The missing pillow troubled me.

Sometimes I look at the bed in which my wife and I now sleep. I am haunted by the possibility that my sons may one day stare at this bed and see only one pillow.

IN MARRIAGE, the sexes meet. At dinner, in bed, expectations encounter reality. A man looks into a woman's eyes, and she into his. In their eyes, manhood and womanhood are most vividly reflected. It is there that many illusions die.

Roughly half of those who walk to the altar of marriage eventually walk into divorce court. This is no mere statistic; it is a way of life. Divorce cannot be dismissed as a "social problem." Since divorce is so expensive, both emotionally and financially, why do so many of us want it? If our families are so precious, why do we so often let them be broken? As a social problem, divorce is incomprehensible. We cannot understand why we inflict such pain on ourselves and on our children unless we recognize that divorce is not a problem.

On the contrary, divorce is a solution. It "solves" the problems of masculinity and femininity. This is what lurks behind the clichés that a couple "didn't get along," "grew apart," "moved in different directions," "no longer had anything in common," or were, in legal terms, "incompatible." All are evidence that our masculinity and femininity do not fit together. In such a world, divorce is not an unfortunate accident. It is sexuality's safety valve.

The divorce between husband and wife is, after all, only the legal "fork in the road." The first splitting, as we have seen, occurs much earlier. It is the divorce of the masculine from the feminine in both husband and wife. In childhood, each sex sacrifices part of its potential in order to prove itself. At maturity, we assume that we will become whole again through joining with the other, through union with the other.

The basic question, then, is not what is wrong with those marriages that end in divorce. Nor is it what is wrong with the institution of marriage. Rather, what is wrong with our assumptions about masculinity and femininity? When a marriage unravels, each couple has its own reasons. They may involve lovemaking, child rearing, money, or scores of other conflicts. But under the surface, the dissolution almost always involves, in the words of one marriage counselor, "the wife telling the husband that he is not a man and he accusing her of not being a woman." That should not surprise us. How can marriage work when manhood and womanhood do not?

We spoke of divorce in our encounter with the Breadwinner. There it was the divorce of work and home into two separate worlds, the social "fork in the road" that foreshadowed the marital one. When the number of divorces increased fifteenfold between 1870 and 1920, America grew worried. By the Roaring Twenties, when one out of seven marriages was dissolving, worry became alarm. And by the "me" decade of the seventies, with almost one out of two marriages ending in divorce, alarm turned into numbness. The exception had almost become the rule. The deviant had virtually become the norm.

The emotional reality of family life has shifted. So many children have been raised in broken families and so many adults are surrounded by separated friends that we no longer presume commitment. We presume uncertainty. Even those who are happily married wonder whether they will be next.

Postwar fiction mirrors these fears. Take the Maples' marriage, for example, chronicled by John Updike in a series of short stories that began in the *New Yorker* in 1956. Every phone call, even the most innocent night out, fans suspicion.

In "Your Lover Just Called" (1966), Mr. Maple, home from work with a cold, answers the phone. The caller hangs up. He goes into the bedroom and says to his wife: "Your lover just called."

"What did he say?"

"Nothing. He hung up. He was amazed to find me home."

"Maybe it was *your* lover."

With each suspecting the other of infidelity, mistrust corrodes the marriage. In "Eros Rampant" (1968), the mistrust takes its toll. Richard Maple is having nightmares, awakening in the middle of the

night soaked with sweat. He is terrified by the thought that he does
not know his wife's lovers.

Will they divorce? The question is meaningless. They are already
divorced, not legally, but emotionally. It is from such homes that a
generation came of age, questioning sexuality with such urgency. A
few made the leap of faith and embraced liberation. But many more
quietly determined to seek alternatives to the traditional family,
which no longer worked.

Although there is no typical marriage or divorce, there is a standard
pattern of miscommunication in many marital tragedies. No one has
described it more personally than the man who spends an hour a day
with millions of American women, Phil Donahue, whose morning
talk show is carried by over two hundred television stations. Columnist Erma Bombeck calls him "every wife's replacement for the husband who doesn't talk to her." As he is the first to admit, he too was
once such a husband.

When he married at the age of twenty-three in a solemn high
nuptial mass, he believed it was forever. Marriage for young Phil was
by definition a "binding commitment." It must be "without question
forever and ever, amen." Within six years he and his wife had five
children; a decade later they were divorced.

"When, at age 39, I became legally and spiritually 'sundered,' "
recalls Donahue in his autobiography,

> I thought of my professional ambition and how costly it had been to
> my family. I thought of how I had been married to my job instead of
> my wife ... I wonder, at age 39, how many other males of the fifties
> had likewise sleepwalked into (and sometimes through) parenthood
> and marriage ... I thought about the early years, after the wedding,
> and what an insensitive and lousy lover I had been ... I thought
> about my childhood and education and how nothing, absolutely
> nothing, was ever said about human relationships.

Donahue shares his "bewilderment as to how my wife had 'suddenly' become so very unhappy." She had, of course, been unhappy
for years, but he had never noticed. The fact that he did not even notice, Donahue admits, "is itself evidence of my consuming professional ambition and only one indication of how little energy I was

really giving to my responsibilities at home." Until the divorce, Donahue "honestly thought that being a father meant giving presents at Christmas and birthdays, occasionally changing diapers, occasionally spanking and occasionally babysitting for the little woman's night out."

The traditional cure for such marital ailments was feminine self-sacrifice. Women were supposed to be the martyrs of marriage; they were persuaded to view their martyrdom as fulfillment. But this prescription for sick marriages is no longer popular. Even when taken in its sugar-coated form, it is a hard pill to swallow.

Anita Bryant tried. A graduate of Marabel Morgan's Total Woman course, Bryant believed her purpose was to serve her husband and God. In the seventies, she was the nation's most visible saleswoman for this image of family life. She led the crusade against homosexuality, the Equal Rights Amendment, and other feminist causes. Under the guidance of her husband-manager, Bob Green, a fundamentalist Christian, she became a spokeswoman for the anti-gay movement. She symbolized traditional femininity for millions of Americans who felt threatened by changing values of sexuality.

But behind the Total Woman image was a darker reality. Anita Bryant was hooked on Valium in the sixties; when she kicked that habit, she became dependent on sleeping pills and alcohol. Her husband was "jealous of every man we met," she admitted after their divorce. "I was always so embarrassed. I felt like a caged animal, smothered, stymied, and I saw that he was miserable too." Nor does she have kind words for the sexual roles of the Moral Majority. "Having experienced a form of male chauvinism among Christians that was devastating, I can see how women are controlled in a very un-godlike, un-Christian way. The problem is that most men are so insensitive to women's needs ... There are some valid reasons why feminists are doing what they're doing."

Ironically, this most strident critic of homosexuality recognized that she had been a victim of heterosexuality. Like many straight people, she used gays as convenient scapegoats for her own dissatisfaction. While shocked at the unnaturalness and sinfulness of deviancy, she remained silent about the oppressiveness of normalcy — silent, that is, until her own marriage shattered.

Behind this tragedy was a philosophy of feminine subservience. It is a mistake to dismiss Marabel Morgan's Total Woman attitude as nothing more than a fluky weekend workshop for wives of the Dallas Cowboys, as did most press and TV coverage. It represents the traditional coping strategy of generations of women who have tried to accommodate themselves to the obdurate contradictions of masculinity. As Phyllis McGinley put it: "We are the self-immolators, the sacrificers, the givers."

Beneath this wife-as-martyr theory, however, is not reverence and admiration for men, but a cynical stereotype of male narcissism and immaturity. The Total Woman recipe for eternal marital bliss can be boiled down to this: Be your husband's ideal mother. Cater to him. Indulge him. Bolster his ego. Treat him like a child. Whenever there is conflict — he wants to go to a football game, you want to go to your best friend's wedding — do what he wants. Adore and praise him as if he were a first-grader returning home proudly with his first finger painting. Be his dream come true: someone who mothers him and with whom he alone can have sex.

It is no oversight that children are all but invisible in Morgan's prescription for wedded bliss. There is no room for them. The husband is the child. If Morgan addressed the wife's other role of mother, her model of marriage would be exposed for the sham it is. In practice, women cannot tolerate taking care of children all day and catering to their husbands' whims all night. The result is often depression. A young mother, one of scores of chronically depressed women interviewed by Maggie Scarf, tells of feeling turned off by her husband's immaturity. What irked her was that not only did he fail to share parenting, but he "felt that I wasn't giving him enough attention . . . that I didn't have enough time for *him*. That I was ignoring him, not concentrating on him as I'd done before. But you know, I was needing *his* support — and what he wanted from me was *babying*. I found him incredibly egocentric! I felt as if this were another child here, pulling at my skirts, demanding my praise."

In such marriages, infantilization is mutual. His babyish emotional dependence on her is matched by her total economic dependence on him. She is only one divorce (or one heart attack) away from financial helplessness. Only he prevents her from joining the roughly seven million middle-aged women in America who, as columnist Joan Beck put it, "gambled by becoming full-time housewives, 1950's style, and lost." They are euphemistically called "displaced homemakers," a category many young women are determined never to join. To avoid it, they must reject the "he provides, she nurtures" model of marriage, which represents interdependence at its worst.

The marriage contract is usually unwritten, its clauses unconscious. *He* is more skilled in the ways of the world, in mapping out a career, at making things happen and getting results in the hurly-burly world of the marketplace. *She* is sensitive to people's feelings, skilled in the inner workings of intimacy. *He* will manage their public existence, the rational and calculating planning of life; *she* will manage their private existence, the emotional and nurturant aspects of life. If *she* is troubled about her work, *he* will help her; and if *he* is troubled about his feelings, *she* will help him.

Were marriages machines, it might work. But they are not machines, they are relationships. The "perfect relationship" of the newlyweds ultimately proves unworkable. They want to experience not being merely masculine or feminine but being fully human. So they part. They resume their search. But this time they are looking not only for a mate, but for the part of themselves they left behind. And sometimes they don't even know it.

The rules of this game are bizarre. They force both partners in marriage into molds that make no sense. Marriage law reflects the game's absurdity. Reviewing the history of married women's legal status, one judge commented sardonically, "A woman's responsibilities and faculties remain intact from the age of maturity until she finds a mate; whereupon incompetence seizes her and she needs protection in an extreme degree. Upon the advent of widowhood she is reinvested with all her capabilities which had been dormant during her marriage." As the judge pointed out, there is no reason why a woman should be less competent in the prime of her life than when she is young and single or aging and a widow. The only reason that her abilities should be so drastically reduced upon becoming a wife are sexual. She has put herself in the provider's hands.

If a husband and wife consciously and mutually choose their respective roles of provider and nurturer, then these roles may serve them well. But when this division of labor is acquired unconsciously and breeds resentment and anger, it produces symptoms of terminal marital illness.

The most obvious symptom is violence. English common law, which has directly influenced our own, considered the husband and wife to be "one person in law: that is, the very being of legal existence of the woman is suspended in marriage." Learned jurists warned that, although men owned their spouses, they should be prudent in their "domestic chastisement." In tones of genteel moderation, they adjured the husband from "using any violence to his wife except in so far as he may lawfully and reasonably do so in order to correct and chastise his wife." We may strike her, but only infrequently; we may beat her, but only for her own good. This is our legal heritage.

Although the statistics vary, the most responsible estimates are that one out of six marriages involves wife abuse. When Congresswoman Barbara Ann Mikulski introduced the Family Violence and Treatment Act in the fall of 1977, she claimed that one fourth of American couples engage in violence during their relationship. But whatever the figure, it is as much an indictment of marriage as are the divorce statistics. Behind the numbers are women (and sometimes men) who are permanently scarred, if not physically, then emotionally.

"We had the nicest family in the world," said fifteen-year-old Peter Malone, whose father is a bank executive. "I had a successful mother, a successful father, a brilliant sister — only my father had a funny little habit of beating the hell out of his wife every once in a while." It was the family secret. They hid it so well that they even lied about his mother's bruised face (the clumsy woman kept stepping on rakes, bumping her head on the dashboard, running into doors). When the family happened to watch a TV program one night in which a man beat his wife to death, no one said a word. "What's that got to do with us?" said Peter, mocking his parents' deceitfulness. "That's about poor people, sick people. Not about the rich, happy Malones."

Anyone who thinks that Peter's plight is rare should read the literature on wife beating. Read it not for its statistics, which vary widely, but for its case studies of countless frightened, helpless, sometimes crippled women. Observe how a man can talk about his wife's "cute baby face" and minutes later beat her across the face with his belt. Ponder how easily these men redirect their frustrations toward their wives. Recall every man you have known who beats his wife, every movie you have watched in which men beat women. Consider the fact that, in the time it takes you to read this page, another woman will be beaten in her home.

Another symptom of the unhealthy marriage is mental illness. Just as women are the most common victims of physical violence, they are also the most common sufferers from mental anguish. Studies consistently reveal that a married woman is more likely to be in mental distress than a married man. In *The Future of Marriage,* Dr. Jessie Bernard summarized the data: "More wives than husbands report marital frustration and dissatisfaction; more report negative feelings; more wives than husbands report marital problems; more wives than husbands consider their marriage unhappy, have considered separation or divorce, have regretted their marriages."

Might this be due, some men inevitably ask, to women's complaining nature? Apparently not. Among single people, the reverse is true. Single men are more likely to be in distress than single women. In examining the relationship between sex roles, marital status, and mental illness, one researcher found that the rates of mental illness among divorced and widowed men were higher, often considerably so, than among women in similar circumstances. The evidence, at least as interpreted by some feminists, shows that the institution of marriage works better for husbands than for wives.

Such an interpretation overlooks, as we have seen, men's mortality rates. Men tend to hold in their emotions. They have been trained to be good soldiers. Under stress, they try to hide what they feel. They suppress their feelings until their gut, their back, their lungs, or their heart betrays them. Traditionally, men have forced themselves to work. The Breadwinner's ethic does not permit a man to recognize his own emotional distress. Evidently, the housewife's does.

Maggie Scarf talked to hundreds of women in order to understand why six times as many women as men suffer from depression. She expected to find that teenage women and older women would be most prone to this debilitating mental condition. To her surprise, she found that depression struck most often in the early thirties. "That's when most marriages tend to break up," Scarf reported. "A lot of depression in the 30's comes from feeling trapped in a relationship. A woman begins to feel, 'I was cheated.' "

The hollowness of marriage is not only expressed in violence or in clinically diagnosed mental illness. It is also evident in the two favorite pastimes of men and women: conversation and sex. Both can be the bases for intimacy, but both can also undermine it.

At one time or another, each of us has eavesdropped on conversations between a man and a woman. Studies of such verbal exchanges consistently reveal that men control the conversation. We do so by interrupting more often (96 percent of the time, according to one study), by switching subjects arbitrarily, and by scores of conversational tactics that are no secret to any woman. It triggers troublesome questions about whether male-female communication is an exchange of thoughts or an exercise in power. And it suggests why so many women compare marriage to a trap. For them, the structure of a conversation becomes the structure of their lives. As Holly Near sings, "I'm lonely when you're gone but I'm lonelier when you're home."

As we make conversation, so we make love. According to most chronicles of married life, sexual routinization is the bane of married life. The stock image of middle-aged marriage is not of passion ripened, but of passion withered. Men, it is assumed, seek new objects of desire. They already possess their wives, and they cannot desire what they already have. As recent feminist fiction clearly shows, the feelings are often mutual. "Even if you loved your husband," complains Isadora Wing in *Fear of Flying*, "there came that inevitable year when fucking him turned as bland as Velveeta cheese: filling, fattening even, but no thrill to the taste buds." It was not a question of whether the early Eros of courtship and romance would diminish and disappear. It was merely a question of when.

Does one stay married and preserve appearances or divorce and try again? This is a personal choice that, in our liberated culture, husband and wife can make freely. If a marriage disintegrates quickly enough, all a husband and wife must divide are their house and possessions. But if they have had children, their choice is far more difficult. It is the same question that bedeviled Solomon: How can one cut a child in half?

Until recently, the courts had a simple answer: the child belonged to the mother. This knee-jerk judicial response angers many men, and rightfully so. It is sexual discrimination against men. As myriad new men's rights and fathers' rights organizations argue, it should have no place in a court of law.

But men must realize that this is not the whole story. We have been told about the divorce, but not about the marriage that preceded it. Among the righteous defenders of fathers' rights today, who was also an advocate of a father's responsibilities?

Some divorced men will admit that they were not ideal husbands. They will acknowledge, as does the angry father who lost his three daughters, that they were busy, preoccupied; that they "didn't set the right priorities"; or that they were "not sensitive enough to my wife's needs." But they refuse to recognize the connection. They refuse to understand that most mothers have been awarded by the courts what they had all along — the daily responsibility for their children's care. Advocates of men's rights are correct: the current interpretation of the custody laws is unfair and needs reform. But if we expect the law to change, we must expect ourselves to change as well.

Men claimed the world of work and power and relegated women to home and children. Since our wives were dependent on us financially, we thought, in fact, we could still control both worlds. But when in divorce they actually take home and children, we cry foul. We cannot accept the fact that when a mother retains custody, it "merely ratifies the existing state of affairs," in Christopher Lasch's phrase. The "emotional desertion of the family by the father" becomes a physical reality. That joint custody is preferable cannot be denied. But if we intend to argue for joint *custody* in broken families, we had also better advocate joint *care* in those that are still intact.

For some men, particularly those in so-called men's rights organizations, alimony and custody are the key issues. According to them, this is the new battleground between the sexes. Unfortunately, their anger clouds their vision. How the spoils of divorce will be divided, while important, is not the crux of the matter.

Parenting is not a war that one side wins and the other loses. A child is not booty. The time to develop our fatherly instincts must come before divorce. The time to show we care about our children should begin when they emerge from the womb, not when they are contested in court. If we had learned to face them then, perhaps fewer of us would end up facing the judge instead.

In the seventies, fathers were finally encouraged. In 1974, Dr. Benjamin Spock had some new advice for fathers: "I feel that a father during the hours when he is at home, in the morning, in the evening, and on weekends, should put in as much time as the mother on child care." And in the 1976 edition of his classic, *Baby and Child Care*, he put it more strongly: "I think that a father ... will do best by his children, his wife *and himself* if he takes on half or more of the management of the children ... when he gets home from work and on weekends ... This is what sons and daughters need to see in action if they are to grow up without sexist attitudes." It was an admirable journey by this veteran pediatrician, a journey that many men half his age have not dared to make. And although a new breed of how-to-parent books are now available, most of us still need something more powerful than print to make us nurturant fathers. We need something as miraculous as life itself.

13 Fatherhood

The Closing of the Circle

The child is father to the man.
— Wordsworth, *My Heart Leaps Up*

Fall

When the nurse said, "It's positive," my confusion began.

"We're not ready to be parents," I told Shelley.

"Maybe you're not," she said, "but I am. I love you and I want this baby."

I loved her, too. But a baby? Shelley and I had only been together a year. I was only twenty-five.

"It would be a mistake to have this baby," I said. "We both have too much we want to accomplish right now."

"You did everything you could to get me pregnant," Shelley said, stating the obvious. "But now you're unwilling to deal with it. You want the baby to pay for your mistake?"

"But what if you had an abortion?" I probed. "Then, you know, in a couple of years . . ."

"Why don't *I* have an abortion? *No!* Why don't you figure out why you're so scared to have a child!"

For days I felt suspended between two contradictory images of the man I wanted to be. Like most men, I wanted to prove myself by marrying and having children. How else could I demonstrate that I was solid, stable, responsible, and mature?

But I also wanted excitement. When a man gets married, his friends often say that he is "hooked" or "tied down." I had no intention of spending my life behind a stack of bills, much less of dirty diapers. Getting married and having kids meant "settling down" or, worse, getting "in a rut." It meant no longer "keeping my options open."

"It's just too soon to have children, Shelley," I insisted after days of agonizing uncertainty. "I want to be free to work, change, grow. With a child, I would lose that freedom."

"What kind of freedom requires ending your child's life?" she asked. Bewildered, her eyes searched mine for a clue. "I love you more than I have ever loved anyone; I won't let you lie to yourself. You won't feel free if I have an abortion. You'll only feel more trapped."

"Trapped? By what?"

"By your fears."

"What fears?"

"Only you can answer that."

Winter

"We offer two basic policies, term insurance and whole life. I personally recommend whole life. It allows you to convert your policy into cash if—"

"Just a second," I said, interrupting the veteran insurance salesman. "I could use a cup of coffee. Let me get you one, too." But the coffee was merely a ruse to talk to Shelley.

"Hey, you let this guy in. How'd he say he'd gotten hold of my name?"

"From obstetrics. At the clinic. Insurance agents check whatever listings they can find of approaching births."

"Vultures!"

"Oh, come on now, it's just their job."

"I know, but for them to —"

"Lower your voice. Just talk to him for a minute. Tell him you don't want any life insurance if that's how you feel." More seriously she added, "You and I should talk about that sometime, though."

I poured the coffee and returned to the den.

"Sorry," said the salesman, "but I couldn't help overhearing. The only reason we seek you out is that we know how distracted you can be when having your first child. I've got three, by the way," he added with well-practiced intimacy.

He resumed his explanation of the unique benefits of his company's whole life policy. It was not until he began to compute the amount of coverage I needed that my resentment reignited.

"Just hold it right there," I said. "You're figuring I need fifty thousand dollars' worth of insurance. I'm wondering why the hell I would want *any.*"

"I understand your feelings," he said. "We don't like to think, do we, that we will pass away someday?"

"I don't need insurance agents to remind me that I'm mortal. What I don't understand is why. Yesterday I didn't have insurance; today I've *got* to have it."

He stared quietly at his folded hands, as if he were a minister advising a wayward son. "Let me speak personally here. What makes today different from yesterday is that you have taken on social responsibilities. Tomorrow, I assure you, you will take on even more. While I advise single individuals to buy insurance, I can respect them if they decide not to. After all, they're not really hurting anyone, are they?" He let a moment of silence pass in order to underscore the word. "I cannot, however, condone such a decision on the part of a man with a wife and child."

I stood up. "Sir, I didn't invite you here. I don't want to buy into your protection racket."

He picked up his briefcase and went out the door without a word.

"Exploiters," I said, fuming to Shelley as she made dinner. "Now that I'm about to be a father, I'm supposed to be a sucker. If I care about you and the baby, I'm supposed to be begging for life insurance. And after life insurance, it's a washer and dryer, then the baby's dresser, changing table, crib, clothes, stroller. Soon we'll feel like we have to buy a house. I swear, this country works as if capitalism was a logical consequence of sperm and egg!"

"I've meant to tell you," she said softly, "that I *do* think we need a washer and dryer. Now I'm not saying we need all that other junk, but I —"

"What's wrong with the Laundromat?"

"Sweetheart, we'll have a *baby.* We'll have three times as much laundry."

"A washer and dryer? Where are we going to put them — in the bathtub?"

"Either we get a washer and dryer or you'll be at the Laundromat twice a week. Now, get ready for dinner. I've made something special."

When I returned, I found Shelley putting candles in her Hanuk-kah *menorah*, which, until that night, had only gathered dust in the cupboard.

"Revival time?"

"Just thought we'd have candlelight at dinner, that's all."

"Fine with me." I thought no more about it until I returned to a darkened dining room.

The table was set for two, complete with wineglasses and a beautiful meal. Shelley wore a scarf over her head and had a box of matches in her hand. She began singing in Hebrew, slowly lighting each of the candles. I closed my eyes and felt peace enter the room. I went to my wife and embraced her, understanding then that a baby did not simply enter one's life. A baby changed it.

Spring

Shelley is lying on her back on a table in the delivery room. She is in the traditional position, holding her legs up. She grabs my hand.

"I can't push like this, lying flat. It feels like I'm trying to push him uphill instead of down."

The table does not lift up. Supporting her back with my arms while standing beside the table doesn't work. Every time she pushes, my arms give way. So I straddle the table, sitting behind her. My torso and arms cradle her sweating body.

"Push now, *push!*" coaxes the midwife for the hundredth time. "Now hold it, hold it, keep up the pressure. Good girl."

"Come on, lover," I whisper. "You're almost there now. You're doing great." I try to sound confident, but I am as scared as she is. Am I doing what I am supposed to? Why am I here? Am I just in the way? I'm tired. How long will this go on?

"The kid won't come out, Mark. He just won't come out."

"He is a pain in the ass, isn't he?" I smile. She tries to smile back but the next contraction stops her. She pushes, harder and harder.

"Keep it coming, keep it coming," the midwife encourages. "Push him out. You don't want him in there anymore."

"I don't want him in there," Shelley half-screams, "but he won't come out!"

"Yes, he will. You can do it. Push!"

I hold Shelley tightly. The doctor, looking worried, tells the nurse to pass him the fetal heart monitor. He carefully checks the baby's heartbeat. The doctor looks at us and sees our fear. He checks the heartbeat again.

Suddenly tears are streaming down my face and the midwife is placing our baby in Shelley's arms. I had stared unflinchingly at his entrance into the world, yet I never saw him emerge.

He is born, yet the second of birth was eclipsed by tears of awe. They spring endlessly from my eyes. It is as if from each lovemaking a tithe of joy had been taken, and now, all at once, they are being given back.

"Care to hold him now?" asks the midwife.

My arms shake, yet the baby is completely calm. I bring him to my shoulder, his head against my neck. Our child is alive. Alive!

When I look at Shelley her face seems luminous. My love for her overwhelms me. I feel a gratitude so pure that it illuminates my soul. Before, I thought the soul was a place that only theologians mapped. But the soul is not a place at all. It is an intensity of being.

My son screams. I sway, rocking him slowly, and he is calmed.

"Come kiss me," Shelley calls. Still holding our son to my shoulder, I step to her side and kiss her. "Who do you think he looks like?"

I have no answer, I have not yet dared to look him in the face. I take him from my shoulder and lean him back. I have seen him somewhere before. I witness him not as a father witnesses a child, but as light witnesses color. Without me he would not be; without him, what could I see?

I look into his calm blue eyes, which are seeing life for the first time. Once again, so are mine.

IN THE LATE forties, a generation of men had just survived a bloody war. In victory, they returned to their wives and sweethearts. Soon, they expected children. It was a bumper crop, now known as the baby boom. But none of these fathers, neither the former infantryman nor the West Point officer nor the GI from Des Moines, saw their children born. They were forbidden to enter the delivery room. If they asked why (and few bothered), the answers should have sounded shallow to the hardened ears of veterans.

Until well into the sixties, fathers were told they were nervous

Nellies, barely able to drive to the hospital much less attend the delivery. Having coped with the stresses of battle, they were nevertheless deemed emotionally incapable of coping with birth. Whether he is "short, thin or fat, or any race, or color, or creed," wrote a woman in the *New York Times Magazine,* an expectant father "tends to pace, chain-smoke, and talk to himself out loud." The fear that he will not get his wife to the hospital in time "gives the expectant father nightmares." Added a doctor: "A prospective father behind the wheel is more dangerous than a drunk on the Fourth of July." As late as the mid-sixties, this demeaning stereotype went unchallenged.

If obstetricians thought at all about the father's useless vigil in the waiting room, they deemed it inevitable. "Bring along a book, a magazine, a batch of crossword puzzles, or a solitary game," Dr. George Schaefer advised fathers-to-be. And if his job involved paperwork, Schaefer suggested that he follow the example of an accountant who whiled away the hours "determining how much tax money would be saved over the years as a result of the new dependency claim that was on the way."

How could such emotional distance pass for so long as normal? Crossword puzzles during delivery, the newborn as dependency claim — what kind of fatherhood was this? Of all those in the hospital, didn't the father know his wife better than anyone else? How could anyone, much less the father himself, believe that he was useless? If a father were irrelevant to his child at birth, when would he become relevant? If he couldn't be expected to support his wife then, when could he be?

In those days, only rarely did men try to stay by their wives' sides. To do so, they had to offend the hospital and even break the law. Because the hospital refused to let him into the delivery room, one father in the sixties was unable to witness the birth of his first child. When his wife became pregnant for the second time, the couple were determined to stay together for the birth. Just before the hospital attendants wheeled her away, the resolute father pulled out a pair of handcuffs. He locked one on his right hand, the other on her left. According to the news reports of this bizarre event, the father did indeed witness the birth. (So, by the way, did the father-to-be in California who barged into the delivery room and refused to leave until three policemen, dressed in sterile surgical gowns and masks, carried him away.)

But such stories are oddities. For every man who forced his way in, there were thousands of fathers who simply gave up. Some accepted it unquestioningly. Others spent their time, as one father in the late sixties put it, "sitting in a plastic chair with aluminum arms, thumbing witlessly through a fourteen-month-old *Good Housekeeping* and inwardly cursing all the mindless, faceless people who stand in the way of my participating in the birth of my child."

Why was childbirth out of bounds for fathers? None of the myths — that we would faint, go out of control, interfere with doctors, be upset by the sight of blood — were based on fact. "There is almost no rationale for these beliefs," concluded Dr. Arthur Colman and Libby Colman.

Some critics of the hospitals' policies blamed the power-hungry medical establishment. Indeed, some obstetricians themselves admit that their profession deserved criticism. "We obstetricians are so clever with our tools and gadgets that we have rewritten the obstetrical drama in a way as to make us the stars instead of women," said one young doctor. "We even accept the congratulations of husbands and then wonder why women are resentful of men."

Dr. Robert Bradley, a veteran obstetrician, delivered babies for years without giving much thought to fathers. But all that changed when an attractive patient, whom he had just helped give birth, pulled him down and kissed him gratefully. He enjoyed her admiration until he reached the waiting room. There sat her husband, Bradley recalled, "frightened, anxious, and distraught." And so he began to wonder: "What on earth was this lovely woman kissing *me* for? Why was I the object of her gratitude as a labor coach while her young lover sat useless in the waiting room? . . . The more I thought about it, the more ridiculous it seemed." Ultimately, it spurred him to write *Husband-Coached Childbirth.*

The obstetrician's high-handedness need not have been an insurmountable barrier. It was not decreed by God. It was erected by men, and if men had opposed it, it could have been overcome. But for decades it remained inviolate. Did men collude in their own exclusion? Did we not *want* to witness the birth? Were we afraid of it, looking for an escape? Perhaps we wanted to run away, but from what?

Social science offers no definitive answers to this question. The only clue we have is embedded in the experience of childbirth itself. It is the one time in married life when the wife's role must be central. A man is irrelevant in childbirth unless he can be of service to his wife.

His role hinges on whether or not he can comfort his wife. He must respond to the cues of her body, which is under stress. He must know how to focus on her needs and fears despite his own natural anxieties.

Because giving birth is often quite painful (and always potentially so), a woman may involuntarily tighten muscles that should remain relaxed. She may hold her breath tensely instead of breathing deeply. She may be frightened by the unfamiliar faces and surroundings of the hospital. If she feels overwhelmed, she may panic and lose control. The sensitive husband may help by massaging the part of her body that is involuntarily tense. He may time her contractions. He may simply hold her hand and offer encouragement. He may give her at that moment what he expects from her at all other moments — support.

He may, but then again he may not. What determines a husband's usefulness is his sensitivity. This is why birth can be a moment of truth for husband and wife. The truth may not always comfort. It may be an event that deepens love, or exposes its shallowness.

"The stress of labor and delivery is too profound to support falsehood," wrote the Colmans. "Former tensions are more likely to be exaggerated than reduced by the intimacy of the process."

Childbirth does not come with guarantees. It does not make all couples who share it feel closer to each other. Unfortunately, it pushes some apart.

"Peter was excited about the birth of our first child," said one woman about her ex-husband. "He read all sorts of books about it and had lots of ideas about the right way to do it. When it turned out to be more difficult than he expected, he became anxious. He got very pushy. He was so involved in his own feelings that he forgot about mine. I vowed to myself that I would not let him near me the next time I gave birth."

Their experience of childbirth was not the cause of their divorce, but it did reveal clearly what was wrong with their marriage. Peter was unable to play a supporting role. He did not know how to put aside his own ego, even for a few hours. He needed to be in control, and childbirth did not allow that. For some men, this is unbearable.

To some degree, every man feels this sense of helplessness, but how we respond to this feeling varies. In times of stress, such as childbirth, our responses reveal who we are. Everyday life occurs against the background of a society in which men are expected to take care of themselves and our inability to nurture others can remain hidden. But the delivery room brooks no ambiguity. The mother's and newborn's needs are paramount. The father's come last. At no other point in married life is it so patently obvious that the husband should serve the wife, not vice versa.

From this perspective, we can see why hospital regulations were a blessing in disguise. Refusing to allow men past the waiting room door constituted a convenient cover-up. We were thus allowed to avoid confronting our own inability to place ourselves in the role of caretaker and supportive helpmate. We were let off the hook. We could escape to the waiting room and avoid exposing our underused capacity for nurturance and care. We did not avoid the delivery room because we were afraid to see our wives' blood, sweat, and tears. We avoided it because we feared being found out. We were afraid to reveal to ourselves, and to our wives, that we could not minister to them.

Three psychologists took month-old rhesus monkeys away from their mothers and placed them in a cage with adult males. The male rhesus monkeys, known for their detached and indifferent attitude toward infants, became devoted fathers. They not only groomed the infants but played with them as intimately and as often as did their female counterparts.

It seems doubtful, then, that human males are biologically destined to be remote and uncaring toward infants. "Our research has discovered," the psychologists concluded, "a substantial potential for nurturant parental care in as relatively inflexible a creature as the male rhesus monkey." If monkeys have it, don't we?

A mother's body is her baby's home for months. Her breasts will nurse her child for many months more. She can experience her connection to her children through her body. We cannot. We are ineligible for the nine-month training course that every mother undergoes. We are not equipped to nurse a child upon our chests. If we want to give birth to children, we can do so only through our empathy. Interestingly, childbirth is an experience that may enable our empathy to deepen.

Studies of the mother-child relationship indicated that women who are alert participants in the births of their children bond more quickly and deeply to their infants than do mothers who did not experience the actual birth. This is equally true, it seems, for fathers.

Observation of fathers during childbirth has convinced researchers that men can bond with babies.

Fathers described witnessing birth as an experience that makes them feel more connected and involved with the child than they had ever imagined they would be. "Up to now, I didn't really feel that involved," said one new father shortly after the birth of his first child. "I really didn't have much strong feeling one way or the other. It was just my wife was pregnant and I was happy for her and that's just about as far as it went. But after witnessing the birth I did . . . a complete switch, just a complete switch! I just felt tremendous about it. And I was surprised because I thought I wouldn't take too much interest in it until it was old enough to be a small human being. But it already *is* a human being."

Becoming a father does not mean merely having someone else's birth certificate in your drawer. Fatherhood is a state of mind, a potentially new dimension of experience. Most of us have never played with dolls, nursed infants, or played with them for more than a few minutes at a time, have never ministered to the sick, the dying, the physically dependent. We have never explored the vast territory of care. Fatherhood offers an opportunity that we have never had before and, once our children are grown, may never have again.

Birth is a critical crossroads in any marriage. For men, it is the moment when our sex partner becomes our children's mother. Birth allows us to confront more graphically than at any other time the reality of our wives' motherhood. Whether the sight inspires us or repulses us tells us much about our masculinity.

If we suffer from what psychologists call exaggerated masculinity, we will have a tendency to "regard women as *either maternal or sexual, but not both.*" If so, we will try to cling to our adolescent fantasies of our wives as sex objects by avoiding seeing them as maternal beings. We will not want to see with our own eyes that the vagina is not only our erotic playground but also a child's birth canal. We will also place our wives in a double bind in which either they are not "sexy enough" or they are not "good mothers."

Birth can help us to outgrow this one-dimensional and ultimately self-destructive attitude. By witnessing the woman who inspires our passion become a mother, we may integrate more harmoniously our maternal and sexual images of women. Our wives, after all, want to be both good lovers and good mothers. They can be both only if we let them, only if we are as turned on by bodies that bear and nurse children. Parenthood is an opportunity to explore a deeper level of beauty, one that cannot be photographed, only felt.

Men who remain in the waiting room not only miss the spiritual beauty of birth, they also miss its pain. Few men have ever experienced as much pain as many women do in childbirth. Some births, of course, are quick and easy, but most are not. Especially if women are awake and aware, the birth process hurts. It is a time when women discover reserves of strength and endurance that they, and their husbands, never knew they had. It is a time when we can see that women, too, can be brave. It is a time when we can marvel at their strength.

No one sensed this more clearly than John Lennon. As he said shortly before his death, he did not want to be "looked upon as a sex object, a male, macho rock-'n'-roll singer. I got over that a long time ago . . . I like it to be known that, yes, I looked after the baby and I made bread and I was a househusband and I am proud of it."

Proud of taking care of children — it is still the exception to the rule. Most men who do so feel the burden of society's expectations that they do "men's work." One young man, whose college major was elementary education, was devoted to working with preschool children with learning disabilities. But after graduation, he realized that his occupation brought him perilously close to the division of the sexes. "I wouldn't say I have to justify what I do to other men," he said defensively. "I mean, it's a free country. But I do have to *explain.* Other men'll say, 'Oh, that's interesting,' but they obviously don't know what to say. In the back of their minds is the question: Hey, I wonder if this guy couldn't make it in a *real* job."

Real, of course, means masculine. A man who stays home with the kids or who chooses a career in early education is still considered bizarre. When James Levine told other men that he taught nursery school, they would ask, "Yes, but what are you *really* going to do?" Being with children, particularly young ones, is simply not "men's work."

For many years, social scientists agreed. Fathers were virtually ignored until the sixties, when they were finally "discovered" by psychologists and sociologists. They were still not considered nurturers, however. Fathers were considered valuable in preventing delinquency, in establishing proper "sex-role identification," and in fostering academic and professional achievement. They were still not expected actually to *care* for their children. It was not until the seventies that studies of fathering broke through the barrier of bias and began to catch up with the profound changes occurring in American society. These studies documented that fathers who were involved in childbirth classes and childbirth itself felt more positive about the experience; that fathers who were involved in the births were later more involved in child care; and that by the age of four weeks, infants responded differently to their fathers than to people outside the family. In other words, social science began to discover that a father-infant bond did exist — if only men would let it.

What price did we pay for ignoring so long the nurturant dimension of fathering? Future historians may one day tell us. Certainly, the consequences of the divorce between men and early childhood extend far beyond the delivery room and the playroom. Nothing — not politics, religion, science, or art — would be the same if men spent more of their lives in the infants' and toddlers' world.

One cannot help but wonder how differently some of our political leaders might act if they had ever spent time caring for children — not visiting them to give the press a "photo opportunity," but cleaning, feeding, dressing, and loving them. Instead, men are cut off from children, both by personal fears and by our culture's mores. We lose touch with life's beginnings, and our own. It requires almost an act of rebellion for men to discover — and to admit, as David Steinberg does in *fatherjournal* — that an infant can reveal to a full-grown man "a new level of loving, something I have been able to share with him that I hadn't allowed with anyone else."

If this is, indeed, rebellion, then more and more men are becoming rebels. Fatherhood is moving back from the periphery to the center of many men's lives. The word *nurturance* is being liberated from psychology textbooks and permitted to roam in daily conversations. *The Nurturant Male,* for instance, is a new men's magazine. It is reclaiming for men a quality that was in danger of becoming an exclusively feminine attribute.

Cultures change slowly. There are few landmarks by which progress can be measured. But one certainly is the bill, passed by Congress almost a decade ago, that reads in part:

To provide for hospitals to allow the biological father to attend the birth of his child if the woman consents.

Be it enacted by the Senate and the House of Representatives of the United States of America in Congress assembled That any hospital, clinic or similar establishment set up for the purpose of fostering, restoring or observing a person's health and which receives Federal funds under a grant, contract or loan or which has loans guaranteed under any Federal program shall allow the biological father to be in attendance during all phases of childbirth if consent is first obtained from the woman involved.

It is not in itself a revolution. But it is one of those documents that symbolize fundamental change. Before, a man had to ask himself if he wanted to share in the birth of his children. Now, a man has to ask himself if he does not want to. Birth is only the first step in the journey of fatherhood, but the direction we take will influence all that follows. Now, at last, we are free to choose which step it will be.

Visit any middle-class community during the day. Go to the park or the supermarket, the elementary school or the backyard. You will see children in women's hands. The men are at work, which for children simply means gone. Boys from birth to puberty are in the hands of women. This was the first lesson that postwar parents taught their children about sexuality: Mom is here; Dad is not. Mom's job was her children; Dad's job was something and somewhere else.

"I was always busy," recalled one typical father interviewed for *Men's Bodies, Men's Selves.* "If office work didn't take up my time, it was a local committee or the volunteer firefighters." Now his children are grown and he regrets "ending up a total stranger to my children . . . I wish I had those growing years back again."

Nixon's former aide John Ehrlichman, now retired to New Mexico after serving time in jail for his role in Watergate, writes in the morning and devotes the afternoon to his stepson. "I'm a full participant and I really enjoy it," he said. For him, it is round two. "I missed being home a lot when my kids were that age. I was building a law practice, and this is a second chance, really, and I'm very grateful for that." Unfortunately, a man's second try at fathering does his first set of children little good.

Ambition, responsibility, power — they lead even men with the strongest family ties to sacrifice family for career. If they change, it is often because of domestic crisis. After recovering from alcoholism through intensive therapy, Joan Kennedy observed that one of the benefits of her absence was "how close my husband, Ted, has grown to Patrick . . . He learned that he could cut back on the numbers of hours he worked in the Senate in order to be home with Patrick when he was sick or to watch him in a play or cheer him in a game and still be better off both at work and at home."

In the House of Representatives, Gary Myers simply could not accept the tensions. After leaping from his $24,000 salary as a steel plant foreman to a $57,000 position representing his district in Washington, he decided he would rather be a foreman. "The amount of time it takes to do this job is just not compatible with how much time I want to spend with my family," he told the *Washington Post*. Faced with eighty-hour work weeks and weekend trips back to his district, Myers found himself "feeling guilty knowing that I was unable to participate in family life," he told *People* magazine. Although to Capitol Hill sophisticates his lines sounded corny, to many young fathers they struck home: "I just wanted to know my kids before it was too late." From the *Washington Post* to *People,* his cautionary tale was prominently displayed, as if to warn the next generation of ambitious young men about the unexpected trade-offs of masculine success.

Even lower-level officials feel the burden. David Breneman lasted less than three months as a deputy assistant secretary at the Department of Health, Education and Welfare before he resigned. "High-level government jobs can wreck marriages," he said after retreating to private life. His fourteen-hour days meant he rarely saw his children, and even on the weekends he was at the office. "Government people are going to have to be childless," said his wife, Judy. "It'll be almost like celibacy, like being a priest. You'll marry the job."

"I don't want your families breaking up just because you feel loyal to me," former President Carter told his Cabinet after taking office in 1977. He admonished them to "see your children and spouses." He had been sensitized to the issue by Vice President Walter Mondale, who, as chairman of the Senate Subcommittee on Children and Youth for many years, had examined the impact of government policies on family life. But by the time the long-awaited White House Conference on Families convened in the final year of Carter's administration, the pattern had repeated itself. Families of administration officials had come apart at the seams. In one of the more publicized breakups, David Breneman's hard-driving boss, HEW Secretary Joseph Califano, found his work habits discussed in the morning paper. The secretary's seventy-hour-plus weeks, friends of Mrs. Califano told the gossip columnists, were part of the problem. No presidential admonition could dislodge a pattern rooted so deeply in the masculine role.

Wherever power resides — not only in government, but in business, the media, and in academia — men scramble for it. The rule is: sacrifice everything for success. And we do. The Gary Myerses and David Brenemans are the exceptions that prove the rule. They sacrificed power in order to be husbands and fathers. It is a price few men have been willing to pay.

According to Bertram S. Brown, a Washington psychiatrist whose clients occupy powerful positions in Washington, family problems were not always so severe. The man married ambition; his wife married him. But now women won't accept this. Men who can't say no to the demands of their bosses are losing their families. In the competitive male race to the top, no one dares say no. No one dares to leave for home first, to risk being thought of as the shirker or as lacking endurance.

As Alan Alda illustrated as a senator in *The Seduction of Joe Tynan,* men will numb themselves to their failures as family members until their families leave them no choice. Only when the adolescent rebels or the wife dissents will the father acknowledge the consequences of his physical and emotional absence from home. He has striven for power and success in the world only to find himself besieged at home.*

In Alan Saperstein's award-winning novel, *Mom Kills Kids and Self,* such a man returns home from work one day to find that his wife has killed their two sons and then herself. For two days, he lives in the house in half-crazed shock until the police find him. During those

---

* *The Seduction of Joe Tynan* and similar movies about the fatherhood dilemma prompted film critic Pauline Kael to remark in the *New Yorker:* "These pictures express the belief that if a man cares about anything besides being at home with the kids, he's corrupt . . . Alan Alda is a weak, corruptible fellow because he wants to stay at home communing with his daughter about her adolescent miseries." But Kael is merely knocking down her own straw man. The movies are not implying that kids should mean everything to men, only that they should mean more to men than they do now. After all, at the end of the film, Alan Alda is addressing a national political convention *and* reuniting with his wife and daughter.

forty-eight hours, he recognizes for the first time in his life what kind of father he has been. Senseless with grief, he addresses the corpses: "All right, let's make up for lost time. Who says it's too late?" And he tries to play catch with his dead son, saying, "The important thing is never to take your eye off the ball." His seven-year-old for once doesn't "beg me to play a game knowing my answer would be a tired, 'Maybe later.'"

"Today I will give you your bath," he announces as he carries another corpse into the bathtub. He had never bathed his children, but instead always sat in the living room reading the evening paper while his wife struggled with the kids upstairs. He had told himself that their baths were not urgent. After all, the children had always seemed clean. "The baths could wait," he had reasoned. "The children could wait. Somehow everything got done without me anyway."

The jacket copy of *Mom Kills Kids and Self* obviously exaggerated when it suggested that "a familiar newspaper headline suddenly becomes the case history of us all." But few fathers could read it without admitting that it struck uncomfortably close to home. Not only do most of us not share equally with our wives the responsibilities of child care; we barely have time to help. After our nine- to twelve-hour absence, not much time is left. And if we have time, we lack energy or patience. When we are home, we are either dressing, eating, and rushing out the door or dashing in tired, needing to relax and unwind. The structure of the Breadwinner's day is a built-in barrier to intimacy between father and child. Confronted by it, we do what human beings do so well: adapt. Children stifle their feelings for their fathers; fathers numb themselves to their capacity for nurturance; and both lose themselves in other things.

Men's ambivalence is so strong, however, that even though we do not want to have primary care of our children, we are determined that they bear our names. No matter how distant we are from them, we want them to be our heirs, our hedge against mortality. Why else would we so adamantly resist any effort to loosen our legal hold on their identities?

When a Florida couple, Steven Stitt and June Rice, gave birth to their first son, they wanted to name him Austin Rice-Stitt. But the Florida Department of Health refused to register their son's birth under that name, ruling that the child must take the father's surname only. So Stitt and Rice took the government agency to court. But, in a decision handed down in the summer of 1980, the First District Court of Appeal of the State of Florida refused to overrule the agency's action by a vote of 2 to 1.

At this writing, Austin is a two-and-a-half-year-old without a legal name. His parents, both lawyers, have decided to continue their legal battle. "It's our position," says Austin's mother, "that we can name him anything we like, certainly so far as the hyphenation of our own surnames."

The language of the Florida statute reflects the traditional American practice: "If the mother was married at the time of conception, the name of her husband at such time shall be entered on the certificate as the father of the child, and the surname of the child shall be entered on the certificate as that of the husband." Not only must a child take the man's name, but so until recently must the wife. It is the cardinal principle of patriarchy: both wife and children are joined to the man. It is a one-way street.*

In all the press coverage of the baby with no name, none of the judges would comment further; it is against judicial ethics to comment on the disposition of cases heard by the court. Although it is impossible to know with certainty what went on in the judges' chambers, perhaps the best clues are their names. Robert and Richard sided with the government. The dissenting judge was named Anne.

Thus do unconscious sexist attitudes masquerade as rational, legalistic judgments. And for as long as our blindness continues, our logic and laws will be hopelessly muddled and confused. How can we insist that our children bear our "label" if we do not bear the burden of caring for them and about them? Indeed, many men, like Bob Slocum in Joseph Heller's *Something Happened,* continually try to escape their responsibilities and their children.

"Let me work now," he says to her.
"I want to talk."
"Please. I was working when you came in."

---

* Although it is still infrequently exercised, a woman's right to retain her maiden name after marriage has recently been established. In 1976, the same court that ruled against Rice and Stitt defended the right of a married woman to obtain a driver's license in her maiden name. Challenging a Department of Highway Safety and Motor Vehicles' decision that upon marriage a woman's family name is "absolutely lost," the First District Court ruled that "although it is the general custom for a woman to change her name upon marriage to that of her husband, the law does not compel her to do so."

"You were reading a magazine."

"That's part of my work. And I have to prepare a program for the next company convention and work on two speeches . . ."

"Is it more important than me?"

"It's something I want to get done tonight."

"I want to talk now."

"Not now."

"Why?"

"No."

"Why not?"

"No."

"You never want to talk to me."

"Please get out now."

.

Later the father admits to himself: "I know by now that I don't have too much in common with children, not even my own, and that I dislike getting involved in long conversations with them. I really don't enjoy children for more than a couple of minutes at a time. It is difficult for me to keep interested in what they say and difficult for me to think of things to say that might interest them. So I no longer try." It is an admission of failure, of fatherly impotence. He is cut off from his own flesh and blood.

This is a bleak and tragic vision of middle age. The father is a rigid, autocratic figure. The passion has drained out of his marriage; his work has lost its purpose. His life, lacking intimacy, wears him down. Relationships are brittle, if not broken. The less he grows, the faster he ages.

While middle-aged, middle-class men are often portrayed as paragons of complacency, they are also symbols of self-doubt. Men who have achieved success know well how empty it can be. They have its rewards, but they have also paid its price. With their lives half over, however, many decide to take another path. They decide to stop trying to live up to the old archetypes and begin to rediscover themselves. Often we call this state a midlife crisis.

For a man engaged in this midlife transformation, everything may change at once: relationships to children, to work, to wife, to self. And the changes have a pattern — a revolt against the masculine armor in which he has been encased since adolescence. He wants to break out. He does not want to live the second half of his adult life as he has the first.

As he regains access to the parts of himself from which he became alienated in order to prove himself a man, he may experience what psychologist Roger Gould calls a "very exciting reunion." He wrote: "We hear of men becoming more in touch with beauty . . . requiring more affection, no longer being able to shut out home problems and go off to work because the pain sticks, wanting more intense relationships, being ready to cry, loving and tending their children with greater depth, seeking more sensuality in life, being more ready to make love."

It *is* a reunion, a reuniting of man with his forgotten self. He is reclaiming his anima, becoming whole. It is not androgyny; he is still a man. But he is a *whole* man. Just as the sun and moon may grace the dawn or dusk, so can feminine and masculine coexist in the same sex. Men thus reborn in midlife have a powerful beauty. They can reach to all ages and to both sexes with a generous and nurturant love. They can be mentors, lovers, fathers, and friends, enriching every life they touch.

14 The Lord

Images of the Soul

Our Father who art in Heaven
Hallowed be thy name...
— The Lord's Prayer

Some pharisees asked Jesus when the Kingdom of
God would come. His answer was: "The Kingdom of God does not come in such a way as to
be seen. No one will say, 'Look, here it is!' or
'There it is!'; because the Kingdom of God is
within you."
— Luke 17:20–21

LIKE EVERY MAN, I have my frailties. Among them is that I loathe
having to get up in the middle of the night. Nothing brings out the
worst in me more effectively than chronically interrupted sleep.

Sharing my home with a strong-willed infant was guaranteed to
trigger my neuroses. When our first son was born, we lived in a modest two-bedroom apartment. With just the two of us it had been large
enough, but with a newborn son who awakened a few times every
night for months, it seemed smaller than a prison cell.

Fortunately, Shelley would get up most of the time. For several
weeks, she handled most of the nocturnal chores. But eventually my
groggy wife and her conscience-stricken husband arrived at a more
equitable arrangement. She would handle all crises until 5:00 A.M.,
then it was my turn. Logically, I knew that this was fair and reason-
able. Indeed, I had an easier shift than Shelley did. But emotionally,
it was for me the hardest part of early parenthood. I always felt that
Shelley should be with him, not me.

For weeks I discharged my responsibilities, albeit resentfully. When I stumbled out of bed, it was still black outside. The apartment was chilly. After changing Shane's diapers or fetching a bottle, I would try to get him back to sleep as quickly as possible. When it took more than a minute (which it usually did), I became frustrated. I refused to let myself simply *be* with him because I refused to let go of my subconscious notion that somebody else should be comforting my little child. *Anybody* else but me.

Partly, I am sure, because of the tension and fatigue of being a father, my interest in meditation was rekindled. University towns like New Haven, Connecticut, where we lived, overflowed with spiritual salesmen of all kinds. I had always been put off by the hype of New Age gurus and their devoted followers. (Sri Aurobindo, Sathya Sai Baba, Sri Chinmoy, Baba Ram Dass, Sri Swami Satchidnanda, Chogyam Trungpa Rinpoche — each of these gurus had gained at least one of my friends or acquaintances as a disciple.) But parenthood had created stresses in my life that made me reconsider. I was still irritated by the aggressive marketing techniques of some of the meditation mongers. But I was so eager for the promised cure that I began meditating twice a day for twenty minutes.

I did not, however, enter a higher, more enlightened state of consciousness. Typically, I would come home wearily from work and, sitting in my favorite chair, try to remove myself from the daily cares and petty emotions of my life. But no matter how hard I tried, it didn't work. Worn down by broken sleep, I would often simply doze. At other times I would reflect anxiously on my life. But I never seemed to experience what the gurus said I should. I was disappointed and confused. Was something wrong with meditation or with me? I became so disheartened that I no longer bothered to sit during my after-work time of solitude. I went to bed instead. I no longer said I was meditating, simply napping.

Then one night, after a particularly exhausting day, Shane awoke crying again. He had recently stopped nursing and was feeling especially needy. I rolled out of bed, picked him up, and sat down, cradling his sobbing little body in my arms. For the first time, I did not resist being there. Instead of trying to pretend I was someplace else, I focused on him. I let myself absorb his cries. I wanted to be with him, wanted him to feel my love. I was not in a hurry. If he needed to cry himself back to sleep, I would let him. I simply wanted to hold him, to let him know I was there.

Slowly his cries abated. His body grew still and heavy against my chest. I felt him sink into a peaceful sleep. And as he journeyed, so did I. My destination was not sleep but a luminous, tranquil state of mind. I had not tried to reach that state; it was effortless. I do not know how long it lasted; it was timeless. I cannot even say I had an experience; all I did was let go.

With the light of dawn dancing on the walls, I laid Shane back in his crib and returned to bed. I did not sleep but lay there wondering. I did not know then, nor do I know now, whether that state of being I entered was what others call meditation. All I know is that the path to it was different from what I had expected. I had always thought of it as a "higher" path, a lofty, even celestial excursion beyond the realm of daily life. But it wasn't that at all. The path I took did not require escaping from my ordinary life but entering it. It did not require denying attachments but accepting them.

From all that I had read and heard, I had thought that meditation meant ceasing to care. For me, however, it meant finally *daring* to.

I say "dare" because caring demands courage — not rip-roaring, physical courage but the moral and spiritual kind. Had it not been for my son and of course my wife, I would have remained a coward. I write this not to boast of my growth but to share a dilemma that is more common than we think. In my mind, I held ideals — being fair with my wife, being nurturant with my child. But in my heart I had deep, primitive urges that contradicted those ideals. Nothing is more tragic than to witness a man whose actual behavior negates his stated beliefs.

My college friend Rick was such a man. He was never without a tidbit of advice gleaned from his readings of Zen or Sufi masters. He usually arrived around dinnertime at the ramshackle farmhouse that I shared years ago with several friends, and each time he would have a different book under his arm. But never food. He never cooked, never cleaned up, never even expressed his thanks to those of us who had done the cooking. It was as if he thought his radiant presence repaid our repeated hospitality.

At the time, I thought Rick irritated me simply because he was a hypocritical freeloader. But now I must admit that his arrogance bothered me so because it exposed my own. The truth is that neither Rick nor I, nor most men, are raised to serve. We are raised to achieve. If anything, our goal is to be served: by mothers or wives, by secretaries and assistants, by waitresses and stewardesses. One of the signs of a man's success is that it is the job of other people to serve him. Although successful politicians call themselves public servants, they rarely act that way. We want to be leaders, not servants; heroes, not helpers.

As a boy, I attended a Presbyterian church in which service was deemed a Christian virtue. Everywhere else the preeminent masculine virtues were achievement, toughness, intelligence, and success. In church I heard the opposite: that the meek would inherit the earth and that we should all serve the Lord and humbly do God's will. But even within the church, men seemed to reserve one kind of service for themselves and another for women. The ministers were always men. So was the treasurer. The secretary was a woman. So were the Sunday school teachers.

My friends and I grew up thinking that religion was rather sissy. It wasn't manly to be too interested in spiritual matters. A man could say he believed in God, but he shouldn't feel it too deeply. If he were to say that he felt God move within him, or that he meditated, or that he was seeking a spiritual path in life, or if he did anything that suggested that he was too involved in a spiritual quest, we found him odd.

Women had greater freedom. They could talk about God; if anything, that made them more feminine. After we young men reached puberty, we began to put distance between ourselves and the church. We did not want to be seen in those long, white choir robes. Not anymore.

The church lost me and my male friends because it seemed too tame. We wanted to prove our manhood, and the church offered us no opportunity. Other than asking us to memorize Bible verses and to sing tenor or bass, it offered no challenge. Other than wearing a coat and tie on a hot summer day, it asked for no sacrifice. It asked only for reverence, compassion, forgiveness, patience — the sugar and spice of piety.

No wonder the ranks of young men in the pews thinned so quickly during adolescence. The church lost us to more masculine callings. We left the church because it seemed so soft. We went off to prove — whether in a back seat or at boot camp, whether on the job or on the baseball diamond — our hardness. We wanted to be in control, not in God. We didn't want to be the meek; we wanted to be winners.

When I showed my friend Jim, a minister, an early draft of this chapter, he was struck by my self-evasion. "There's a lot of good information here, Mark," he said bluntly, "but where are you?

"It seems to me," he said gingerly, aware he was treading on tender ground, "that you're still stuck in your rebellion against Sunday school. When you couldn't believe in the kind of grandpa-type God they showed you, you decided that you weren't interested in religion. But religion is not just what happens in church. It is whatever moves you most deeply, whatever your deepest loyalties are."

Jim's simple words revealed to me why I had been so stuck for so long. The church had taught me to divide the world into those who believe in God and those who don't. In fact, every man has his gods, his deepest loyalties. Whether or not we call them God is not as important as whether we truly know what our deepest loyalties are. They are our ultimate image of manhood, the essence of our heroism.

IN JANUARY 1977, Paul Moore, Jr., the Episcopal bishop of New York, found himself in tears. For the first time, he was ordaining women as priests in the Episcopal church. First he had struggled against it, but finally he struggled for it. Facing the women ordinands, he was overwhelmed by his own emotions.

"We have been through a lot together," he told them from the high altar in the Cathedral of St. John the Divine. "You have hurt me, wounded me. I am sure I have wounded you. But now, thank God, we are to forgive one another and ask the forgiveness of God himself for whatever sins we have committed in conflict. And I want you to know that over the past years I have always respected your integrity and admired your courage. Let us confess our sins against God and our neighbor, and especially our sinfulness in the oppression of women in the life of the Church and the world, and in the wounds inflicted upon one another."

Bishop Moore had changed his mind only after months of meditation. Now he is convinced that the church's decision to accept women as priests was not only right, but of great importance. "It is part of a search for a spiritual reference point beyond gender," he said, reflecting on the difficult decision. "If the liturgy is always spoken by a man's voice, never a woman's, the worshiper cannot help but see God as male. What is of epochal importance is this search for a God who is neither male nor female alone, but contains or transcends both."

As he stands before his congregation, he still wonders about the same question that bedeviled nineteenth-century ministers. "I have often noticed that more women than men always seem to be in church," he said. "I don't have an explanation for it. But the fact that all gods are male has *got* to have something to do with it. Religious devotion comes from the same part of the human being as all other forms of affection. If the objects of that devotion are only male, one cannot fully experience one's own spirituality. Everyone's prayer life is impoverished if we can only relate to a male God."

It is not on behalf of women that Bishop Moore believes that the Church must become more balanced. It is for men's sake as well and for his own. "Ever since women have joined us, I feel a lot more relaxed, more natural," he says. "It is hard to put into words."

Bishop Moore's experience is but one episode in an ongoing religious conflict between the sexes. It has been the focus of countless conferences within every religious denomination and the subject of many books and essays. Written by both male and female theologians of vast knowledge, most of these studies analyze this conflict in terms of the structure of the Church. Some defend the Church's traditional sexual structure. "We can never ignore the fact that Christ is a man ... His role must be taken by a man," announced the Vatican's "Declaration on the Question of the Admission of Women to the Ministerial Priesthood." According to the Church fathers, a "natural resemblance" is required between Christ and the person who offers the sacraments. With a woman in such a priestly role, "it would be difficult to see in the minister the image of Christ. For Christ himself was and remains a man." According to this traditional interpretation, the sex of God and Christ is no minor detail. That God is called the Father and is referred to as "he" are not, to use a National Council of Churches phrase, "accidents of the limitations of human language." They are fundamental to the structure of the Church.

Other equally knowledgeable religious leaders disagree. They believe the structure of the Church must be reformed in order to include women as equals. "How can we agree that 'his role must be taken by a man'?" asks Sonya Quitslund, one of the founders of Christian Feminists. "If Paul and Christ could represent the feminine dimension, why cannot women represent the masculine?" During Pope John Paul II's trimphant tour of America in October 1979, Sister Theresa Kane expressed these same concerns at a formal welcoming ceremony for the pontiff in Washington, D.C. The only churchwoman to address the pope, she spoke of the anguish of womankind and asked that women be included in "all ministries of our Church."

For theologians and ministers, the question of the Church's structure naturally seems central. But a more personal question is also involved. It is a question, not of the structure of the Church, but of man's soul.

Every man raised in the Judeo-Christian tradition must at some point have felt flattered that the maker of heaven and earth was a male.* The earth may be called she, but God is always he. Only pagans worshiped the she-earth; civilized men reserved their devotion for their he-god. On one level, we are worshiping the most holy religious symbol. But on another level, we are worshiping our own sex. "God" not only represents a spiritual being; it represents a masculine archetype. Without intending disrespect for any single religious tradition, we will call this archetype the Lord.

The Lord stands at the apex of a spiritual pyramid based upon an unbroken chain of male command: from the Lord in heaven, to my lord the king, to the lord of the manor, and finally to the lord of the household — the husband. (The dictionary mercifully calls this final usage "archaic.") What all have in common is the prerogative to lord over others or, as *Webster's* puts it, "To play the lord; domineer."

We have already seen how men have played the Lord both in

---

* To varying degrees, other religious traditions — including Judaism, Islam, Hinduism, and Buddhism — have also been male dominated. Jewish custom, as contemporary Jewish feminists have pointed out, is also patriarchal. Islamic practices strikingly reflect male biases. The practice of purdah and suttee among the Hindus reveals male-centered world views. And even Buddhism, perhaps the least sexist of the great religious traditions, is rooted in an anti-feminine world view.

public and in private. But we have yet to explore the religious roots of our masculinity. What we call faith in God may often inspire true compassion and service, but it has also helped to buttress an irrational male self-righteousness. Men who unconsciously emulate the Lord as an image of manhood can become arrogant, enthralled by their own holiness. Instead of inspiring humility, our beliefs can be used to justify being callous, judgmental, and unloving. Instead of believing in the goodness of all men and women as God's children, the Lord can despise and even destroy the Philistines, those men of different faiths. At his worst, the Lord can become so zealous about saving the souls of others that he loses his own. He can launch crusades against Satan with such vengeance that his own evil is indistinguishable from his adversary's. He represents domination, not service; power, not nurturance.

This unconscious image of the Lord is embedded deep within men's souls. Throughout history, it has led men — even those who wore the vestments of the church — to behave in ways that later generations would condemn as diabolical. Indeed, our "holy" ambivalence toward women reveals more about our souls than most sermons from the pulpit.

From the very beginning, the Judeo-Christian tradition has linked woman and evil. When second-century theologians struggled to explain the Devil's origins, they surmised that Satan and his various devils had once been angels. They were banished by God from heaven for committing a heinous crime: carnal relations with the daughters of men. Their name testified to their sins: *angeli fornicatores*. Illicit sex and the powerful allure of women's bodies lie at the heart of the cosmology of heaven and hell, God and Satan. Despite its logical flaws (when Satan tempted Eve in the Garden of Eden, there were as yet no daughters of men), the explanation survived for centuries. Men's ambivalence toward women — as objects of hate (the witch) and objects of worship (the Virgin) — is an unconscious dynamic that has confounded man's spiritual quest throughout history.

In 1484, the long-standing Christian belief in the link between women and Satan burst into flames. Pope Innocent VIII issued a special papal pronouncement directed against witches, many of whom were women who allegedly fornicated with Satan. As Jesus Christ, the Son of God, served as his Father's emissary on earth, so the witch served as the Devil's. The pope's decree provided the Church's official blessing to the fires being kindled throughout Central Europe that would claim the lives of a million or more witches, evil spirits that inevitably took a feminine form.*

The grisly history of witchcraft is now common knowledge. Among feminist and gay critics of the Church, recounting the horrors of witch trials has become a predictable exercise. Some of Christianity's critics seem to believe that the evidence of witch hunts alone establishes the irredeemable sexism and spiritual bankruptcy of our "patriarchal" religious tradition. To them, official Christianity and misogyny are virtually synonymous.

This one-dimensional portrayal of evil, woman-hating churchmen, does justice neither to Christianity nor to masculinity, however. In fact, men have far more complex and contradictory feelings about women. We may despise them, but we also worship them.

The witch hunts of the fifteenth century followed a period in Church history during which the Virgin Mary was raised to the status of a goddess. As early as the eleventh and twelfth centuries, the Virgin had become the object of a popular groundswell of Mariolatry, or the worship of Mary. As one historian described it, her followers "placed the Virgin on a higher emotional plane than the purely masculine Trinity." The Almighty God was even addressed as "god, son of Holy Mary." Wrote Amaury de Riencourt in his panoramic study, *Sex and Power in History:* "This new Gospel of Mary, carved in stone in every Gothic cathedral consecrated to 'Our Lady,' swept Western Christendom, compelling the church to sanctify it. Great festivals came into being celebrating the Virgin's life ... In fact, in the thirteenth century, one author bluntly declared that 'God changed sex.' "

---

* The pope anointed as chief inquisitors a pair of Dominican monks, Jacob Sprenger and Heinrich Kramer. They composed a document describing witchcraft called the *Malleus Maleficarum,* or *Witches' Hammer,* which went through nineteen editions. Of its seven rambling chapters, six were about sex. "A woman is beautiful to look upon, contaminating to the touch and deadly to keep," argued its two celibate authors. Since "all witchcraft comes from carnal lust, which is in women insatiable," women have turned to the Devil for fulfillment. It is through women that the Devil works his evil designs on the world. Witches are capable, for example, of causing impotence and castration. Being by nature more carnal than men, and "feebler both in mind and body," they naturally come under the Devil's influence more easily than men. It is a durable paradigm, a protofascist mind set that lurks behind our own century's most heinous crimes. It entitles good men to destroy other human beings, because the victims are in league with satanic forces. The assassin can thereby portray himself as a hero — a savior, so to speak, of mankind. Even the greatest legal minds succumbed to such vanity.

This popular movement portrayed the Virgin Mary as the ultimate healer and the quintessence of love and charity. Since it posed a threat to the Church, the Church fathers repeatedly attempted to discredit it. "The woman is subject to the man on account of the weakness of her nature, both of mind and of body," wrote Thomas Aquinas in his *Summa Theologica*. According to him, the Virgin was conceived in sin like every other mortal and was redeemed by her son, Jesus. "Man is the beginning of woman and her end," said Aquinas, "just as God is the beginning and end of every creature."

The centuries-old biases of the Bible were used to buttress such patriarchal arguments. One text — "The head of every man is Christ, the head of every woman is her husband, and the head of Christ is God" (1 Corinthians 11:3) — was often cited to justify establishing a hierarchy in which woman was twice removed from God. "The women should keep silent in the churches . . . If there is anything they desire to know, let them ask their husbands at home" (1 Corinthians 14:33–35). And again in 1 Timothy 2:11: "I permit no woman to teach or to have authority over men; she is to keep silent."

But the devotion to Mary among the masses was deeply rooted. Heavy-handed Bible verses were not enough to counteract it. People seemed to need a feminine symbol of goodness, mercy, and nurturance. An exclusively male Trinity did not satisfy this yearning. Mary moved them more profoundly and more spontaneously than the male saints promoted by the Church. They wanted to be saved, not only by a man, but by a woman. Until the end of the fifteenth century, the Madonna appeared everywhere. She was the Regina Coeli, Queen of Heaven. Only the witch hunts finally ended her reign. Masculine images once again prevailed in the Catholic church as well as among the emerging Protestant groups.

The officially sanctioned murder of millions of diabolical women, on the one hand, and the extraordinary devotion inspired by the Virgin Mary, on the other hand, reveal a vital contradiction. If women were evil in the Christian mind, then why did a woman — Mary — also symbolize the ultimate in goodness?

To answer this question we must shift our focus. We have seen how our unconscious ambivalence toward women was reflected in our images of the holy Virgin and the evil witch. But we also have a similar ambivalence about our own sex.

If women's souls were capable of superhuman purity and subhuman depravity, so were ours. At one extreme, we were saints; at the other, sinners. God epitomized the former; the Devil, the latter. The structure of our souls resembled a ladder reaching from heaven to hell, and every man occupied a rung. Every act of our lives either raised us a notch above those around us or lowered us similarly. We were engaged in an enterprise, partly conscious and partly unconscious, that involved spiritual heroism. The more we resembled the Lord, the more likely we were to be saved. The less we resembled him, the more likely we were to be damned. In the case of salvation, we would live forever in a radiant celestial paradise with God (portrayed throughout history as a white-bearded holy "boss" and his angels as white-gowned holy "secretaries"). All its residents lived without any pain or suffering. In the case of damnation, we would live forever in a dark, underground hell with the Devil (invariably dark-haired, short, and heavyset) and other sinners. All its residents lived without any joy or pleasure.

This supernatural, manmade universe was created and ruled by a merciless, vengeful Lord. There were no goddesses or Holy Mothers in this hypermasculine world view. We were all, in the words of Jonathan Edwards's fiery sermon, "sinners in the hands of an angry God." The Almighty "abhors you," Edwards told his terror-stricken congregation in Enfield, Connecticut, on July 8, 1741. "His wrath towards you burns like fire; he looks upon you as worthy of nothing else but to be cast into the fire . . . you are ten thousand times so abominable in his eyes as the most hateful and venomous serpent is in ours." As the historian Perry Miller observed, Edwards sounded "more fiendish than Christian" and evoked a male God who "stands aloof, a being compacted essentially of wrath."

First in Northern Europe and then in the New World, this Protestant world view prevailed. Feminine images of deity were completely discarded and the need for them was repressed. The feminine side of man's nature, Jung's anima, was banished from the Church and excommunicated to the unconscious. Femininity and divinity had to be kept separate. God the Father, God the Son, the disciples, the prophets — all were men. From God to the village preacher to the head of the family, spirituality was to be kept firmly in the hands of the first sex. Only a man could embody the Lord.

This fundamentalist world view is often dismissed as hocus-pocus by modern, secular men. But if we are to uncover the subconscious roots of our own masculinity, we can learn much by studying its most extraordinary features. The subordination of women represented man's attempt to deny them spiritual power. In addition to denying women, it denied death. Whether sinner or saint, everyone lived forever. This afterlife, furthermore, denied the most basic truth: joy and suffering, pain and pleasure, are intertwined in the human heart. Not surprisingly, the settings for these black-or-white hereafters were otherworldly. The verdant earth, the Great Mother of so-called primitive faiths, was also denied.

History itself is evidence of the extraordinary power of this man-made belief system. It enabled us to feel in control. It appeared to put the great existential questions of life conveniently to rest. It answered many of man's unconscious needs. But the unconscious is a weak foundation on which to build a belief system. It was constructed upon a profound denial of women, death, the earth, and, indeed, life itself. No wonder feminist writers now mock our masculine self-deception, as did Phyllis Chesler in her satiric version of the all-male creation:

> In the beginning there was the word. It will tell a fabulous lie so often and with such force that everyone will believe it. Soon, no one will even notice the deception.
> "Listen, children, here are the facts: Your real Mother is me — your Father!"
> It was God the Father who gave birth to Adam, and Adam the Man who gave birth to Eve, and God the Father who created Christ.

Chesler and other critics of patriarchal religion are not mocking the belief in God. They are asking us instead to believe in a God that transcends sexuality.

It is not only feminists who ask why God must be so dogmatically masculine. Humanistic theologians, when probing the frontiers of religion, have also advocated demasculinizing our images of God. Paul Tillich, for example, raised the question of "whether there are elements in genuine Protestant symbolism which transcend the alternative male-female and which are capable of being developed over against a one-sided male-determined symbolism." He did not write this to satisfy current feminist critics; it was written a quarter-century ago. It was not written to be fashionable; it was then a minority point of view. Tillich raised the question of God's sexual identity because, as a theologian, he sensed that theology was incomplete. The conception of a single, mortal human being requires both a mother's egg and a father's sperm. Why on earth, then, should our symbols of spirituality be exclusively male? Why should our conceptions of divinity be any less miraculous than life itself?

Ultimately, it is not a question of reforming the Church's structure or terminology. It is rather a question of daring to delve deeper into our own inner lives. Each of the masculine archetypes described in this book, including the Lord, requires the denial of the feminine. Each depends on denying the independent creative power of womanhood (its so-called masculine side) and on denying the tender, vulnerable dimension of manhood (its so-called feminine side). In the Frontiersman's relationship to the earth, the Breadwinner's to his family, the Soldier's to violence, and the Expert's to knowledge, domination displaces service. While claiming, like the medieval witchhunters, that we are *serving* God (or some other noble goal), we are in fact worshiping our unconscious masculine hero images.

This is why the search for a spirituality that seeks alternatives to the image of a masculine Lord is so vital. It symbolizes the quest for a new heroism that embraces rather than denies the feminine and that seeks service rather than domination. Such a spiritual quest is intensely personal. As Bishop Moore admitted, it is "hard to put into words." But perhaps he felt "more relaxed, more natural," after women had been ordained because he could accept a part of himself, and a part of God, that had for so long been denied.

In the beginning, we come from our mothers. In the end, we return to the mother earth. A man's spirituality cannot be complete unless it embraces the full meaning of these truths. If our spirituality cannot embrace femininity, then it remains incomplete, unrealized. Spirituality in a man does not require a denial of the feminine. On the contrary, it is an affirmation of femininity as an essential part of ourselves — and of our God.

PART III

In Transition

HEROES TODAY are not born. They are packaged. They are thrust upon us by marketing strategies. In place of legends, we create personalities. Instead of gods, we manufacture superstars. Instead of admiring greatness, we worship celebrity.

It is a consumer's heroism, and the shelves of our cultural supermarket are crammed to capacity with competing brands. We are free to purchase the heroism that best suits our fancy. It is one of the final freedoms of the pluralistic, individualistic society: to each man, his own store-bought hero. It is far better than totalitarian heroism, where the imposition of a single demigod with a touched-up, aging face hangs in every shop and home. But consumerist heroism can also be oppressive.

As the old images of manhood fade, new ones emerge. Betty Friedan, in her sympathetic portrait of the new masculine attitudes, calls it "a deceptively quiet movement, a shifting in direction, a saying 'no' to old patterns, a searching for new values."

But no sooner have such men emerged than an image of them begins to be marketed. When *Cosmopolitan* reprinted Friedan's thoughtful, perceptive analysis, it was under the headline: "And Now ... the Liberated Man." The article featured a full-page photograph of the "new man" kneeling on the sidewalk with a boy. Laughing together, the man holds a briefcase; the boy, a soccer ball.

It is touching until one reads the credits. The photograph was by Bruce Laurence; styling, by Sharon Simonaire; the man's clothes, by Alexander Julian; the briefcase, from Bottega Veneta; the boy's jacket, from Au Chat Botte. It is not a picture of father and son caught in a moment of intimacy. It is a synthetic image that promises, like all the old images, to become larger than life. The man portrayed will become the post-feminist Superman, a magical juggler of roles who can afford stylish suits and Italian leather briefcases but who still plays ball with his son.

Replacing one icon with another is hardly liberation. Merely switching images like TV channels alters the message but not the medium. Producing and consuming images is a multibillion-dollar industry. Fortunes are invested to bring us glossy, charismatic models of masculinity and femininity. Surrounded by this well-hyped cast, we may neglect our own firsthand experiences. We relate more to these images than to our friends. We are more often in communion with the media than with our own senses. It is easy to evade the difficult, sometimes traumatic search for our own identity by adopting one prescribed by someone else.

Why do we seem to need images so desperately? Perhaps they provide security. They help us to define ourelves and to locate ourselves in the universe. They make us feel less fragile and alone. Pretending to be the Frontiersman, Breadwinner, Soldier, Expert, or Lord is an attempt to find safety. Each is a bulwark raised against profound, existential fears.

Throughout this book, we have explored many of these fears. But by accepting and sharing our fears of insecurity and vulnerability, we can move beyond these images. Since the old archetypes no longer work and the new ones are untested and unclear, we must each choose our own direction. Forced to change, yet uncertain of our direction, we must break new trails. Old landmarks have been eroded. Signposts have been effaced. Yet a crisis in masculinity is also an opportunity. It compels us to find new maps of the world we live in. It encourages us to find wise traveling companions. It inspires us to learn to read the compass of our heart.

15 Heroism

The Emerging Masculinities

> The deep, nourishing and spiritually radiant energy of the male lies not in the feminine side, but in the deep masculine ... The kind of energy I'm talking about is not the same as macho brute strength ... it's forceful action undertaken, not with compassion, but with resolve.
> — Robert Bly

AMERICA SEEMS TO BE perpetually engaged in its ritual elections. We are constantly either preparing for, engaged in, or recovering from these sacred rites of white American males. Every four years, with a tedious frenzy, we pick one of our brothers to be the President. The most recent line-up of candidates was typical: Reagan-Bush (Republican), Carter-Mondale (Democrat), Anderson-Lucey (Independent). All are white, middle-class, college-educated males. Regardless of who won, power would remain within this elite.

Outsiders, such as blacks and women and the poor, frequently criticize the sociosexual cadre of which I am a member. Unlike blacks, Hispanics, and women — roughly two thirds of America's citizens — I could become President of the United States — unless, of course, I break the club's rules.

The rules evolve slowly. A Catholic may be nominated and elected, but not a Jew or a black. A candidate's manly eyes may moisten, although he is not yet allowed to weep. He may be divorced and remarried, but preferably not single, and absolutely not gay. He should have served in the armed forces; if not, he should act as if he did. He must not admit to ever having been depressed, nor should he have ever had psychological counseling. He must have no connection whatsoever to socialism, and he should praise competition. He is required to pepper his speeches with sports metaphors and always to advocate being tough. An American action may be ill advised but never a mistake. Like a human computer, he should memorize statistics and explanations for everything. No candidate may say, "I don't know." And regardless of how intelligent he is, he must mechanically blame the other political party for everything that is wrong in America — except, perhaps, the weather.

I know the club's rules well. Many of my friends and classmates and neighbors are members, but I do not agree with those anti-male fanatics who believe that the "best and the brightest" are fatally flawed. Ambitious, well-educated white men, busy scrambling for seats close to the centers of power, are just as capable of change as anybody else. Neither their sex nor their comparative success inhibits them. They can become leaders worthy of respect if only they become more aware than their forefathers were of the forces that have shaped their personal and collective history. If they do so, they will at last become what they have always claimed to be: public servants.

What sort of leader do I want? Since the nod of his head can initiate Armageddon, I want him to be free of the unconscious desire to prove himself a man. I do not want him to dismiss as effeminate everyone who counsels caution or mediation or who favors nonmilitary responses to conflict. If he ever has to decide whether or not to "push the button" in a crisis, I want him to perceive that crisis accurately — to recognize it as the killing of America, civilization, and perhaps the planet, not as a presidential test of manhood.

Each man picks his own leaders. What follows are some of mine. For each profiled here, there are thousands more. "You can write about me," one of these men told me, "but don't turn me into an ideal. I'm not." None of us is. The men who symbolize the emerging masculinities are not superheroes; they are real men with ordinary human faults. They are everyday heroes.

THE ESSENTIAL quality of the emerging masculinities is embedded in the phrase itself. It is not singular, but plural.

Men are not formed in molds. To replace an old stereotype with a new one would be pointless. The range of masculinities and femininities is wide, so wide that the qualities overlap. Who could wish that all men were passive any more than one would wish that they were all aggressive? The transformation of sexual identity now occurring is an opportunity to acknowledge and respect diversity. We have had enough experiments in regimentation and in totalitarian definitions of the "new man." What we seek, then, are new men, who not only differ from past archetypes, but who also differ among themselves.

The emerging masculinities are unlike the old, not only in their emphasis on diversity, but because they are not based as much on tradition as on experience. Too often tradition is invoked to justify the latest twist in sexual roles. The traditional role of the housewife was not traditional at all. It was an invention of the Industrial Revolution. So many changes have occurred so rapidly that relying on tradition is tantamount to refusing to question all widely shared biases. It is far better to acknowledge, as many men now do, that the meaning of masculine and feminine must be determined by every man and woman and couple based on their own experiences. Although the past must be studied, to deny the teaching of our own experience is to deny the only contemporary, personal instruction available.

The emerging perspective on sexuality, then, is not moralistic but experimental. It does not decree that women with young children shall not work outside the home; nor does it reverse the rules and claim that women who devote themselves to their homes and families are unliberated. Instead of a codified set of expectations, we are now ready to examine for ourselves what works and what does not.

In such a culture, the encounter of man and woman may be more enthralling than ever. It will certainly be less preconceived, more spontaneous. Couples may write their own scripts, construct their own plots, with unprecedented freedom. Whether the encounter is between strangers on a bus, colleagues in a meeting, or lovers in bed, a man and a woman are free to find the fullest range of possibilities. Neither needs to act in certain ways because of preordained cross-sexual codes of conduct. As a result, they may discover, and thereafter continually rediscover, new ways of being together.

Freed from the burden of continually promoting their sex's superiority, men who embody the emerging masculinities can develop a deeper awareness of the mutuality of the sexes. Just as two men faced with a common task can divide responsibilities according to their talents and personalities, so can a woman and a man who are free of unexamined notions of what manhood and womanhood must be. They can replace these stale and deadening prescriptions of sexual behavior with greater freedom. No automatic assumptions will be made that men are achievement oriented or that women are nurturance oriented. Each will be free to experience both.

As these emerging masculinities gain strength, men will no longer feel compelled to keep masculine and feminine roles separate. We can allow them to be shared. The lines of responsibility, such as his for making money and hers for taking care of the children, can soften. Most jobs are more rewarding if they are freely chosen and do not consume one's whole life. Men will be more balanced breadwinners if that responsibility is shared. Women will be more balanced caretakers if that responsibility, too, is shared. And as they are shared, they will be transformed. Some couples may wish to reverse roles completely; others may retain clearly divided roles. But if the freedom to choose is increased, the outcome, whatever its form, will be liberating for both men and women.

These more personal and more fulfilling arrangements can develop because men will no longer need to be the ultimate decision makers. Instead of claiming that he is rational and she emotional, men and women together can develop a more holistic understanding. Narrowly rational approaches to problems are ultimately as superficial as blindly emotional reactions. The very separation of these terms is a symptom of the destructive patterns that developed in our culture. The emerging masculinities will share a greater willingness to expand the boundaries of what we have called rational thought to include spiritual, sexual, psychic, and bodily experiences. We will recognize that other ways of knowing may bring wisdom and meaning into life that the rational may never know.

Finally, the emerging masculinities are not inherited images with which men identify unconsciously. They are rather living emblems of a kind of masculinity to which men consciously aspire. They are signs pointing toward a fuller, more humane understanding of sexuality, reflections of a more loving mutuality between men and women, other men, and the earth itself.

It is still too soon to tell whether these new emblems will survive and flourish. But from diverse sources comes clear evidence that they are struggling to take root in our culture, for there can be no doubt that the old archetypes are being challenged.

The emerging masculinities may not replace the old. But they will certainly change them.

The Healer

Being considerate of other people, like being considerate of the earth, has not been highly valued. We desperately need masculine role models that make being considerate just as important as being tough.
— Denis Hayes

Twenty years ago, only specialists knew the term *ecology*. Today it is a household word. Legions of men and women have stepped forward to protect and to heal the earth. Some call themselves environmentalists or conservationists. Others call themselves stewards of the land, or its custodians. But they are all searching for a more gentle relationship with the earth. In their own lives, they are seeking, in Gary Snyder's phrase, to "live lightly" on this amazing, fertile planet.

Men in the forefront of this emerging masculinity do not speak of themselves as "King of the wild frontier," as in the Davy Crockett ballad. Nor do they claim the title "master of the wilderness," as Daniel Boone's biographers called him. "We think of ourselves as the earth's students," says Denis Hayes, a former director of the Solar Energy Research Institute in Colorado. He has embodied the Healer for more than a decade as the founder of the national consciousness-raising events Earth Day (1970) and Sun Day (1980) and as the author of several books advocating a wiser, more sensitive use of the earth's resources.

"The people in the environmental movement," says Hayes, "do not think man is entitled to use the earth for instant gratification. We need to learn how to be considerate of her needs. It is enlightened self-interest, really: we want to be able to continue enjoying our relationship to the earth and to watch our children enjoy her too."

Hayes is aware that the energy-environment debate has become polarized — and sexualized. Now a resident of Golden, Colorado, Hayes resents it when national environmental groups are dismissed by aggressive developers as "Eastern environmentalists." He believes the slur implies that those who respect the earth are all flabby, office-bound city folk, while those who want to plunder the earth are robust, daring outdoorsmen. "I've been concerned about the sexual dimension of the debate for some time," Hayes continues. "I told Amory Lovins [the author of *Soft Energy Paths*] that he shouldn't use the terms 'soft' and 'hard' to describe the alternatives. I knew that 'soft' would immediately trigger a negative sexual response. I like the terms 'sensitive' or 'gentle' or 'sustainable' better. I'm calling my next book *Smart Energy* for this very reason. I am trying to use a vocabulary which won't push any of those unconscious buttons."

It is not only the earth that men must learn to treat more gently, according to Hayes. He feels men tend to be inconsiderate in other spheres of their lives as well, particularly toward women: "Being considerate of other people, like being considerate of the earth, has not been highly valued. We desperately need masculine role models that make being considerate just as important as being strong. Consideration and sensitivity should not be seen as sissified traits, but as noble ones."

The Healer's voice is still rarely heeded. The image of the Frontiersman still mesmerizes much of our culture. Many men still counsel a more aggressive, exploitative approach to the earth. We must find stronger, more powerful machines, say today's Frontiersmen. If we leave scars, we will cover them. If we leave poisons, we will bury them. Whatever the earth has — oil or coal, land or water — we have a right to take. If we cannot take it gently, we must take it by force.

The Healer stands opposed. A growing chorus of voices now calls for a "new reverence for the land" and "a new ethic." They prize the traits of "simplicity, neighborliness, humility." They use the word *husbandry.* They advocate self-restraint, saying, "We must come to terms with ourselves." They propose a policy of thinking before acting, of asking what the "environmental impact" of any action will be. They assert that we can grow food without destroying the earth's soil; that we can produce without polluting air and water; that we can be men without doing violence to the earth.

The environmental movement and feminism have overlapped and fueled each other because they are both political and personal. The Healer emerges as a masculine emblem because the Frontiersman's violence has been directed, not only at the earth, but also at his own species, even those he loves.

Tom Mosmiller lives in California, where the Frontiersman once flourished. He is not involved in conquest, however, but in dealing with its consequences, for he works at a shelter for battered women and children. His job is to counsel the men who do it.

"Of course men who batter women differ," says Mosmiller. "But one common theme is that these men feel worthless — or helpless. And they take out those feelings on their loved ones."

I found myself trusting Mosmiller easily. His face is etched with gentleness. His body is at ease, and his eyes radiate warmth. He moves slowly, deliberately, calmly. Like a modern Johnny Appleseed, he seems to sow good will. But Mosmiller, now in his mid-thirties, was not born into this state of grace.

"My father was an angry man," he says. "I don't remember him hitting us kids or my mom, but the threat was frequently there. Violence was in the air. Like most of the men in the neighborhood of Baltimore where I grew up, he was a worker without much future. When he got depressed about his life, he'd get drunk. He'd swagger around the house, calling himself the Duke, as if he were John Wayne. I was afraid then that he'd hurt one of us."

Unlike many men who were raised by fathers they could not respect, Mosmiller describes his father more in sorrow than in anger. Although his father was not the kind of man his son wants to be, Mosmiller still loves him, forgives him, and brings this forgiveness into his counseling.

"A lot of people think I work for a feminist counseling center only because I want to protect women. And I do," Mosmiller says. "I don't want them to get beaten up. But I also work with abusive men because I care about *them*. They may not have any scars showing, but inside they're just as torn up as the women they hurt. I want to help them get in touch with the gentle, caring, sensitive person inside them. They don't like the kind of men they have become. My commitment is to help them change."

A number of men's organizations exist around the country whose primary purpose is to end violence against women. Like the Boston counseling service Emerge, these centers recognize that men are socialized to be violent and that violence is a legitimate expression of anger. This embryonic movement against violence believes that men can change, and it calls on all men to work for this change.

A St. Louis group called the End Violence Fund has translated the movement's concerns into simple slogans. The fund raises money for its counseling efforts by selling bumper stickers and T-shirts with messages such as NEVER ANOTHER BATTERED WOMAN or SUPPORT NONVIOLENCE IN MEN or GENTLENESS IS STRENGTH. One of the fund's T-shirts bears a logo similar to the one emblazoned on Superman's uniform — except its has a big red letter G, for "Gentleman."

In addition to his counseling, Mosmiller is part of an editorial group scattered across the country that issues the quarterly *M: Gentle Men for Gender Justice.* It has something that the glossy, professional, profit-making men's magazines lack: a new, more humane vision of masculinity. Or, as Mosmiller puts it more modestly, *M* is a "step in the right direction.

"The men's movement, and that includes our magazine, is still unclear about the kind of man we're striving for. We know what we don't like about traditional masculine roles. But discovering alternatives is not so easy. I am beginning to see, though, a second generation of men's writing that is making these alternatives come alive. Men are no longer just parroting feminism but are starting to reach into their own souls. They are beginning to speak in the first person, out of their own experience."

Mosmiller's commitment to end men's violence is both political and personal. "Before getting involved with the men's movement, I spent several years as an antiwar activist. I was opposed to the way America tried to throw its weight around in the world. Finally, I saw that the problem was deeper than foreign policy. It was a problem of men. We were not only violent in Vietnam. We were violent in the way we used the earth, violent in the way we make energy, violent in the way we play games, even violent in our own homes. We are violent in almost everything we do. That's what we have to change first. That's where we have to start."

The Companion

Our marriage had to work for both of us or it wouldn't work at all.
— James Fallows

The quest for an alternative to the Breadwinner is a quiet, private search. In the tender regions between husband and wife, a personal exploration is now occurring for new ways of sharing the responsibilities of the human family. While some men still rest their identity on bringing home the family's income, others are seeking another emblem of manhood. They would rather be a loving companion, part of a mutual, interdependent relationship.

The Companion (*com:* together; *panis:* bread) is "one who eats bread together with another." The symbol of life, daily bread, is not won by one and given to the other. It is made by both and eaten by both. The Companion recognizes that building a fulfilling marriage and family requires many skills and many tools. Like bread itself, life tastes better when it is shared.

"I watched my father and men like him work their lives away," says one young lawyer who recently became the father of a baby boy. "Those men never really knew their children, and they had little time for their wives. My dad would say he was doing it all for us, to make us happy. But I think he was running away from us, from any possibility of intimacy. Well, I don't want to be like that. I am trying to organize my practice so that I can see my children. What's the good of providing for a family if I never am with them?"

The emergence of the Companion is reflected in studies showing that fathers are spending an increasing amount of time with their children. According to James Levine, such studies also indicate that men are becoming increasingly supportive of their wives' working, both in terms of their attitude and in terms of the amount of housework they do.

Levine and his fellow researchers, Joseph Pleck and Michael Lamb, believe that a new fatherhood is emerging in America, and they are studying how social institutions are encouraging and enabling men to take more responsibility for their children. In health care, they observe profound changes in birth practices and hospital procedures. In law, they find rapidly shifting interpretations of child custody. In employment, their research focuses on paternity leaves and corporate policies for men and women. In education, they gather evidence of how schools and colleges are reexamining sex roles and family life. In mental health, they find more spirited debate among therapists about what constitutes feminine and masculine behavior. Finally, in religion, the authors are observing how churches and synagogues are beginning to provide support groups to deal with stresses on family life.

In a period of transition, the search for a balance between the Breadwinner's and the Companion's virtues will not be easy. Judged solely on his curriculum vitae, which includes his job as President Carter's chief speechwriter, James Fallows might seem like the model of an ambitious, career-oriented Breadwinner. Before reaching the age of thirty, he was ensconced in the Executive Office Building across from the White House and earning $47,000 a year, working beside the most powerful men in the country. Since he put in close to an eighty-hour week, he was with his wife and young son far less than he would have liked.

But Fallows did not blindly subordinate his family to his career. "Just when my journalism career was starting to come together," he recalls, "I left Washington to follow my wife. I had been working on the *Washington Monthly* and had begun to get articles published in other magazines. But Debbie was not happy in Washington. She was tired of taking jobs she didn't really like. She realized that in order to do what she wanted in her field, linguistics, she'd have to get her doctorate. Unfortunately, the program she liked best was at the University of Texas in Austin. Although the work I wanted to do was in the East, we moved south.

"I am hardly a martyr. But at first it was very hard on me. For a couple of months down there, I felt as if I'd just fallen off the edge of the world. My career seemed at a standstill. What got me through was the belief that to stay married in the long run, both of us had to have lives we enjoyed. Our marriage had to work for *both* of us, or it wouldn't work at all." Now, six years later, Jim can laugh about it. "The joke was that eventually we both came to enjoy Austin more than any other place we've lived."

After working as an aide to a Texas state senator and then freelancing for various magazines, Fallows signed on with the staff of the former Georgia governor when he was in the final stages of his long-shot campaign for the presidency. Fallows then came with Carter to the White House, where he worked at breakneck speed for another two years. Midway through Carter's term, he decided to leave.

"I doubt that our marriage would have survived two more years like that — or at least survived in a healthy form." Instead, Jim turned his basement into an office, which gives him an opportunity to spend far more time with his wife and children than he otherwise could. His workday is divided into two shifts: first, from 9 A.M. to mid-afternoon, when the kids come home; then from 9 P.M. until fatigue sets in. "That way," says Fallows, "I can really be with my kids and still get in a good day's work."

Although Fallows, now Washington editor for *The Atlantic,* is more visible than most men who are emblematic of the Companion, he is by no means unique. In virtually every profession, men are trying to repossess their most valuable resource — time. Without time, intimacy is jeopardized. In particular, those men who have children are trying to redress the imbalance between work and family. These men still want to achieve; they still have their driving ambitions; they still need to earn an income. But freed from their unconscious ties to the Breadwinner, they are less likely to confuse those achievements, ambitions, and income with masculinity.

"The company asked me to run one of our biggest European divisions," said a talented engineer, the father of three children. An outstanding athlete with a keen sense of competition, he wanted to take the job. He wanted the feeling of being in charge. But the promotion had drawbacks, too. "It meant moving from New England to Amsterdam for a six-year stint. I knew that was too long. My wife didn't want to be away from her job that long, and the kids didn't want to be away from the schools and friends they had grown up with. Because it meant a big step up in the company, I said I'd go for three years but no more. They said no dice, and gave the job to someone else."

Like Fallows, the engineer did not find his decision painless, but he did not regret it. "Although it hurt for a while," he said, "I know it would have been a mistake to accept the company's terms. All the promotions in the world are not worth an embittered family."

So widespread is this resurgent commitment to family that it is having a profound impact on the marketplace. New firms specialize in finding jobs for spouses in order to induce otherwise reluctant executives to relocate. Ad campaigns in major publications like the *Wall Street Journal* are now directed at the growing number of businessmen for whom success must be balanced against commitments to wife and children (and to a vital part of themselves). Even the armed services are being forced to cope with officers whose willingness to extend their tour of duty is contingent on their wife's careers. In short, the market is beginning to recognize that men are no longer Breadwinners who can be bought and shipped. They are also Companions, husbands and fathers whose sense of manhood rests on values and commitments that go beyond paychecks and fringe benefits.

Unlike the predictable family of the Breadwinner, the Companion's fits no mold. In some, wives may still stay home with small children. In others, they may work part-time. In many others, wives may continue to work throughout their childbearing years. And in a few, wives are the primary income earners, while their husbands manage the household and work irregularly. Whichever path they choose, the

Companion's family may experience a freedom that the Breadwinner's never knew. Since both husband and wife are free to provide for the family in ways once limited to men *or* women, both are free to create their own professional and personal standards of manhood and womanhood.

The Companion emerges just in time. He arrives as the emotional desolation that surrounds the Breadwinner is becoming unbearable. The Companion promises to reconnect manhood to its emotional roots. He is a positive symbol of manhood that women, whether feminist or not, can respect. He is an emblem for men who want to define themselves, not as the one who wins the family's bread, but as one who shares it intimately with those he loves.

The Mediator

Unless we become more conscious of how to mediate conflicts, violence will become epidemic.

— Roger Fisher

No masculine archetype will be harder to dislodge than the Soldier. Even now, when conservatives and liberals alike concur that total war would be unwinnable, the image of the Soldier is still invoked whenever our nation's leaders feel insecure and confused. In January 1981, in a world transformed by the changes of the past half-century, President Reagan focused his inaugural address on the heroism of an American soldier in World War I who was killed in action. This anachronistic image of male resolve is always the last resort of speechmakers who can imagine no more compelling alternatives.

But even as the Soldier defends his territory in the masculine mind, a new emblem of masculinity is taking root in the cracks of the war system. Courage is being redefined. It no longer hinges on how much violence a man can inflict, but on how much he can prevent. No word captures this emerging masculinity more accurately than mediator (*mediare:* to stand in the middle).

The Mediator does not require that life be a battle, nor does he equate heroism with fighting valorously. Rather, the Mediator's heroic calling is to stand between the opposing armies. His goal is to enable the adversaries to coexist and, if possible, cooperate. He is not necessarily a pacifist, although a growing number of men so describe

themselves. Nor is he dogmatically committed to Gandhian nonviolence — although, again, men frequently avow such commitment. He
is simply no longer enamored of violence.

"Have you ever heard of an army base in Texas called Fort
Bliss?" Shepherd Bliss asks me. "Well, it's named after my family. I
come from a long line of military officers. I've done my stint too: five
years in the army." In my mind, I shorten his hair and remove his
professor's spectacles, but it is still difficult to imagine this organizer
of the seventh Conference on Men and Masculinity as a soldier in the
U.S. Army. Many men who have rejected the masculine hero-image
of the Soldier have never been near a military base. But Bliss spent
most of the first twenty-five years of his life on military bases. Perhaps
this is why he speaks with precision as well as passion about why the
Soldier is obsolete. He has received his doctorate in political science,
but when he talks about the Soldier, his tone is personal.

"When I saw my father recently," he recalls sadly, "I happened
to ask him where he was when I was born. He told me that his unit
was on maneuvers less than an hour away from our home in Santa
Monica. He went to the colonel in charge of the maneuvers and told
him that his wife was on the way to the hospital. 'Could I have the
rest of the day off, sir, and join her?' my dad asked him. 'Hell, I've
had six kids,' the colonel replied, 'and I was out of town for every one
of them. Now rejoin your platoon, soldier!' Dad said it was six weeks
before he ever saw me."

As a young man, Bliss was of course eager to prove himself. He
joined the army, ready to prove he was as much a man as any of his
illustrious forebears. But now, as he approaches forty, his goals have
changed radically.

"I've kept waiting and waiting for American policy-makers to
show that they learned something from our mistakes in Vietnam. But
I've concluded that they haven't learned anything. The problem goes
beyond politics. It's a question of character.

"I think the loss of the war in Indochina is probably the most
important fact in understanding American masculinity today. Our
pride was wounded. Then the Iranians rubbed salt in those wounds
by holding Americans hostage. We felt helpless . . . and we didn't like
it. Now I think Reagan is rallying those emotional energies. He is returning to a cult of toughness which, if not checked, could lead to
war."

Bliss has stopped teaching political science. He is committed to the men's movement, a network of men who share a different vision of masculinity. "I've shifted my energies entirely," he says. "Men need to find new ways of coping with conflict. I think the men's movement is the best vehicle for organizing an alternative to a foreign policy based on violence."

Bliss is one of countless men who, having been trained for war, are now beginning to train themselves for peace. Among the most popular courses on many campuses are those teaching negotiation and mediation. Students sense that resorting to violence is not an option for them as it was for their parents. Universities, institutes, and scores of independent groups offer training courses on nonviolent conflict resolution. "We have to turn them away at the door," says Roger Fisher, a professor at Harvard Law School.

"Let's face it," says Fisher, who has consulted on strategies of conflict resolution for the State Department as well as the military academies. "Conflict is a growth industry. On every level — family, community, national, global — people are standing up for what they consider to be their rights. But the rights being declared often conflict with someone else's. Unless we become more conscious about how to mediate conflicts, violence will become epidemic."

With his colleague William Ury, Roger Fisher wrote *Getting to Yes*, a primer on negotiation techniques that has already proved useful in settings ranging from a Kentucky coal mine strike to the Israeli-Egyptian peace process. Stop choosing between soft and hard positions, argue Fisher and Ury. Learn to take positions based on principles. "The critical ingredient is that the mediator is empathic, not judgmental," stresses Fisher. "Being empathic with the other side does not mean giving in. It means discovering what they think their real interests are. Until you do that, conflict is inevitable."

Trained as an anthropologist and a generation younger than Fisher, Ury is even more specific about the human qualities that characterize the Mediator: "I would say that among the most important personality traits which characterize good negotiators are *patience*, sticking with the process even when it is complicated; *empathy*, being able to see the world through someone else's eyes; and *sensitivity*, listening and dealing constructively with other people's emotions and your own. The ineffective negotiator is more or less the opposite. He is able to think only of his own problems, he can't handle emotions, and he wants to win quickly."

Ury recognizes that the key attributes he mentioned — patience, empathy, and sensitivity — are often called feminine qualities. "Many men have what I would call an engineering mentality," he says. "They think there's a technically correct solution and they want to look for it while ignoring the human factor. Such an approach almost never works."

Both Fisher and Ury consider their techniques useful in resolving even minor personal disputes. But it is clear that their original motivation grew out of their concern about nuclear war. "Clearly the most pressing danger in our time," says Ury, "is the mechanism we have created for destroying ourselves." Adds Fisher, "In World War II, it was possible for the stronger party to physically impose his will on his adversary. But even the biggest advocates today of nuclear arms build-up don't expect us to be able to impose our will on our adversary acre by acre. The only way one nuclear nation can win today is by changing the way another nuclear power thinks. In other words, it's a negotiating problem — which requires a very different attitude." This in turn requires a different image of man.

We are not, as the Soldier's world view suggests, merely competitive animals with a primitive urge to dominate. We are a species designed to cooperate. As Alva Myrdal, the renowned Swedish disarmament specialist, reads the evidence, the conclusion is clear: "Cooperation, the need and willingness to give mutual support, is a genuine human behavior trait."

The anti-nuclear movement is another illustration of the Mediator's creative nonviolence. Even those who disagree with the movement's objectives must recognize that its supporters are a breed apart from many of those of the sixties. The various regional alliances (such as the Clamshell Alliance in the East and the Abalone Alliance in the West) require that all participants undergo training in nonviolence. When they stage a demonstration at a nuclear power plant, they are not an anonymous mass of protesters. They are a disciplined body organized into clusters and sharing a commitment to peaceful resistance. As one West Coast organizer puts it, "We're trying to stop a violent technology, so it only makes sense to oppose it nonviolently."

What is striking about these activists is that they have overcome the unconscious masculine equation of courage and violence. Unlike isolated pacifists of earlier generations, they share a bond with other men who have redefined masculinity. Perhaps no one put it better than Gandhi himself, a man whose teachings are finding an expanding audience. "Nonviolence and cowardice go ill together," he said in 1939. "I can imagine a fully armed man to be at heart a coward. Possession of arms implies an element of fear, if not cowardice. But true nonviolence is an impossibility without courage."

As in any transition, the old reasserts itself just as the new is taking hold. As this is written, the Pentagon is being promoted as they key to our security and is being offered a larger share of our nation's productivity. But at the same time, the culture the Pentagon claims to protect is seeking alternatives to violence. After generously funding military academies throughout our nation's history, Congress is now being asked to fund a peace academy. Scores of parliamentarians from more than twenty democracies recently gathered at the United Nations to call for the creation of a peace system, a combination of international mediation and peacekeeping forces as an alternative to the arms race. From Buckminster Fuller to George Kennan, from the Club of Rome to the Paris Group, far-sighted individuals and organizations are calling forth a different image of earth and of man. We are not soldiers in opposing armies, but passengers on spaceship earth.

Enter the Mediator. He sees conflict, not in terms of winning and losing, but in terms of inventing peaceful solutions of mutual benefit. As husbands and wives know, it is possible to settle disagreements in a way that strengthens the relationship. The Mediator believes that this skill applies to all conflict. These skills — sensitivity, empathy, compassion, flexibility — are now as important as any of the Soldier's virtues. "The survival of the fittest" no longer prevails. It is now, in Jonas Salk's phrase, "the survival of the wisest" — or holocaust.

As arms mount on every frontier, the Soldier no longer enthralls. The nature of heroism shifts. Men emerge who have ceased to revere proficiency in violence and instead respect those who prevent it. It is a nobler kind of heroism because it has a future.

"Of course the nuclear threat is growing," observes one political scientist, who has helped organize peace studies curricula for several colleges. "It would be easy to get depressed. But I see signs of hope as well. The insanity of it all is triggering a new awareness. Until recently, men always believed that wars were caused by their enemy —

whoever that happened to be. But now that belief is waning. We are beginning to realize that we have to change *ourselves* — and that is a big step forward."

The Colleague

I'd been captain of this, manager of that, sergeant of that. I thought I knew all about how to manage people. But ... I had a lot to learn.

— Rob Ayres

Instead of the Expert, that archetype of hierarchy and authority, the symbol of the Colleague has begun to attract men's allegiance. The Colleague (*com:* together; *legare:* choose), who represents an alternative perspective on human potential, was spawned by dissatisfaction with a world of omniscient experts and ignorant citizens. Instead of letting the Expert decide, the Colleague advocates that all those affected by a decision should choose together. Instead of the boss defining the employee's job, they can define it together. Observed Stewart Brand in the latest (1980) *Whole Earth Catalog,* "A realm of intimate, personal power is developing — the power of individuals to conduct their own education, find their own inspiration, shape their own environment."

The key word is *access*. The book metaphorically called it "access to tools." The kind of access women want is access to what has been male: jobs, power, responsibility, leadership. Men, meanwhile, want access to what they have forfeited: intimacy, nurturance, friendship, mutuality.

The Colleague has been emerging in many different forms. In publishing, it crystallized in the phenomenon of *The Whole Earth Catalog.* In academia, it emerged as the interdisciplinary approach or, more radically, holistic studies. (Others called it integrative, systems-oriented, or multidimensional.) In business, the Japanese approach has become a subject of intense interest to American management. Emphasizing collective effort rather than individual achievement, the Japanese corporation enjoys efficiencies that its American counterparts have never imagined.

In personal lives, the revival of the do-it-yourself ideal has gone far beyond home remodeling. From education to health care, from distribution to sports, the cult of the Expert is being challenged.

Whether self-education, self-care, self-help food co-ops, or self-moti-
vated exercise, a renewed belief is flourishing in the possibility, indeed
the necessity, of making every person knowledgeable concerning the
issues that affect him.

Nowhere is the emergence of the Colleague more striking than at
the center of the American economy: the corporation. "When I came
to this company over a decade ago," says Rob Ayres, a senior personnel manager at a $3.3 billion-a-year company, "there was no strategy
on how to deal with gender. Most people didn't even know how to
talk about it, myself included. Even when the Equal Employment
Opportunity Commission sanctions started coming in from Washington, we thought the only thing that we had to change were the numbers. So we hired more blacks and women. Finally, around 1977, we
began to realize that it wasn't just a question of changing the numbers but changing ourselves."

We are sitting in Ayres's office. The walls are metal partitions
covered by blackboards and drawing pads showing organizational
charts and projects in progress. I had wondered whether this thirty-
six-year-old corporate manager would have much to say about
changing images of masculinity. But I quickly learn that he has far
more to say than our interview permits.

"About four years ago," he explains, "the company finally began
to take the gender issue seriously. We made a fundamental decision to
start at the top of the house, with the senior managers. We began
having awareness sessions. It amazed me that if you can change the
way people think, then everything else begins to change too.

"When we started out, our approach to affirmative action here
was a deficit model: blacks are less than, women are less than, et cet-
era. Like most companies, this one was run by middle-aged white
men with a white, male, locker-room mentality. But thanks to these
training sessions, in which all of the senior managers participated, we
began to break out of our stereotypes. I'd been captain of this, manager of that, sergeant of that. I thought I knew all about how to manage people. But these workshops dealing with gender showed me I
had a lot to learn. The changes have been fantastic."

What effect have these changes had on the company — and on
him?

"Some of it's personal: how we behave at meetings, say, or our
hiring procedures. But you can also see it in the numbers: more

women are getting hired and promoted. Ten years ago, very few women were senior managers. Now we have quite a few. Sometimes the men under them will still try to pull the old tricks, like going over the woman's head about a gripe and coming to me. But I won't play into it. Or somebody will say, 'Gee, it seems like women are getting all the jobs.' To which I say, 'You worried about your promotion, Jack?' Some men still cling to the old sexist thinking. You know, that if you're white and male, you're entitled, and all these blacks and women mean that you're giving up your entitlement. But when I think where this company was just a few years ago, I think the progress is remarkable."

As he talks, I am impressed with his frankness and openness and tell him so. "I couldn't have had this conversation with you in the mid-seventies," Ayres admits. "I would have given you some bullshit about how great our programs were. I would have been all over you to show you how smart I was or how liberal I was. I think I've learned something from women's ability to share their emotions and be vulnerable. I've been in a lot of scary situations, physically intimidating, like in the army. But that's nothing compared to the courage you need to open up your feelings in front of the people you work with. Over the years I had developed all sorts of reasons for not saying what I really felt. I'd given up my freedom. But this experience at work helped me to regain that freedom. Even my wife noticed it."

Ayres is silent for a minute. I think he is shifting gears, preparing to get back to work. "One more thing," he adds in a much more businesslike tone. "I've said a lot about why I think what we've done here is right. But don't get me wrong. We've also done it because we believe it's profitable. It's just raw economics. If a company's going to grow at, say, 30 percent a year, you can't do it with all white males. You've got to widen the circle. And the better the races and sexes get along, the more efficient your company is."

As Ayres walks me through the maze of offices and out to the entrance, we talk about sports. Years ago, as a college student in Chicago, he was a star soccer player. Now his seven-year-old daughter is playing on a local team. "I went to one of her practices the other day," Ayres recalls, "and I saw her crying. That day, she was the only girl at the practice. Her coach and I asked her what happened. She said the boys were making fun of her and were saying girls can't play sports. So the coach got everybody in a huddle and told them that's not how a team behaves. That it's the sum of its parts. That everybody who plays their best, whether a boy or girl, deserves their teammates' respect. I was really impressed. The coach was teaching them at the age of seven what most of us here at the company began to learn only after we'd grown up."

Ayres's company is not alone. Dozens of major corporations have begun the complex process of raising their consciousness from that of a white, male, locker-room mentality to the level of the Colleague. At Ayres's company, they call it "enlarging the winner's circle." Enlarging the circle, however, changes the meaning of winning itself.

For the Expert, being best or first is based on excluding as many kinds of people as possible from the inner circle. The Colleague's goal is to enable men and women as diverse as America itself to work together as equals. The Expert is so determined to be better than others that he loses the ability to be equal. The Colleague thrives on cooperative, egalitarian efforts. The Expert's identity hinges on knowing more than others, and he therefore forfeits his capacity to teach. Although the Colleague seeks to develop his skills to their fullest, he values sharing his knowledge as much as acquiring it. The Expert breaks knowledge into specialized segments and hungers for the feeling of reigning supreme in his cerebral fiefdom. Attempts to demonstrate the interconnectedness of knowledge, whether called holistic or interdisciplinary, are dismissed by the Expert as unsystematic and undisciplined.

The Colleague uses knowledge more humanely. He does not measure his intellectual virility in terms of being the leader or the boss. He would rather be a mentor and a friend. He respects expertise, but he knows that its value depends on its being shared and joined to the knowledge of others. He admires excellence — except when it is used to dominate others. He cherishes knowledge — when it is used to enlighten, not to mystify. Having seen the hollowness of egoistic success, the Colleague does not subordinate his relationships to his goals. His relationships are among his primary goals.

The Colleague does not hate competition, but neither does he worship it. He recognizes it as part of manhood, as valuable as cooperation and compassion. Unlike the Expert, who needs to put women (and whatever is feminine) beneath him, the Colleague respects women and accepts the feminine as part of himself. Indeed, he is open to learning from women precisely because they are different from him.

The creator of *The Whole Earth Catalog,* a former paratrooper now in his forties, Stewart Brand once participated in a peyote ritual among the Navajo. "The amazing part of it," he says, "was that the person acting as the spiritual guide was a woman. It was the first time I'd ever been in a religious ceremony led by a woman. I think it made the whole experience much more powerful for me."

Brand assembled his gargantuan books with a group of researchers, many of whom were women. They worked together, not only as boss and employee, but also as colleagues. Indeed, Brand is grateful to feminism for having cleared away some of the misconceptions and prejudices that had for so long separated men and women. In his view, feminism "has reduced the bullshit factor of being alive. The whole dating system works better now. Men and women work better together. The two favorite human pastimes, sex and conversation, have improved enormously. Life is more exciting when men and women are free to be themselves."

Although he respects knowledge, Brand is not enthralled by the Expert. "I have always preferred the symbol of the doubter myself. I think of him as a sort of a cross between a scientist and a Buddhist monk. A man who questions everything, who takes responsibility for finding his own truths."

Technical breakthroughs and spectacular inventions may still be achieved by solitary Experts, but it is the Colleague's qualities that are needed to make the specialized, technological world more humane. Wherever creative ideas are being explored for organizing society to foster human growth, the Colleague is at work. He is the enemy of unnecessary hierarchy, the champion of shared leadership, the architect of a meaningful workplace. He knows that until the power-oriented boss mentality is overcome, even so-called revolutions will merely replace one kind of oppression with another. In an information society, the Colleague symbolizes a new attitude toward knowledge, a new intellectual ethic. If the Colleague were to choose a slogan, it might well be the title of the book on collective self-management recently issued by Vocations for Social Change: *No Bosses Here!*

Once disenfranchised by the Expert, women are now being welcomed by the Colleague. After declining and almost disappearing, midwives are once again being trained to deliver babies. They are now working hand in hand with doctors who recognize that midwifery complements their profession. Women are entering medicine itself, and between woman patient and physician new bonds of trust are being built. As women enter the domains once called masculine, men are also entering those fields once called feminine. Men no longer shun nursing and child care, no longer avoid elementary schools, no longer keep their distance from the stove. The old walls between the sexes are being chipped away, enabling both men and women to begin to explore areas of knowledge that had been closed to them.

Few Experts have affected more human lives more intimately than Dr. Benjamin Spock. For more than a generation, numerous editions of *Baby and Child Care* have been consulted by millions of middle-class parents. Yet, at the zenith of this pediatrician's career, he stopped playing the almighty Expert and became the Colleague. He changed many of his views on child rearing and family life because he began listening to women's criticisms of his work.

"I took an awful beating from feminists," Spock recalls. "In 1972, when I spoke before a national women's conference, Gloria Steinem stood up and called me 'a major oppressor of women in the same category as Sigmund Freud.' *Time* magazine said, 'Spock hung his head in shame.' Truth was, I just couldn't think of anything to say to such a hostile audience."

Now living in Arkansas with his wife, whom he calls an ardent feminist, Spock remembers how difficult it was to reexamine his own views: "It took me two or three years at least to digest all the criticism I got and to admit that I was a sexist, like almost every man I know. I have since apologized and corrected many of the foolish things that I've written or said over the years."

Spock now believes that both parents, when at home with their children, should share equally the responsibility for their children's care. "A father grows and gets satisfaction from functioning as a father," he says. "He not only gets closer to his children; he gets closer to himself. I am glad that men now recognize that they can nurture, too. A lot of men got that message in the late sixties and seventies. It has been one of the women's movement's greatest contributions to men's lives."

The Nurturer

Learning to nurture — whether as fathers, husbands, coworkers or friends — is the hardest change for men to make. For us to do this would be a revolution.

— James Levine

"Now I would like you all to join me in prayer," says the young woman in the pulpit to the congregation gathered in the historic New England church. "I wrote it as a variation on the Lord's Prayer."

> Our Mother
> Who is sprung from the earth
> Hallowed be Your Name . . .

And the congregation prays.

The male image of the Lord, rooted as deeply in our minds as in our history, will no doubt remain. But other spiritual symbols are joining it to enrich and deepen our experience of God. Instead of an image of power, we witness emerging symbols of nurturance. The closing words of the Lord's Prayer are "the kingdom and the power and the glory." But when this woman wrote her "Prayer to Mother," she changed them to read "the beauty, the passion and the truth of love." They are the words of the Nurturer.

"Prayer to Mother" grew out of the young woman's own spiritual quest. "We pray to God as Lord and Father and Son," she tells me. "But we never speak of God as Lady or Mother or Daughter. Well, I am a mother with daughters. I want to know that side of God, too."

Her prayer is but one element in a women's service, designed and led by the women of the congregation. The senior minister, whose bass voice has since midcentury echoed in the sanctuary of this venerable church, is seated in the pews, listening. It is the assistant minister's turn this cold Sunday in January to lead the hour of worship, but he too is sitting in the pews. He has stepped aside so that the women of the congregation might hear their sisters speak of God. When I ask him why, he says, "The best way to get beyond the image of God as a cold, stern, judgmental old man is to let women have equal access to the pulpit. I am convinced that it can only deepen our spiritual lives."

Unlike the Lord, who leads men to believe they must save others, the Nurturer inspires men to empower others. The difference is humility. The patriarchal image of the Lord, a celestial being without needs or failings, breeds arrogance. The Nurturer cannot assume this posture of moral superiority. Painfully aware of his own limitations, he is less judgmental about those of others. He refuses to pack away his self-doubts in closets of ideology and is therefore less likely to preach sanctimoniously about what is right for others. He is less likely to claim the right to intervene in the affairs of other nations (or of the other sex). He respects devotion to principle and commitment to cause. But his respect becomes suspicion when one person, group, or nation proclaims itself to be the savior of, or the lord over, others. He loves his God, but not with the self-righteousness that triggers holy wars. He loves his country, but not so slavishly that he sacrifices his own judgment.

As a teacher, the Nurturer does not feign omniscience. As a therapist, he does not monopolize mental health. As a religious leader, he does not treat his congregation as if he alone were pure. And as a man, he does not pretend that he is closer to God than are women.

"When I'm leading services now," explains Rabbi Michael Luckens, "I find myself changing the words in the middle of a reading. I try to make the service nonsexist by referring to God as 'she' as often as 'he.' " His task is not always easy, particularly with one conservative, small-town congregation that he serves. As he tells me, "One of the elders of the synagogue came up to me once and said, 'Look, rabbi. If the language has been all right for thousands of years, if generations of Jews before us have used it, why must you change it now?' I told him that Judaism is evolving. The way my parents expressed their faith is different from the way I do, and my son's will be different from mine. What remains static eventually dies. When they ask me why I believe women should be called to the Torah and counted in the *minyan* [prayer quorum], I tell them very simply. I tell them I don't work for the complete equality of women because I am a feminist. I work for it because I am a Jew. I want Judaism to continue to grow and change, to serve *all* its people."

The Reverend James Robinson, the minister in whose church the women's service was held, shares Rabbi Luckens's commitment. "I want women to participate as equals in our church, not just for their sake, but for men's," he says. "I am afraid masculinity can easily get in the way of spirituality. Men have been under pressure to avoid feeling vulnerable, weak, or dependent. But those very feelings are the ones which may bring us most powerfully into contact with a spiritual being greater than ourselves. I want the men in my congregation to discover this dimension of spirituality. It is one of the reasons why I want women to conduct our service."

What makes the Nurturer's emergence so vital is that he has inspired changes not only in church, but in men's daily lives. Men who are emblematic of the Nurturer are freeing themselves from their unconscious striving for dominance, both over women and over other men. They are freeing themselves to explore any dimension of life without fearing that they will appear soft or effeminate. They may be who they are and express their own feelings without sexual self-censorship.

The Nurturer does not conceive children with the belief that someone else must take care of them. He sees himself as responsible for their growth as for their birth. He subscribes to Jesse Jackson's motto: "You're not a man because you can kill somebody, but because you can *heal* somebody. You're not a man because you can make a baby, but because you can *care* for a baby." The Nurturer does not view spending time with children as doing them (or his wife) a favor. He considers it a basic part of his life. The Nurturer symbolizes men's capacity and commitment to practice what Erik Erikson has called generativity, the antithesis of narcissism. It is the commitment to foster the growth of something beyond oneself.

James Levine's life reflects men's struggle today to discover the Nurturer within themselves. The father of two children, Levine speaks frequently around the country to groups interested in the new fatherhood and changing sex roles within the family. Because of these achievements and because he spends more time with his children than most men, many people who know him naturally consider him a paragon of the emerging masculinities.

But Levine is not infatuated with his liberated public image. He does not boast about his accomplishments or complacently portray the role of the new man. On the contrary, he is still engaged in discovering his own capacity for nurturance.

The year before our interview had been one of the most difficult of his life. Levine had just moved to New York to take a job as the director of Program Development at the Bank Street College of Education. As for most newcomers, it was a strain to break into a new position. For the first time in their marriage, Levine's wife was not working but had returned to graduate school. In trying to offset the loss of his wife's income, Levine found himself taking on outside assignments. Instead of spending quality time with his children, he found himself increasingly preoccupied.

"I felt miserable that year," he recalls. "It wasn't till we went on vacation that I figured out why I was feeling so bad. I was starting to act just like my own father. Sure, I was spending more time with my kids than my dad ever did with us. I'd make dinner or get them off to school. But I would rarely just *be* with them. Like my dad, I felt as if I was always behind the eight ball."

Pencil in hand, I asked him about his father.

"When I was a boy I wished my father had more time to play with me," he says. "But he was always working, even when he didn't have to be. I think he considered the family just another business. He had his big business — he worked in sales for a textile company. And he had his small business — his family. At home he was always the planner, the efficiency expert, the executive. I remember once he compared himself to that character in the 'Li'l Abner' comic strip, General Bull Moose — you know, the one who was always giving orders. He was successful, of course. No doubt about that. But the price he paid was that he wasn't able to be with us. I don't remember him ever really being with me, ever entering *my* life. That's the kind of man I was raised to be, but it's not the kind of man I want to be.

"What I realized this past year was that I am caught between the two. My father and his generation represented a model of masculinity that doesn't work for me. Yet I and my generation haven't found new models. That's the real tension in men's lives today — and in my own."

Levine's office reflects this dilemma. Children's toys are stacked beneath his desk for times when his son or daughter is with him during the workday. The walls are peppered with posters, news clippings, and other symbols of masculine reappraisal. On his door hangs a picture of a muscle-bound wrestler cradling an infant. It is from a public service ad that the Swedish government has promoted to encourage fathers to take paternity leaves. Above the desk is the wrestler's American counterpart, a burly middle-aged man named Crusher

Lizowski. Wearing an apron and holding a mixing bowl, Lizowski is the centerpiece of the Future Homemakers of America ad campaign. ("Nobody makes fun of me," he says.) Near the typewriter is mounted an excerpt from an interview with John McPhee, the versatile *New Yorker* journalist, in which McPhee says, "The best part of my day is getting up and driving my daughters to school."

It is not easy for Levine to share his personal feelings with me, a virtual stranger. But, still playing the interviewer, I push him further. While sharing little of myself, I ask him why it is so hard for him — and for most men — to nurture.

"Making money takes time and energy," he replies. "But I think the deeper reason is our attitude. I think of it in terms of holding on and letting go. If I complete a project — give a lecture or write an article — that's something tangible. I can hold on to it. Men are used to having these kinds of rewards. We want credit for the things we do, and we always find time to do them. But to be with my kids, I had to let go. I had to stop looking for tangible rewards and worldly achievements. I had to get in touch with myself, with the experience of just being with them.

"There are a lot of important struggles going on now in America. But none is more important than this one. In some ways, learning to nurture — whether as fathers, husbands, or friends — is the hardest change for men to make. For men to do this would be a revolution."

Finally, my pencil stops moving. As I interviewed scores of men for this book, I have always scribbled notes. It is the interviewer's job. But Levine's words touch me so directly that I no longer want to record them. I want to respond, to thank him. By sharing his growth with me, he has helped me to grow. Like so many men who have opened themselves to me, he has nurtured me.

Indeed, all the men whose lives reflect the emerging masculinities have enriched my life. They have influenced me without ever trying to have power over me, without ever needing to dominate. They affected my life because they have the power to be themselves, the power to nurture.

Men who are imbued with the emerging masculinities do not all dress, think, or vote the same. You cannot recognize them by their job or their education or their political affiliation. But nonetheless you will know them when you meet them. They are the men who do not make you feel besieged, but befriended; not depleted, enriched; not used, understood; not dominated, served.

Cast a glance backward at these emerging masculinities — Healer, Companion, Mediator, Colleague, Nurturer — and you will notice one striking similarity. The human qualities they symbolize transcend sexual identity. They reflect awareness of the earth, of work and family, and of the human body, mind, and soul, an awareness that any man or woman can develop. To heal, nurture, or mediate is neither a masculine nor a feminine role. To be a companion or a colleague is not the monopoly of one sex or the other. These traits are based on values; they are not sexual, but ethical.

This is the ultimate difference. Unlike the old archetypes, which were for men only, the emerging masculinities are not. They are, in fact, emerging humanities.

Afterword

AFTER THIS BOOK was published in 1982, I no longer had to pursue my subject. It pursued me.

Writing *A Choice of Heroes,* I had to struggle to find the best sources, the most revealing interviewees, the most insightful experts, and the most divergent viewpoints. But after publication, I could not avoid them. All kinds of organizations concerned about gender issues asked me to speak. People from every walk of life sent me fascinating materials I had not seen before. Experts called me with words of praise or, more often, criticism. And audiences for my speeches and my media appearances provided me with perspectives as wide-ranging and disparate as America itself.

The experience was bittersweet. On the one hand, I was grateful to be able to learn so much about American men. But on the other hand, I regretted that I was able to have this experience only *after* publishing this book.

Since *A Choice of Heroes* has remained in print and is being reissued in a new edition, I have a chance to share some of what I have learned from my unusual public education. Reflecting on what has happened to men's consciousness during the past decade and what may happen in the next, I once again see two interactive spheres of change, the private and the public.

In Private: Reaffirming the Masculine

In the late twentieth century, we face a crisis in masculine identity of great proportions. The devastating dimension of this phenomenon . . . affects each of us personally as much as it affects our society as a whole.
　— Robert Moore and Douglas Gillette,
　　King, Warrior, Magician, Lover

Since 1982, audiences from around the country have thrown hundreds of questions in my direction — some like bouquets, others like grenades. But two questions, above all, haunt me. They are both evidence that what I wrote was not the end but only the beginning of my inquiry.

The first question came from a college student on a small campus in upstate New York in the spring of 1985. He shook his shoulder-length hair out of his eyes and said politely, "Mr. Gerzon, I'm more confused after reading your book than I was before I read it. Now, maybe there's something wrong with me. But I just don't see how what you wrote applies to me."

With some encouragement, he went on to explain that he had two goals after graduation: first, to join the air force and become a fighter pilot; second, to be a househusband. He was perplexed, he said, because his first goal grew out of an old archetype of masculinity (the Soldier) and his second goal grew out of an emerging archetype (the Nurturer). "How can I have two goals that are so contradictory?" he asked innocently. "Is it just because I am confused?"

His question demonstrated to me that something was amiss in my book. The five-by-five set of historic and emerging archetypes of masculinity was very neat, providing a tidy structure for the book, but, as evidenced by this pilot-househusband's quandary, it was a little *too* neat.

I had taken five dimensions of masculinity that had been denuded of what in our culture we often call the feminine and that therefore had lost their full humanity. I had then contrasted them with what was missing — that is, with the missing "feminine" qualities. I had written as if men should somehow endeavor to let go of the former, "macho" qualities and to embrace the latter, more "liberated" virtues. Although I made the proper cautionary comments, carefully warning about the risk of substituting one set of stereotypes for another, my presentation lent itself all too easily to precisely such misuse.

Unfortunately, my young questioner had fallen into this very trap. He felt that choosing his heroes required him to select one set or the other. In fact, the book's title, *A Choice of Heroes*, first appeared on a 1967 *Life* magazine cover emblazoned with competing portraits of the traditional hero, John Wayne, and the emerging anti-hero, Dustin Hoffman. Men's challenge, it implied, was to take one path or the other, when in truth our challenge was to combine the virtues of both in ways that were uniquely authentic to each of us. My questioner thought *A Choice of Heroes* was asking him to throw out the old and grab the new, when in fact it was inviting him to weave these emerging masculine potentialities into a more humane fabric of gender.

If this young man were standing before me now, I would tell him pointblank: The test of manhood is not true-or-false. It is not even multiple-choice. It is not even a test. It is a journey of self-discovery.

To make matters worse, if a white, American, college-educated male found my archetypal choices too unconvincing, imagine how confusing they were for a *non*-white, *non*-American, *non*–middle-class reader. As Dr. Peggy McIntosh, associate director of the Center for Research on Women at Wellesley College, pointed out to me, the structure of the book was based on overgeneralizations drawn from the lives of white heterosexual males. "Your book was refreshing and ahead of its time," she said. "But the weaker part of it from the outset was that it was not sufficiently sensitive to racial, ethnic, and economic diversity. It is very much a white man's book, a very European-American look at *some* of the changing faces of masculinity. A man only a few generations out of slavery, or a man whose parents crossed the border from Mexico, might have a lot of trouble relating to your archetypes."

Even though the opening page defines the intended audience as "white, college-educated, heterosexual men," I agree that a one-line disclaimer does not let me (or, for that matter, the current men's movement) off the hook. Today, not only men of color and gay men would find my book too narrow. So would the young pilot-househusband and his fellow students, who have begun to combine old and new images of masculinity in ways that could never before have been imagined.

The younger generations have celebrated stars such as Michael Jackson and Madonna, who symbolize the degree to which a man can manifest so-called feminine qualities and a woman can express the masculine ones. When I met Michael Jackson and shook his hand, it felt soft and tender. When I looked into his eyes, I saw a gentleness and vulnerability that amazed me. From his surgically altered face to the well-turned curls on his forehead, from his slender form to his soft, quiet speech, he is the epitome of what Robert Bly calls the "soft male." When I met Madonna and shook her hand, it was firm and hard. Sitting at lunch with her, I was struck by her muscled strength and her tough talk. For all her eroticism, she has the strength and power and forcefulness traditionally associated with male stars. Make a comment with which she disagrees, and she will cut you off like a marine drill sergeant. Unlike Michael Jackson, who averts his eyes demurely when meeting a stranger, Madonna stares straight to your guts.

Despite these two examples of new gender roles, many stars continue to embody the old ones. But this only serves to underscore my point: Men are no longer choosing between A and B, between John Wayne and Dustin Hoffman, between the competing clichés of "traditional" and "liberated." They find themselves (just as women do) facing myriad choices. Whether reflected in styles of dress, big-screen heroism, real-world achievement, or everyday lifestyles, choices abound. Every man is on his own.

Which leads me to the second memorable question, which came just a few months ago from a man in his twenties who had just completed a men's weekend that I had staffed. He caught up with me as we walked in the hills near San Diego.

"What I don't understand is, *why now?*"

He paused, waiting for my reply. I asked him to say more, since I did not know what he was talking about.

"I read your book eight years ago, when I was still in college," he explained. "Back then, there was almost nothing on the shelves. Nobody was talking about this stuff. Now it's everywhere — best sellers, audiotapes, TV shows, men's workshops like this one, you name it! So why did it finally break out into the open?"

I certainly could not argue with his perception. It was indeed true that a small and apparently ineffective men's movement had grown into a cultural ground swell in only a decade. When I wrote *A Choice of Heroes,* the men's consciousness-raising movement was still on the periphery of Western culture. Now, in the United States, Canada, and England, it is moving decisively toward center stage.

I brushed him off by suggesting that we discuss it the following day, when we were more rested. As soon as the words were out of my mouth, they rang hollow. At the time I thought I was being evasive because I was exhausted from witnessing two dozen men dive into the swamp of their pain and emerge, after back-to-back twenty-hour days, with power and a new clarity about what it meant to be a man. But the truth was: I was not sure whether I had an answer. There is an element of mystery in the upsurge of men's awareness. For those of us who have been active in men's work for a decade or more, it is both heartening and mystifying that the message is finally finding its audience.

Let us review some of the relevant history, gathering clues to this mystery along the way. The early men's movement was destined to marginality. In both of its polarized manifestations, one called pro-feminist and the other called men's rights, it was a child of feminism.

On the left were the pro-feminist men, who accepted the feminist charge of macho oppression. They recognized the basic truth that masculinity had become divorced from femininity in ways that were a disservice, if not an insult, to women and to men. Aware of their sins, the men who joined this early movement tended to align themselves with political causes and personal characteristics that represented a critique of what was masculine and an affirmation of what was perceived as feminine. Thus the pro-feminist men's movement focused on feminist issues; it most often spoke out against rape, against wife-beating, against sexual harassment, against pornography, and of course against restrictions on abortion. Strongly influenced by a sizable gay minority, as well as by the genuine sympathies of the heterosexual majority, the pro-feminists also prided themselves on providing one of the few places in American society where men of different sexual preferences could meet in a friendly, open-minded atmosphere.

On the right, the men's rights movement stressed the ways in which our society's gender stereotypes discriminate against men. With considerable vehemence, their spokesmen pointed out that it was men who died in battle, whose lives were on the average eight years shorter than women's, who faced extraordinary hurdles in getting custody of their children in divorce court, who carried the primary burdens and stress of breadwinning, who were expected to have the money to underwrite courtship and the courage to initiate it, and so on. When thoroughly assembled and eloquently presented, their lengthy litany of injustices, which often failed to distinguish the petty from the profound, was persuasive evidence that some kind of movement was needed to express men's interests.

But as reactions to feminism — the first positive, the second negative — both these approaches had limited appeal to men *as* men. The ability of the men's movement to attract men in the mainstream was inherently weak. Both were, to borrow Adrienne Rich's phrase, "of woman born." Neither had existed before the feminist movement; neither would have emerged without it. While the movement's left wing went into the streets and joined the parade in support of feminism, the right wing stayed on the sidewalk and shouted counterslogans. Neither wing of the early men's movement put forward a compelling agenda that directly appealed to mainstream men in terms of their own masculinity.

Although support for both the left and the right can be found in the pages of this book, I was more closely aligned with the former than the latter when I wrote it. One of the book's great strengths was that it did not blame women or men. It made it clear that men had much to learn from women's wisdom. As Dr. McIntosh put it, "*A Choice of Heroes* is useful because it analyzes constructed roles and shows how men were taught to live up to those constructs. That opens the door for seeing that these constructs can be changed — that our ideals of manhood and womanhood can be *re*constructed. To find this in a book by a man in 1982 was very rare."

But if the book's strength derived in part from its pro-feminist orientation, so did its great weakness. When I advocated that men support their wives during childbirth, I advised them to overcome their fears and enter more deeply into this powerful, age-old women's rite of passage. When I urged men to spend more time with their children, I encouraged them to develop their "feminine" qualities of nurturance. Even in describing how straight men could express physical tenderness toward and an emotional bond with their buddies during wartime, when it would be taboo to do so away from the battlefield, I assumed that this was yet another expression of the feminine side of men. Like the early men's movement I was wearing the blinders of the time.

Birthing children, rearing sons and daughters, comforting injured buddies — why did I see these behaviors as reflections of men's feminine side? Why did I not recognize that they were expressions of what is truly, deeply, authentically masculine?

In the early eighties, *A Choice of Heroes* responded to feminism by calling on men to explore their *own* images of masculinity. Robert Bly, Sam Keen, Robert Moore, Douglas Gillette, and the other gifted writers whose books have been part of the recent wave of men's literature have now taken a further step. The spokesmen of the nineties do not begin with feminism. They begin by asking, "What do *men* feel?" — a question that, a decade later, has finally brought the men's movement to Main Street.

In the highly charged world of sexual politics, this in some ways defiant reassertion of the masculine has confounded both male and female defenders of feminism. The resurgence of a more self-confidently masculine movement sent a shudder of fear through those who suspected they were about to be served old macho wine in new bottles. They became suspicious when they heard Robert Bly urge men to get in touch with the inner "wild man," when the word *warrior* was invoked positively rather than negatively, and when they read accounts of retreats at which men painted their faces, adopted animal names, wore masks, formed clans, and made loud grunting noises as they prowled through the woods.

Like professional football, at which feminists have scoffed for years, this emerging "wild man" wing of the men's movement might have been dismissed as the harmless, puerile expression of over-grown adolescents trying to prove their manhood. Its critics might have been satisfied with ridicule and derision. Instead, it elicited fear and condemnation as it challenged basic feminist assumptions about men. Critics of both sexes were clearly angry that men were being invited to explore their wildness, which the critics suspected was yet another pretext for men to regress to violence and domination. For example, Betty Friedan (who assigns this book in her classes and has repeatedly invited me to speak) describes what she derisively calls the "so-called men's movement" as if it is nothing more than regression. She believes the movement's message to its members is: "Feminism has made a wimp out of you. Get back to your cave man." As such, she has said publicly, it is a reactionary definition of masculinity, "based on dominance."

Critics are correct in believing that something fundamental has changed. Men are no longer basing their behavior primarily on women's views. Marching side by side with their feminist sisters to create a just, egalitarian, nonsexist world order is no longer the first order of business on the wild men's agenda. Instead, men are off in the woods, at gatherings that are off-limits to women, creating secret all-male rituals, beating strange-looking drums, reading myths about hairy men who lived in swamps (Bly's *Iron John*), healing their "father wounds," and exploring "deep masculinity."

I am part of this movement. I have witnessed its value to me and to other men, young and old, black and white and brown, millionaires and bus drivers. And I defend it. Yet I understand why it often seems silly, even ludicrous, to outsiders. There is a strange, arcane vocabulary, including frequent allusions to ancient gods such as Dionysius and Pan, and references to archetypes such as the King and the Magician. Conversations are punctuated by shouts of "Ho!" and other ritualistic phrases. Suddenly men are calling each other Brother David or, in some cases, Brother Eagle. Weeping and screaming is not only permitted but expected. And literally everyone seems to be "in recovery" from something.

Unlike the well-groomed men wearing jackets and ties who meet in hotel conference rooms, would-be wild men, with their scruffy clothes and unshaven faces, look like overgrown, unkempt Boy Scouts. Why do they feel such a strong need to exclude women? Why can't they be more open about what they are doing? Why do they need these old myths and stories? Why do they adopt all these Native American rituals, including drumming, using animal names, and making masks? And what is really so liberated about all this farting and burping, anyway?

These questions cannot be answered until we recognize that they are rooted in a fear of the masculine — a fear which I unfortunately used to share. Although I found myself on the lecture circuit as the author of a "men's book," I had only begun to outgrow my well-ingrained biases about masculinity. In retrospect, I can see more clearly that I was in fact afraid of the masculine. I had seen the historical horrors that men had committed on each other and on women. Personally, I had witnessed the cruelty of men to other men. Even after writing this book, and even after encountering many brothers whose love and tenderness I learned to trust, my fear of men remained.

I became aware of this most clearly when, in 1989, my friend Ken Druck, the author of *Secrets Men Keep*, encouraged me to attend a Chicago-based men's workshop called the New Warrior Training, which he said was "without a doubt one of the best things around." In spite of his recommendation, I resisted doing the training. First of all, the word *warrior* was not a positive one for me. It connoted making war, not making peace, and I could not imagine any positive reason for resurrecting the word. Add to that the structure of the training (forty intense hours packed into a single weekend), its reputation (tough and confrontational), and the aura of secrecy around it (no one, including Ken, would divulge much), and I had plenty of reasons to succumb to my suspicions that these "new" warriors were in fact a regression to the old. Would they gang up on those who didn't conform to their New Warrior party line? Would their so-called initiation rituals involve physical intimidation or violence? Would the all-male setting encourage anti-feminism and derogatory comments about women? Would we wallow in a shared sense of victimization by fathers who were (a) absent, (b) workaholic, (c) alcoholic, (d) abusive, (e) unemotional (check one)? And would there be a lot of posturing and struggling for dominance but very little genuine intimacy?

I was not alone in my suspicions. Carol Bly, the ex-wife of the author of *Iron John,* publicly questioned the integrity of the movement her husband's work had helped to launch. Calling it the "men's *separatist* movement" (a word that, for some reason, feminists never applied to their own movement), she shared her fear that male bonding was little more than "permission to regress." As she saw it, instead of working for peace ("which is a highly civilized, humble, thought-requiring kind of work"), the wild-man wing of the men's movement was whipping up the same old macho frenzy. (Her fears remind me of how men often reacted in the sixties and seventies when they were excluded from women's consciousness-raising groups. Unable to witness such gatherings firsthand, men could project whatever fantasies they wished onto them — projections that would never risk contact with reality.)

My curiosity, plus some fortuitous timing, finally helped me to overcome my fears. The New Warrior Training was first offered in California only a few hours' drive from where I live. (In itself, this is noteworthy — that a consciousness-raising movement should be born in America's heartland and only later spread to the trend-setting East and West coasts.) Not only were my fears allayed, but some of my deepest hopes were realized. Men — all kinds of men, too, including those who had never even heard of Betty Friedan or Robert Bly — came together with honesty, respect, and compassion. We entered our pain and moved through it into a deeper and more authentic kind of brotherhood than we had ever known. Together we formed a bond, not as in war, based on hating a common enemy, but based on loving one another and ourselves.

I learned to cherish the very word that had triggered my fears — *warrior*. The training did not ask us to become warriors of napalm and B-52's but warriors of the spirit. We were not told by a commanding officer what our mission was. We were challenged to know, and to live up to, the mission that was in our souls. We were not instructed to be fearless, which is inhuman, but to put our fears on the tip of our "swords" of truth. We were shown that true warriors fight the inner dragons first, so they can be sure that the external dragons they fight are real, not imaginary.

In the searing heat of our honesty and vulnerability, a profound layer of my stereotypes melted. I recognized that what is missing in typically macho male behavior is not just the feminine but, even more important, the deep masculine. Among men, wildness does not have to mean savagery; it can mean playfulness, raw energy, joy, and sorrow. Confronting men does not have to lead to violence; it can lead to deeper intimacy. After the civilized veneer is pulled away, the heart of masculinity does not have to be *Lord of the Flies*, or even *Lord of the Rings*, or any lord at all. The heart can be warm, wise, tender . . . and whole.

Watching in amazement as two dozen men broke out of the straitjacket of their cultural conditioning and became more loving human beings, I recognized that I had let myself come perilously close to losing sight of the beauty of my own gender. As a creature of my culture at a particular time in history, I had so deeply recoiled from what was wrong with our brand of heroism that I had lost touch with what was right. When we are not posturing and posing and pretending — when we are "deeply and vulnerably ourselves — we are beautiful. The beauty rests not just in our strengths but also in our wounds; not just in our muscles but in our souls.

Men who attend such gatherings make themselves vulnerable. They dare to explore their weaknesses and pain in public. They risk letting down their defenses and being seen in all their frailty, ignorance, and fear. Expressing their feelings authentically in the company of other men, sometimes for the first time in their lives, they may look and act awkward and foolish.

One does not have to be an expert marksman (or markswoman) to be able to hit such an easy target. Even the most inexperienced and uninformed male journalist can covertly enroll in one of these gatherings and then churn out a sophomoric, sarcastic memoir that asks: "How did I get to this place, crawling around with a dozen middle-aged men with smelly feet, snorting and mooing and sniffing?" Sadly, male reporters have actually stooped to lying about who they are and have violated the trust of other men in order to go undercover for their cheap brand of journalism. After accepting the privilege of witnessing this deep, therapeutic work and actually signing agreements promising confidentiality, they have turned around and sold the experience to the highest bidder.

This journalistic rape takes advantage of men who are easy prey. Unlike someone being interviewed by a journalist for a story, these men have not given their consent. They are not speaking prepared lines or posing for "photo ops." On the contrary, their wounds are raw; their pain is unconcealed; their shadows are in full view. To expose them in the media without their knowledge is just as inappropriate as taking secret photos in a hospital trauma unit.

Just as early feminists who staged bra-burnings made excellent fodder for the press, so men with painted faces romping in the woods have become an all-too-easy stereotype. Both then and now, the point is not that these women and men are in rebellion against bras and ties, respectively. The point is that they are symbolically ending one era and beginning another. Women's flaming undergarments (a girdle, as Betty Friedan has pointed out, might have been a better choice than a bra) made sense only in the context of women's oppression. Similarly, tribes of "wild men" make sense only in the context of the real worlds in which men live:

> Men walking down the sidewalks of Manhattan, sweating in their suits, ties, leather shoes, and calf-length socks, violating their body wisdom and their common sense to honor some unwritten code of dress

> Men in the locker room of their local athletic club, each wanting to share his dreams and dreads but talking instead about

whether the San Francisco 49ers will make it to the Super Bowl

Men at work, talking about deals and business plans, promotions and paychecks, but never, never howling at the idiocy of the bureaucracy that surrounds them or grieving for their sacrificed ambitions and lost dreams

Men at home, trying to be "good husbands" and "good fathers," measuring themselves against a standard they cannot see, trying to provide their children with a family experience they themselves never had

Men standing in front of the mirror, watching wrinkles appear and hair disappear, trying so hard to stay tough and trim and upbeat but seeing a sadness around the eyes, a sadness reflecting fears of decline, fragility, illness, impotence, despair, and loss

Men flying multimillion-dollar planes at breakneck speed above the clouds, proudly dropping bombs on villagers below who cannot even see their attackers.

Men in the movement are doing what they do on weekends because these are the worlds in which they live during the week. Evoke the underlying pain that so-called real men ignore, and the ridicule and sarcasm stop. The smart-ass grin is wiped off men's faces. Their defenses drop. They become quiet — quiet because their hearts are opening.

If we, whether male or female, enter with compassion into the pain and craziness of the world in which men live, making fun of those silly men off playing in the woods is beside the point. They no longer seem so forbidding. On the contrary, it is clear that they are healing their wounds. They are learning to trust other men because they have too often been trained to mistrust. They take animal names because they want to get back in touch with their instinctive nature. They are being wild because they feel that they have been so systematically, sometimes cruelly, tamed.

The men's movement is growing now, growing beyond belief, because our culture is finally creating settings in which we can reintegrate the feminine and the masculine — that is, in which men can dare to feel *everything*. At the Wild Man workshops in Texas or at the New Warrior Training in Illinois, Wisconsin, and California, and at other healing workshops throughout the country, *every* man, from the macho construction worker to the straight-arrow executive to the gay banker, can be a man. Being liberated from sexism does not mean that we become more homogenous, less androgynous. It means that we can become more ourselves. It means that we broaden and deepen what *masculine* means.

To the question "Why now?" we at last begin to see the outlines of an answer. The men's movement is no longer offering a narrow new definition of liberation, whether pro- or anti-feminist. It is opening its arms to all kinds of men who are willing to be authentic with other men. It is embracing its brothers — and it is welcoming its sons.

I was so moved by the New Warrior Training that when I returned home, I asked my seventeen-year-old son, Shane, if he wanted to experience it. I asked him because I could tell he was ready to be tested, and ready to be treated as a man among men. What he did during the training and how we grew is his story to tell, but I can say here that it was powerful for both of us and helped us to heal some of the deepest wounds between us and to reopen powerful channels of love. Shane's younger brothers are now curious as to what this men's initiation is all about. And Shane is passing on the word to his friends and their fathers.

Despite its strength, the men's movement is still young, fragile, and vulnerable. Only ten years ago, there were no workshops like the one Shane and I shared. As recently as a decade ago, Ron Hering, the fifty-five-year-old cofounder of the New Warrior Training, was just beginning to rethink masculine roles. He recalls walking into the University of Wisconsin bookstore in 1983 and scanning shelf after shelf of books about women. "There were literally hundreds of books in the women's studies section," says Hering. "But there were only six books about men — and two of them were about picking up women! There was a real vacuum, which your book helped to fill."

Although Hering had some kind words about *A Choice of Heroes*, he too recognized that it was internally askew. "Being present for the birth of your child is not just reclaiming the feminine," he told me. "It's reclaiming your deepest, most primal energy. Anything that is so powerful, so natural, so bloody, so life-and-death is part of our masculine heritage too. Your book tended to equate men's becoming more whole with men's becoming more feminine, but that is only one direction in which they need to grow. The other is toward the deep masculine."

Sam Keen, the author of *Fire in the Belly* and the father of a young daughter, makes precisely the same point. "When I pick up my daughter to cuddle her, by what stretch of the imagination is that a feminine act?" he asks. "That's as much a part of my maleness as riding my horse down the side of a mountain at breakneck speed."

Because the men's movement is encouraging men to grow in *both* directions, more men are beginning to trust it. "There's still a core of men who don't want to feel or to look at themselves," Hering says, basing his conclusion on his work as a business consultant as well as a New Warrior trainer. "But I think that core has shrunk from a majority to a minority. Although the men's movement is still widely misunderstood, it is clearly here to stay. Men are saying: 'I'm hurting. Something's wrong. What is it?' And they're looking for answers."

Talk to leaders of the men's movement: management consultants, doctors, metalworkers, therapists, ex-marines, auto company executives, professors. Read Robert Bly, or Sam Keen, or Moore and Gillette, or other authors of the recent crop of men's literature. You will find something that is all but missing in this book, just as it was missing in the culture of the seventies and early eighties. You will find a reaffirmation of masculinity's deepest, most nourishing roots.

When my son completed his men's training, he had received a gift — a gift to all our sons and grandsons, not just from me, but from a quarter of a century of men's work. Although younger than feminism, the movement is nevertheless old enough to have elders. It is old enough that we are now being called into a deeper awareness of our manhood by our fathers. There are men who have done enough work on themselves to be able to initiate younger men into manhood. This gift of male love instead of being passed down from grandfather to father to son has become endangered. In our culture this chain of love has reached the breaking point. To witness the strengthening of that chain in my family, and in the families of scores of other men and in our culture as a whole, has given me even more hope than the dismantling of the Berlin Wall. That wall, after all, was only in Germany. The wall between men is everywhere.

The women of the sixties, we must remember, had several generations of feminism behind them. The early men's movement, however, was an orphan. It is only now, in the nineties, that the slow, patient, sometimes misguided, but always persistent seeding of the fields of masculinity is about to yield its first major harvest. In previous decades, men who felt alienated from the standard, lock-step, John Wayne image of masculinity tended to remain isolated and alone. Now they are going public.

In Public: Searching for a Politics of Masculinity

If some girl wants me because I was there, that's kind of shallow — fun, but shallow.
— Lance Corporal Richard Musicant, a Desert Storm veteran

After reading *A Choice of Heroes* for an educational seminar, Bill Chalmers, a teacher in Juneau, Alaska, titled his paper "I Want You to Know that I'm No Hero." In his essay, which he kindly forwarded to me, he described the feelings of a man who had left the old definitions of gender behind. For him, rejecting the old archetypes was old news. He had never been enamored of the Frontiersman, the Soldier, or the Expert. His disinterest in the Breadwinner was so strong that he left a high-paying job in order to return to his first love, teaching. And he let go of the Lord when he dropped out of the seminary, hoping only "to live long enough to receive communion from a female priest."

But liberation had not brought him happiness, only isolation. Because of his metamorphosis, he had lost his male context. "I can no longer sit with the boys over a pitcher of beer at the Maplewood Bowl — to my knowledge, we don't congregate, at the Maplewood Bowl or anywhere else. Perhaps it's because we're too busy living our two lives: erasing the old with the left hand while writing the new with the right."

Like so many men in the nineties, Chalmers is not satisfied with liberation. He wants friends. He wants a tribe. He wants "a gathering of men," as Bill Moyers titled his PBS interview with Robert Bly. Instead, he is alone with his wife and kids. He has found no new ways to congregate or, in the current jargon, to bond. "There is for me," he laments, "no longer any cozy cave of manhood into which I wish to crawl."

The good news is that men are finally constructing new caves. As we realize that we need clans, that we need brothers, that we need male elders, men's groups are taking root in communities throughout the country. Thousands of men in dozens of cities join Robert Bly and Michael Meade for readings and drummings. As thousands of men are initiated by the New Warrior Training and many other workshops, a community of men is at last forming.

But the bad news is that many men aren't part of this. The old caves are still there. So are the old myths, the old heroes, and the old warriors. Yes, Robert Bly has his followers. But so does General Norman Schwarzkopf. Denis Hayes, the founder of Earth Day, is a hero to many. But so is Lee Iacocca, whose gas-guzzling machines continue to pollute our world. It's still the Soldier versus the Mediator, the Frontiersman versus the Nurturer.

Let's look first at the Frontiersman, a hero who symbolizes the exploitation and control of the earth. On many fronts, this archetype appears to be in retreat. The environmental movement is stronger than ever. It is no longer a passing fad but a social force. Ecology is not just an academic discipline. It is now a word that appears on supermarket shelves and on the tongues of schoolchildren. Clearly a new archetype is emerging.

Challenging the Frontiersman, the Healer (which is what I call the new "green" hero) wants not to exploit the earth but to sustain it. "Sustainable development," a term known only to specialists a decade ago, has now moved into the mainstream, as more and more people come to understand that the ethic of the Healer is the key to human survival.

If any single event shows how far we have come from the Davy Crockett/Daniel Boone syndrome, it was the 1991 Academy Awards presentation, when Kevin Costner's film *Dances with Wolves* received seven Oscars. Here was a film that graphically showed what our heroes of yesteryear did to the buffalo and other creatures of our vast and bountiful continent. The film showed scores of carcasses lying raw and bloody across the prairie, the animals killed only for their fur or, worse, for sport. Costner's choice of heroes was clear. He wanted to follow the ethic of the Healer, who used only what he needed and left the land rich and verdant, ready to sustain future generations until the end of time.

But just as it is a mistake to conclude that the househusband should triumph over the pilot, so it is unwise to wait for the Healer to triumph over the Frontiersman. From the perspective of the past ten years, that is not how history will unfold. As I have argued in detail in *Coming Into Our Own: Understanding Adult Metamorphosis*, the environment is still deteriorating, not improving. It shows every indication of continuing to do so. So, within each of us and within our culture, the Frontiersman and the Healer must meet. They must talk with each other and find common ground. Just as the National Resources Defense Council worked hand in hand with McDonald's to end the extraordinary waste of paper and plastic in thousands of fast-food outlets, so must these two archetypes enter into dialogue and work together. Like the Native Americans before us, we must become partners with the land, using our superior technical knowledge to extract greater value from the earth while still respecting its integrity.

Like the Frontiersman, the old archetype of the Soldier also seems to be in decline. Until recently, still suffering from the effects of the unpopular war in Vietnam, the Soldier was not an image that inspired male enthusiasm. To make matters worse, the Communists, who had served for over half a century as the Soldier's ready-made enemy, self-destructed before our very eyes. The Berlin Wall came down. The general secretary of the Communist party in the U.S.S.R., Mikhail Gorbachev, disavowed Marxism, and the Soviet Union began to break up, with each republic seeking independence. As a consequence, cuts that would slash the Pentagon budget were planned in the United States. Bases were scheduled to be closed throughout the country. Weapon systems that would once have been easily funded were under attack. The all-volunteer army was suffering from low morale.

But the archetype of the Soldier is resilient. As evidenced by Operation Desert Storm, the U.S. military code name for the brief Persian Gulf war against Iraq in early 1991, the Soldier archetype lies as deep as any other in the minds of men — and, it appears, in the minds of women as well.

Shortly after the war in the Persian Gulf ended, readers and friends suddenly inundated me with the same news clipping. The story that reminded all these people of my book was *Boston Globe* columnist Ellen Goodman's widely syndicated ode to Norman Schwarzkopf, the military mastermind of Operation Desert Storm. A successful and insightful columnist who loyally champions feminist causes of all kinds, Goodman shouted hosannas for the general. Calling him the "heartthrob of America," she did her best to turn the six-foot-three-inch, potbellied, 240-pounder into a sex object. "Find yourself looking in the personals column for a burly fifty-six-year-old in fatigues with a 170 IQ and a taste for Pavarotti? Desperately seeking a man who is caring but, well, commanding? If you are among the millions suffering from Schwarzkopf withdrawal, take heart. The war may be over, the daily briefings kaput, but the general is not going to fade away.

No, indeed. For months after the war, he was leading parades, standing in front of the White House, receiving awards, and being mentioned as a political candidate ("Do you hear the faint refrain of 'I Like Ike'?" asked Goodman.) Since heroism hates a vacuum, into the vacuum of male role models rode Stormin' Norman. Citing what she considered to be the "search for a new model of male leadership," Goodman concluded that the general "seems like the real thing." And if feminist accolades were not enough, he was even named Father of the Year. "His story is going to have a very, very broad popular appeal," said the president of Bantam Books, who paid a whopping $5 million for the rights to publish General Schwarzkopf's autobiography. "He exemplifies a lot of things that we are looking for in this country: moral centeredness, traditional values, courage, and also a kind of competence and leadership."

But before we enshrine this millionaire general in the pantheon of American heroes, let's admit the obvious truth. We are trying to mythologize him. We are trying to turn him and his war into something more — and better — than they are. We want to transform him into a tall, handsome, rugged John Wayne of the nineties, even though he clearly is not a John Wayne. Somewhere deep in our psyches, foreign policy and archetypal mythology merge. And it is on this level that the Persian Gulf war deserves our attention. Even though it will soon fade from public memory, this war and this general will remain embedded in our minds. We will remember the lesson: The soldier is still a hero.

The Vietnam war lasted for years. Over fifty thousand soldiers lost their lives. And there were no celebrations. The Gulf war, however, lasted only a few weeks. Just a few hundred of our troops died. Yet the celebrations lasted for months, *longer than the war itself*. The New York Sanitation Department had to assign three hundred workers to clean up the mess left from the June 1991 ticker-tape parade honoring the victorious troops. They hauled away an estimated 12 million pounds of confetti, a million yellow ribbons, and 6000 tons of ticker tape — more garbage than was left after the Victory Parade in 1945, celebrating the end of the long and painful years of World War II. That war cost thousands upon thousands of American lives, and millions of innocent people died. The very excess of the Gulf war celebration indicates that we were not just celebrating victory. We were celebrating something else: the resurrection of the Soldier.

But the Soldier as archetype can be no more heroic than war itself. And recent wars, whether in Grenada, Panama, or the Persian Gulf, are anything but heroic. Even some of President Bush's White House aides joked that Operation Desert Storm was "making the world safe for feudalism." After the war, the same royal clique that had controlled the tiny desert state of Kuwait returned to power, resisting as best they could efforts to democratize their oil-rich kingdom. Saddam Hussein remained in power in Iraq — and many Arabs elevated him to hero status. As Kuwait's precious oilfields continued to burn months after the war, the Iraqi dictator rebuilt his army.

Compared to these meager results, the human cost of the war was astronomical. By American estimates, over 100,000 Iraqi soldiers died, and as many as 300,000 were wounded. To those numbers we must add 100,000 dead Iraqi children. Add to this the devastation visited on the Kurds, who dared to rise up against Saddam Hussein, only to be left at his mercy after the foreign troops went home, and we pass the half-million mark. Only then do we begin to see the scale of the massacre in the Persian Gulf.

I use the word *massacre*, not *war*, for a simple factual reason: the United States, Iraq's principal adversary, suffered 389 dead and 351 wounded (one quarter as a result of so-called friendly fire). That means well under a thousand dead and wounded on our side, over half a million on theirs — a ratio of 1 to 5000. To my knowledge, this conflict dwarfs any massacre committed by any American military force. Never before were we so invulnerable; never before were our victims so vulnerable.

Because of the moral implications of this massacre, the military tried to downplay the casualty figures. "General Schwarzkopf decided earlier in the war that his troops wouldn't count enemy bodies and report the totals," reported Walter Mossberg and David Rogers in the *Wall Street Journal*. The practice of making body counts marked the Vietnam war and led to charges that the military was inflating its battlefield successes and celebrating carnage. Aware of this problem, General Schwarzkopf told the press just after the Gulf war began, "I have absolutely no idea what the Iraqi casualties [are], and I tell you, if I have anything to say about it, we're never going to get into the body-count business." Body counts were out. They would be too embarrassing. They would reveal that this was not a war but a massacre. It would show that the Soldier, armed with "smart" weapons, could go berserk without ever breaking out in a sweat.

Instead, we celebrated. The archetype of the Soldier, which had been so severely undermined by the protracted and ultimately paralyzing war in Vietnam, was rescued, revived, and enshrined. Troops returning from the Gulf were not treated with contempt, as Vietnam veterans were. On the contrary, they were accorded a hero's welcome. In fact, they were mistreated in precisely the opposite way from soldiers who served in Vietnam. The Gulf vets were made uncomfortable not because they were not given enough respect but because they were given too much.

When the second squad of the first platoon of Alpha Company, First Battalion of the Fifth Marine Regiment, came home, they were treated like movie stars and given parties, limousines, receptions, honors, awards. But very quickly their satisfaction gave way to a nagging doubt that would not go away: "What had they done to deserve all the hoopla?" When one marine was asked if he had shot anyone, he replied honestly: "Well, no. I sat on an Amtrac for a few days and collected a few prisoners. That's it. I didn't do what those Marines in Vietnam did." Said one of his buddies, "A cook in Vietnam saw more action than I did. I don't want any parades. *I'm no hero.*" As the journalists who interviewed them concluded, "For them, the war lasted seventy-two hours. Then they went home 'heroes' and tried to figure out why."

Again and again, veterans returning from the Gulf made it clear that they felt they were being miscast. A nation that felt bad about masculinity wanted to feel good about it again. So we turned the high-tech massacre into a moral victory. We told and retold the story until we felt better about ourselves. By emphasizing some facts and ignoring others, by burying our heads in ticker tape, we remade a myth. We erased the nightmare of Vietnam so that we could sleep deeply once again.

Since this book may well be read ten years from now, long after our culture has forgotten this "little war," it is tempting to overlook this conflict's long-term significance. But we cannot. The next war will be fought with even more sophisticated weapons from the Defense Advanced Research Projects Agency (DARPA). That agency is working hard to remove soldiers from the battlefield altogether. "The whole idea is to get the human being out of harm's way," says Roger Schapell, the director of Martin Marietta's advanced automation technology group, which is working on military robotics for DARPA. For example, this group is developing the autonomous land vehicle (ALV), which in a few years will be able to penetrate enemy lines while the "drivers" are hundreds of miles away.

With increasing automation, the next time a superpower does battle against a Third World country, the us-against-them, killed-and-wounded ratio will be even more insanely lopsided. We will be forced to recognize that it is not the soldiers who should march down Broadway but their machines. The "heroes" are not the generals but the inventors from DARPA. There will be no risk that anyone will be charged with war crimes, because none of us will be there — only our machines will fight.

Michael Meade, one of the leading figures in the new men's movement, calls American culture passive-aggressive. According to him, the Gulf war illustrated that "the government can aggress, and the people are passive about it. . . . Everybody's going to allow it, and then show up for the celebration, a celebration of brutal dealing of death — the heaviest bombing ever in the history of the world. I don't personally find pride in it at all."

Perhaps now those strange men in the woods with their drums and animal names seem different. Let's listen again as they cry and growl and grunt, reconnecting with their feelings and regrounding themselves in their bodies. Let's watch them as they explore their "wildness" in the company of men they call their brothers. Witnessed against the backdrop of the last war, and the next one, they no longer seem so strange. Indeed, they no longer seem to be the problem at all. Strange and awkward as they may be, they are an alternative to stealth bombers and smart weapons, to the pounding of tank treads and the shockwaves of aerial bombardments. As long as men are drawn to violence, and as long as nations are drawn to war, *nothing is more important than ensuring that men feel their own pain — and the pain of their victims.*

The state of our souls and the state of our culture are symmetrical. Both are divided. One part of us, and one cultural movement, is inspired by a potbellied poet from Minnesota whose book is on the best-seller list. Another part of us, and another part of our culture, is personified by a potbellied general fresh from the battlefield. Neighbor against neighbor, father against son, brother against brother — the ranks of men are split. And ultimately, a house divided cannot stand.

Even as I write about my revulsion at this massacre, I remember my excitement as a Patriot missile shot down Iraqi Scud missiles before they could detonate on Israeli soil. I identified with our high-tech heroes in the same way I admired the hero of the *Star Wars* trilogy, Luke Skywalker. I felt proud that our troops and our technology could contain the violence of a ruthless, cruel dictator who would stop at almost nothing to achieve his ends. I feared Saddam Hussein and wanted his brutality stopped. Thanks to the courage, skill, and daring of our armed forces, his power was pushed back within Iraq's borders.

Yes, men are divided. *I* am divided. I have a Robert Bly inside of me, and a General Schwarzkopf. Yet ours is a culture in which the poets disown their wars and the generals disown their poetry. It is time for healing this split. It is time for a dialogue, time to find the parts of us that can imagine a world in which Bly could be a general and Schwarzkopf a poet laureate. The challenge of the men's movement is to include the veterans not just of the New Warrior Training but of Operation Desert Storm. We must tear down the wall that separates the old masculinity from the new and begin to wrestle with the contradictions that are inextricably part of all our lives.

Broadening the movement, tearing down the wall, healing the split — yes, this will involve venturing into the terrain we call politics. But in the long run there is no alternative for the men's movement. The movement is about telling our truths as men and seeking a world that reflects and honors those truths. In the nineties, this will require that we express ourselves, not only in the woods on weekends but in the marketplace and at city hall and wherever power is used by men.

As my young questioner so poignantly illustrated, the fighter pilot and the househusband are in every man. We need them both, the old and the new, the soft and the hard, the househusband and the pilot. To be truly ourselves, we need them both in our daily lives.

Notes

1. The Frontiersman

16–17   The Indians' statements are from Ake Hultkrantz, *The Religions of the American Indians* (Berkeley, Calif., 1967); T. C. McLuhan, *Touch the Earth* (New York, 1971); and Amaury de Riencourt, *Sex and Power in History* (New York, 1974). See also Norman O. Brown, *Love's Body* (New York, 1966): "The world is our mother . . . to love and penetrate."

17   The ecological wisdom of primitive religion is described in Lynn White, "The Historical Roots of Our Ecological Crisis," *Science* 155 (1967), and by other contemporary feminists.

References to Tagore are from René Dubos, *The Wooing of Earth* (New York, 1980).

17–18   The Illinois editor is quoted in Norman Graebner, *Manifest Destiny* (New York, 1968). The nineteenth-century congressman is from Graebner, as are the comments on manifest destiny.

18   The role of violence in the formation of the American West is analyzed in Richard Slotkin, *Regeneration Through Violence* (Middletown, Conn., 1973).

The William Henry Harrison episode appears in Michael Rogin, *Fathers and Children* (New York, 1975).

The statistics on western migration are cited in Rogin, *Fathers and Children.*

18–19   Tecumseh's remarks are from McLuhan, *Touch the Earth.*

19   The emergence of the Frontiersman archetype is explored in Slotkin, *Regeneration Through Violence,* and in Henry Nash Smith, *The Virgin Land* (New York, 1970).

For a discussion of Henry Nash Smith's comments on Buffalo Bill, see Leonard Kriegel, *On Men and Manhood* (New York, 1980).

Jefferson's remarks are from Smith, *The Virgin Land.*

20   Cooper's character is discussed by Marvin Meyers, *The Jacksonian Persuasion* (Stanford, Calif., 1957).

Vernon Parrington's observations are from his *Main Currents of American Thought* (New York, 1963).

21   Dubos, *The Wooing of Earth.*

      C. G. Jung, *Man and His Symbols.*

      Kriegel, *On Men and Manhood.*

21-22 Michael Horse's remarks are from a review of the movie in the *Christian Science Monitor*, May 28, 1981.

22   Examples of feminist ecology include Nancy Todd's and Evelyn Ames's articles, "Women and Ecology" and "Return to the Feminist Principle," first published in the *Journal of the New Alchemists,* New Alchemy Institute, Woods Hole, Mass.

      Significant books addressing this subject are: Elizabeth Dodson Gray, *Green Paradise Lost* (Wellesley, Mass., 1981); Susan Griffin, *Women and Nature* (New York, 1978); and Theodore Roszak, *Person/Planet* (Garden City, N.Y., 1978). Roszak summarized the views expressed at what he calls "the first major festival devoted to women's spirituality," which took place in 1976.

2. The Soldier

31   James Fallows, *National Defense* (New York, 1981).

32   Ron Kovic, *Born on the Fourth of July* (New York, 1971).

      Phil Caputo, *A Rumor of War* (New York, 1977).

33   Robert Jay Lifton, *Home from the War* (New York, 1973).

      Harold C. Lyon, Jr., *Tenderness Is Strength* (New York, 1977).

35   "Every man . . . his war." Marina Sulzberger made this statement, according to Gloria Emerson, *Winners and Losers* (New York, 1977).

35-36 Julius Caesar, *The Conquest of Gaul* (London, 1951).

36   Comments from Germany, Spain, and Ireland are from Theodore Roszak, "The Hard and the Soft," in *Masculine/Feminine,* ed. Theodore and Betty Roszak (New York, 1970).

      Ruth Hubbard's essay appears in *Women Look at Biology Looking at Women* (Cambridge, Mass., 1980).

37   John Adams's remarks are cited in Michael Rogin, *Fathers and Children* (New York, 1975).

      The role of arms is discussed in Walter Millis, *Arms and Men: A Study of American Military History* (New York, 1956).

      The frequency of wars in American history is documented in Marcus Cunliffe, *Soldiers and Civilians* (Boston, 1968).

The military historian is Cunliffe, *Soldiers and Civilians.*

Alexis de Tocqueville's remark is in his "Pocket Notebook No. 3," in *Journey to America,* ed. J. P. Mayer (New Haven, Conn., 1960).

John Dos Passos's remark is analyzed in Paul Fussell, *The Great War and Modern Memory* (New York, 1975).

38 The "expert on American writing" is Frederic J. Hoffman in *The Twenties* (New York, 1949).

The Vietnam veteran speaks in Jan Berry, ed., *Peace Is Our Profession* (New York, 1981). For similar comments, see also Al Santoli, *Everything We Had* (New York, 1981), and Mark Baker, *Nam* (New York, 1981).

James Jones, *The Thin Red Line* (New York, 1962); discussed in Fussell, *The Great War.*

38–39 Lord Moran, *The Anatomy of Courage* (Boston, 1967). General S. L. A. Marshall's work is discussed in John Keegan, *The Face of Battle* (New York, 1977).

39 Samuel Stouffer's research is discussed in Marc Feigen Fasteau, *The Male Machine* (New York, 1974).

41 Bertolucci's comments are from Joan Mellen, *Women and Their Sexuality in the New Film* (New York, 1973).

42 The Playboy is discussed by Arlene and Jerome J. Skolnick, "The Inexpressive Male — A Tragedy of American Society," in their *Intimacy, Family and Society* (Boston, 1974).

Joseph Heller's *Something Happened* (New York, 1977) is analyzed by Christopher Lasch, "The Flight from Feeling: Sociopsychology of Sexual Conflict," *Marxist Perspectives* (Spring, 1978).

43 From Burke Davis, *Marine!* (New York, 1962). In this biography of General Lewis B. "Chesty" Puller, Puller's wife expresses shock at his reputation for brutality and lust for war. Puller disputes this, saying, "I assure you, Virginia, that never in my life have I ever made a statement that 'I like to fight.' "

Lyon, *Tenderness Is Strength.*

43–44 Rollo May, *Power and Innocence* (New York, 1972).

44 Patton is quoted in Fallows, *National Defense.*

Eddie Graham was interviewed by Emily Rubin, *Boston Globe,* August 17, 1979.

44–45 Lifton, *Home from the War.*

3. War

50–51   William and Henry James's views are discussed in Joe L. Dubbert, *A Man's Place* (Englewood Cliffs, N.J., 1979). This is an outstanding volume on the history of masculinity.

51   Roosevelt's role is analyzed in Dubbert, *A Man's Place.* See also William Henry Harbaugh, *The Life and Times of Theodore Roosevelt* (New York, 1961), and Peter Gabriel Filene, *Him/Her/Self* (New York, 1974).

Elizabeth and Joseph Pleck, *The American Man* (Englewood Cliffs, N.J., 1980). The Boy Scouts are discussed in Jeffrey P. Hantover, "The Boy Scouts and the Validation of Masculinity," in this volume.

52–53   The language of World War I is beautifully dissected in Paul Fussell, *The Great War and Modern Memory* (New York, 1975).

53   The *Ladies' Home Journal* editorial is cited in Filene, *Him/Her/Self.*

The Committee on Public Information's remarks were first published in *Century Magazine* (May 1916); reprinted in Robert H. Bremner et al., *Children and Youth in America* (Cambridge, Mass., 1971).

54   Kilmer's death is discussed in Filene, *Him/Her/Self.*

Thomas Pynchon, *Gravity's Rainbow* (New York, 1973).

The reviewer commenting on war poetry's subversive tendency is Richard Fein, "Modern War Poetry," *Southwest Review,* vol. 47, no. 4 (1962); cited in Fussell, *The Great War.*

55   The changing face of the battlefield is discussed in John Keegan, *The Face of Battle* (New York, 1976); Walter Millis, *Arms and Men: A Study of American Military History* (New York, 1956); and Stanton A. Coblentz, *From Arrow to Atom Bomb* (Cranbury, N.J., 1953).

55–56   William James, *The Varieties of Religious Experience* (New York, 1961) and "The Moral Equivalent of War," reprinted in Bremner, *Children and Youth in America.*

56   Walter Lippmann, "Poltroons and Pacifists," first published in the *New Republic* (January 1916), reprinted in *Early Writings* (New York, 1970).

Farley Mowat, *And No Birds Sang* (Boston, 1980).

56–57   Glenn Gray, *The Warriors: Reflections on Men in Battle* (New York, 1970). See his observations about the "lustful" eye, which finds battle beautiful, and the "Enduring Appeals of Battle."

57   John Huston, *An Open Book* (New York, 1980).

58   Adolf Hitler, *Mein Kampf* (Boston, 1971).

4. Genocide

62   William Shirer's remarks were reprinted in *Review* (February 1981).

63   A more complete list of books published during the 1940s about the authoritarian personality can be found in Theodore Adorno et al., *The Authoritarian Personality* (New York, 1950). The quotations on pages 63–64 are taken from this volume.
Kate Millett, *Sexual Politics* (New York, 1969).

Theodore Roszak, "The Hard and the Soft," in *Masculine/Feminine,* ed. Theodore and Betty Roszak (New York, 1970).

64–65 Goebbels is quoted in Millett, *Sexual Politics.*

65   The Nazis' persistent attitude against women is described in Joachim Fest, *The Face of the Third Reich* (New York, 1970).

The OSS profile is summarized in Robert C. Waite, *Hitler* (New York, 1977).

Adolf Hitler, *Mein Kampf* (Boston, 1971). Unless otherwise noted, Hitler's statements are from this source.

65–66 The material about Bormann's wife and the suicides of Hitler's women is from Waite, *Hitler.* To be exposed to Nazi misogny at its worst, read Otto Weiniger's *Sex and Character* (London, 1906). This young Jew, who killed himself in his early twenties, is the great theoretician whose influence on Hitler is described in George L. Mosse, *Toward the Final Solution: A History of European Racism* (New York, 1978). "Women have no existence and no essence," Wieniger wrote. ". . . Mankind occurs as something or nothing, male or female . . . she is non-moral and she is non-logical. But all existence is moral and logical existence. So woman has no existence."

66   Adrienne Rich, *Of Woman Born* (New York, 1976). Kollwitz's life and work are described in Mina C. and Arthur Klein, *Käthe Kollwitz: Life in Art* (New York, 1972).

67   Feder is quoted in Robert Cecil, *The Myth of the Master Race* (New York, 1972).

The "prophylactic health measure" speech is reprinted in Joachim Remak, *The Nazi Years* (Englewood Cliffs, N.J., 1969).

68   Von Hindenberg's letter and Hilter's reply are also in Remak, *Nazi Years.*

Fred Uhlman, *Reunion* (New York, 1978).

69   Heinz Heger, *The Men with the Pink Triangle* (Boston, 1980).

The Hitler Youth member is H. C. Koch, the author of *Hitler Youth: The Duped Generation* (New York, 1972). Because of the author's background, this volume is of particular interest.

70   The slogan "pinks, punks, and perverts" is discussed in Robert Goldston, *The American Nightmare: Senator McCarthy and the Politics of Hate* (Indianapolis, 1973).

The McCarthyite is quoted in David Caute, *The Great Fear: The Anticommunist Purge under Truman and Eisenhower* (New York, 1978).

Senator Wherry's remarks are from an interview with Max Lerner, *New York Post,* July 17, 1950; reprinted in Jonathan Katz, *Gay American History* (New York, 1976).

McCarthy's study of *Mein Kampf* was first reported in Jack Anderson and Ronald May, *McCarthy: The Man, the Senator, and the "Ism"* (Boston, 1952).

70–71 Harnischfeger and the Malmédy massacre are discussed in Goldston, *American Nightmare.*

71   McCarthy's critics on this issue included Max Lerner and Richard Rovere. See Rovere, *Senator Joe McCarthy* (New York, 1959). Roy Cohn described the sexual slander and counterslander in *McCarthy* (New York, 1968).

5. Holocaust

77   Harold Bell Wright, *When a Man's a Man* (Chicago, 1916). Wright dedicated this "story of manhood" to his sons.

The scene in the ICBM silo is described by Daniel Lang, *An Inquiry into Enoughness: Of Bombs, Men and Staying Alive* (New York, 1965).

79   The sexual undertones of Groves's message to Truman are discussed in Franco Fornari, *The Psychoanalysis of War* (New York, 1974).

Truman's, Churchill's, and Byrnes's remarks are quoted in Robert Jay Lifton, *The Broken Connection* (New York, 1979).

80   Truman's diary entry was reported in an Associated Press dispatch in 1980. The diary was discovered in the Truman Library by Robert Ferrell, a diplomatic historian at Indiana University.

Alfred Nobel's remark is from Anthony Sampson, *The Arms Bazaar* (New York, 1977).

Albert Schweitzer, *Peace or Atomic War* (New York, 1958).

81   The residents of Utah and Nevada speak in "The Downwind People: A Thousand Americans Sue for Damages from Atomic Fallout," *Life*, June 1980.

81–82   These victims' statements are from *Newsweek*, November 26, 1979; *New York Times Magazine*, April 22, 1979; and *Time*, March 12, 1979.

83   Dorothy Dinnerstein, *The Mermaid and the Minotaur* (New York, 1976).

6. Antiwar

91   Arthur Schlesinger, Jr., *A Thousand Days* (New York, 1977).

91–92   Kennedy's Cincinnati speech was reported in the *New York Times*, October 1, 1960.

93   David Halberstam, author of *The Best and the Brightest* (New York, 1969), spoke of "bigger balls" in conversation with the author.

Doris Kearns, *Lyndon Johnson and the American Dream* (New York, 1977).

93–94   David Halberstam is the source for these remarks.

94–95   James C. Thomson's remarks, in conversation with the author.

95–96   Leslie Fiedler, *Collected Essays* (New York, 1971).

96   Susan Sontag, *Styles of Radical Will* (New York, 1966).

Unless otherwise credited, the source for the attitudes of feminists who emerged from the New Left is Sara Evans, *Personal Politics* (New York, 1979).

97   Jane Lazarre, *The Mother Knot* (New York, 1977).

98   Michelle Wallace, *Black Macho and the Myth of the Superwoman* (New York, 1978).

99   Daniel Patrick Moynihan, "The Negro Family: The Case for National Action," Office of Policy Planning and Research, U.S. Department of Labor, March 1965.

James Peters's letters were part of an article by Christina Robb, "Another Draft, Another Resistance," *Boston Globe Magazine*, November 16, 1980.

101   Ellen Goodman's comments are from her column "Equal Rights, Equal Draft: There's More to Win Than Lose," *Boston Globe*.

The comments by Congresswoman Schroeder and Betty Friedan were on the front page of the *Washington Post*, February 9, 1980.

Charles Reich, *The Sorcerer of Bolinas Reef* (New York, 1976).

7. Politics

108   Richard Reeves, "Getting Ready for War," *Esquire,* April 24, 1979.

109   Daniel Yankelovich, "Assertive America," *Foreign Affairs,* March 1981.

Arbatov's remarks are from his speech in March 1981 at the first congress of International Physicians for the Prevention of Nuclear War, at Airlie House, Airlie, Virginia.

The army officer was Arthur Collins, *Washington Post,* October 17, 1980.

110   Alexander Haig's remarks quoted in TOKUM.

111   Lloyd S. Etheredge, *A World of Men: The Private Sources of American Foreign Policy* (Cambridge, Mass., 1978).

112   Amory Lovins, *Soft Energy Paths: Toward a Durable Peace* (New York, 1977).

Margaret Mead's reactions to the terms "hard" and "soft" are mentioned in Lovins's replies to a lecture he delivered in memory of E. F. Schumacher, reprinted in *The Schumacher Lectures,* ed. Satish Kumar (New York, 1980).

In praising a book by the feminist Elizabeth Dodson Gray, *Green Paradise Lost,* Lovins wrote that its "evocative fusion of ecological, spiritual, and feminist values shows why" the sexual reaction is so strong. Dodson's book, said Lovins, "helps us all to liberate ourselves from projecting sexual dominance onto other people — and onto the natural world of which we are a part."

115   The *Ms.* magazine issue on leadership was that of July 1980.

Charlotte Bunch's article appeared in that issue, also.

116   James Fallows, *National Defense* (New York, 1981).

8. The Breadwinner

121   Mary Lavin, "Lilacs," in *Women Writing: An Anthology,* ed. Denys Val Baker (New York, 1978).

124–125   The Daniel Boone legend is discussed in Richard Slotkin, *Regeneration Through Violence* (Middletown, Conn., 1973).

125   Leslie Fiedler, *Love and Death in the American Novel* (New York, 1975).

126   The complaining man is interviewed in Donald F. Sabo, Jr., "Male Sexuality and Social Change," Ph.D. diss., State University of New York at Buffalo.

Studs Terkel, *Working* (New York, 1975).

126–127 The longevity data are from James Harrison, "Warning: The Male Sex Role May Be Dangerous to Your Health," *Journal of Social Issues*, vol. 34, no. 1 (1978).

128 John Stickney, *Self-Made* (New York, 1980).

An excellent account of women's status in American history is Sheila M. Rothman, *Woman's Proper Place* (New York, 1978). The differences between colonial and mid-1900s women's roles are based on John Demos, *The Little Commonwealth* (Oxford, 1971); Ann D. Gordon and Mary Jo Buhle, "Sex and Class in Colonial and Nineteenth-Century America," in *Liberating Women's History*, ed. Bernice A. Carroll (Urbana, Ill., 1976); Mary P. Ryan, *Womanhood in America* (New York, 1975); Gerda Lerner, "The Lady and the Mill Girl: Changes in the Status of Women in the Age of Jackson," in Jean E. Friedman et al., *Our American Sisters* (Boston, 1976).

Alexis de Tocqueville's remarks are from *Democracy in America* (New York, 1966); reprinted in Nancy F. Cott, *Roots of Bitterness* (New York, 1972).

128 The "divorce" of work from home is Amaury de Riencourt's phrase, as explained in *Sex and Power in History* (New York, 1972).

128–129 The "splitting of the national character" is discussed by Ryan, *Womanhood in America*. See also Gordon and Buhle, "Sex and Class."

129 Marilyn French, *The Women's Room* (New York, 1977).

129–130 Peter Gabriel Filene, *Him/Her/Self* (New York, 1974).

130 Cynthia Russet, in her review of Filene's book in *Signs*, vol. 1, no. 4 (1978).

The era of the self-made man has no beginning or end, but both of the following sources point to the 1830s as a critical decade in the formation of this archetype: John C. Cawelti, *Apostles of the Self-Made Man* (Chicago, 1965), and Irving G. Wyllie, *The Self-Made Man in America* (New Brunswick, N.J., 1954).

130–131 The traits of Horatio Alger's good employee are summarized in Cawelti, *Apostles*.

131 Bernard Wishy, *The Child and the Republic* (Philadelphia, 1968).

The first study that documented Horatio Alger's indiscretion, to my knowledge, is Edwin P. Hoyt, *Horatio's Boys* (Radnor, Pa., 1974).

Eli Ginzburg, *Lifestyles of Educated Women* (New York, 1966).

132 See Cynthia Dowling, "The Cinderella Complex," *New York Times Magazine*, March 22, 1981; and Erich Gronseth, "The

Breadwinner Trap," in *The Future of the Family*, ed. Louise Kapp Howe (New York, 1972).

The increase in job-family conflict was reported in *U.S. News & World Report*, July 16, 1980.

Margaret Mead, *Male and Female* (New York, 1949).

133   Child-rearing manuals are described in Ryan, *Womanhood in America*.

9. The Expert

140   Aristotle's statement is from "Physiognomics," in *Minor Works*, vol. 2, trans. W. S. Hett; cited in Boslooper and Hayes, *The Femininity Game* (New York, 1973). It is discussed at greater length in Amaury de Riencourt, *Sex and Power in History* (New York, 1974).

141   Auguste de Candolle, *Histoire des Sciences et des Savants depuis Deux Siècles;* quoted in H. J. Mazans, *Woman in Science* (Cambridge, Mass., 1974).

Regarding cranium measurement, see Jonathan R. Cole, *Fair Science* (New York, 1979), and Stephen Gould, *The Mismeasure of Man* (New York, 1981).

142   Julian Jaynes, *The Origin of Consciousness in the Breakdown of the Bicameral Mind* (Boston, 1976).

143   J. Marion Sims is discussed in J. Barker-Benfield, *Horrors of the Half-Known Life* (New York, 1976).

143–144   Clark and Hall are discussed in Barbara Ehrenreich and Deirdre English, *For Her Own Good: 150 Years of the Experts' Advice to Women* (New York, 1978).

144   The decline of midwifery is chronicled in Ehrenreich and English, *For Her Own Good.*

James D. Watson, *The Double Helix* (New York, 1968).

145   The Biochemist quoted is my father, Dr. Koert Gerzon. I do not have statistics to confirm his remarks, but others in the profession concur.

The best article I have seen is "Nuclear Power as a Feminist Issue," by Dorothy Nelkin, a professor in the Program on Science, Technology and Society at Cornell University. It appeared in *Environment*, vol. 23, no. 1. She summarized the polling data, and her bibliography is excellent.

146   Nietzsche's comments are from *Beyond Good and Evil* (New York, 1966); reprinted in Theodore and Betty Roszak, *Masculine/Feminine* (New York, 1970).

The Schopenhauer quotation is from H. R. Hays, *The Dangerous Sex* (New York, 1964). See also de Riencourt, *Sex and Power.*

Durkheim and Comte are both cited in Cole, *Fair Science.*

147 Freud's comments on women are cited in R. V. Sampson, *The Psychology of Power* (New York, 1966).

147-148 The statistics regarding the APA and the comments of its president are from Nina McCain, "Psychiatrists Split over ERA," *Boston Globe.*

149 Germaine Greer, *The Obstacle Race* (New York, 1979).

Mailer's comments, from *Advertisements for Myself* (New York, 1976), are discussed in Mary Ellman, *Thinking About Women* (New York, 1968). See also Tillie Olsen, *Silences* (New York, 1979), and Honor Moore, *The New Women's Theatre* (New York, 1977).

149-150 The male child-rearing experts are from Ehrenreich and English, *For Her Own Good.*

150 Robert Miner, *Mother's Day* (New York, 1978).

151-152 Luther and Knox are cited in de Riencourt, *Sex and Power.*

152 The feminine qualities of some American ministers are discussed in Ann Douglas, *The Feminization of American Culture* (New York, 1978).

153 The remarks by Henry James, Sr., are quoted in Douglas, *Feminization.*

The comments on Christ's masculinity are cited in Joe L. Dubbert, *A Man's Place* (Englewood Cliffs, N.J., 1979).

10. Boyhood

159 Laurens van der Post, *The Seed and the Sower* (London, 1974).

160 Joseph Pleck, "My Male Sex Role—and Ours," *Win,* April 11, 1974.

161 Talcott Parsons's theory is presented in *Family Socialization and Interaction Process,* ed. Talcott Parsons and Robert A. Bales (Glencoe, Ill., 1955).

161-162 My summary of the state of research into fathering is taken from the excellent study by James Levine, *Who Shall Raise the Children?* (New York, 1976).

162 John Irving, *The World According to Garp* (New York, 1978).

Dorothy Dinnerstein, *The Mermaid and the Minotaur* (New York, 1976).

163 Margaret Mead, *Male and Female* (New York, 1949).

Betty Friedan, *The Feminine Mystique* (New York, 1963).

163-164 Della Cyrus, "Why Mothers Fail," *Atlantic Monthly*, April 1947.

164 Margaret Mead, "Some Theoretical Considerations on the Problem of Mother-Child Separation," *American Journal of Orthopsychiatry* (1954). Although her statement is more than twenty years old, it is still supported by current research.

165 Hans Sebald, *Momism* (Chicago, 1976).

165-166 Levy, Strecker, Wylie, and the maternal overprotection syndrome are discussed in Friedan, *Feminine Mystique*.

11. Manhood

173 These comments on rites of passage are adapted from Mark Gerzon, *The Whole World Is Watching* (New York, 1969). See also Arnold van Gennep, *Rites of Passage* (Chicago, 1960).

174 Pat Conroy, *The Lords of Discipline* (Boston, 1981).

Lucian K. Truscott IV, *Dress Gray* (New York, 1978).

Mark Baker, *Nam* (New York, 1981).

175 Clint Eastwood's comments are from the *Time* magazine cover story devoted to him and Burt Reynolds.

175-176 The data on teenage sexuality are from "Teenage Sex," *Newsweek*, February 1, 1980.

176 Dan Wakefield, *Going All the Way* (New York, 1970).

Margaret Mead, *Male and Female* (New York, 1949).

177 Lisa Alther, *Kinflicks* (New York, 1976).

Judith Rossner, *Looking for Mr. Goodbar* (New York, 1975)

Paul Starr, "Hollywood's New Image of Masculinity," *New York Times*, November 25, 1979.

178 The men's rights leader is R. F. Doyle, author of *A Manifesto of Men's Liberation*, published by Men's Rights Association, P.O. Box 189, Forest Lake, Minn.

178-179 George Gilder, *Sexual Suicide* (New York, 1973), and Michael S. Korda, *Power!* (New York, 1973).

179 The earliest advocates of liberation include Marc Feigen Fasteau, *The Male Machine* (New York, 1974), and William Farrell, *The Liberated Man* (New York, 1974).

My criticism of the lists of do's and don'ts refers to Herb Goldberg, *The New Male* (New York, 1980). His authoritative, often impersonal dictums disturb me because although his message is new, the medium is not. While some of his commandments make good sense ("Cultivate buddyships"), others seem evasive ("Post-pone binding commitments").

The sex role images are from Inge Broverman et al., "Sex Role Stereotypes: A Current Appraisal," *Journal of Social Issues,* vol. 28, no. 2 (1972).

12. Marriage

187   The historical statistics on divorce are from Christopher Lasch, *Heaven in a Heartless World* (New York, 1977).

John Updike, *Museums and Women and Other Stories* (New York, 1972).

188–189   Phil Donahue, *My Own Story* (New York, 1979).

189   Marabel Morgan, *The Total Woman* (Old Tappan, N.J., 1973).

Anita Bryant's remarks are from a UPI interview, as reported in the *Boston Globe,* November 15, 1980.

190   Phyllis McGinley, *Sixpence in Her Shoe* (New York, 1964).

Maggie Scarf, *Unfinished Business: Pressure Points in the Lives of Women* (New York, 1980).

Joan Beck, "The 1950s American Dream Wife," *Boston Globe,* December 1, 1980. Beck suggested, incidentally, that Nancy Reagan symbolizes this type of femininity.

191   Karen de Crow, *Sexist Justice* (New York, 1974).

192   The English common law notion of marriage as ownership is discussed in R. Emerson Dobash and Russell Dobash, *Violence Against Wives* (New York, 1979).

The text of Mikulski's bill is available from the U.S. House of Representatives Printing Office. It was published in *Parade,* October 16, 1977.

The best estimate I can find of the frequency of wife abuse is from Richard Gelles, one of the most respected researchers in the field. In conversation, he dismissed other writers' claims that half of all married women were battered as an exaggeration based on the incorrect extrapolation of figures in one of his own early studies. He feels that the best estimate is one out of six. See his *Family Violence* (Los Angeles, 1979).

193   Jessie Bernard, *The Future of Marriage* (New York, 1978). For correlations between marital status and marriage, see W. R. Gove, "The Relationship Between Sex Roles, Marital Status and Mental Illness," *Social Forces* (1972). See also W. R. Gove and J. F.

Tudor, "Adult Sex Roles and Mental Illness," in *Changing Women in a Changing Society*, ed. J. Huber (Chicago, 1973).

Maggie Scarf, "So Many Unhappy Women: She Asked Why," *New York Times*, August 23, 1980.

194   The structure of conversation was reported by the *Boston Globe*'s Judy Foreman. The researchers mentioned are Candace West and Don Zimmerman at the University of California at Santa Cruz.

195   Christopher Lasch, *The Culture of Narcissism* (New York, 1978).

Benjamin Spock, *Raising Children in a Difficult Time* (New York, 1974).

13. Fatherhood

202   The woman journalist is Joan Cook, "Reducing the Risk for Expectant Fathers," *New York Times Magazine*, July 5, 1964.

George Schaefer, *The Expectant Father*.

203   Arthur and Libby Colman, *Pregnancy: The Psychological Experience* (New York, 1977).

Robert Bradley, *Husband-Coached Childbirth* (New York, 1974).

204   Colman and Colman, *Pregnancy*.

205-206 The studies and the excerpt from one father's recollections of birth are from Martin Greenberg and Norman Morris, "Engrossment: The Newborn's Impact upon the Father," *American Journal of Orthopsychiatry* (July 1974).

207   John Lennon's comment was in an interview with *Playboy*; see *The Playboy Interviews*, ed. G. Barry Golson (New York, 1981).

Levine, in conversation with the author.

208   David Steinberg, *fatherjournal* (Albion, Calif., 1977).

209   The "typical father" comments are in Sam Julty, *Men's Bodies, Men's Selves* (New York, 1979).

John Ehrlichman, quoted in the *Boston Globe*, September 2, 1980.

209-210 Joan Kennedy, quoted in Ellen Goodman's column in the *Boston Globe*. For a darker account of the sexual attitudes in the Kennedy family, see Garry Wills, *The Kennedy Imprisonment* (Boston, 1982).

210   Congressman Gary Myers, in the *Washington Post*, October 29, 1977, and *People*, March 7, 1978.

210-211 David Breneman and Bertram S. Brown, interviewed by the *Wall Street Journal*'s Dennis Farney.

211 Pauline Kael, *The New Yorker*, June 23, 1980.

211-212 Alan Saperstein, *Mom Kills Kids and Self* (New York, 1980).

212-213 The account of Rice and Stitt is from interviews, wire service reports, and legal transcripts.

213-214 Joseph Heller, *Something Happened* (New York, 1974).

215 Roger Gould, "Transformation During Early and Middle Adult Years," in *Themes of Love and Work in Adulthood*, ed. Neil J. Smelser and Erik H. Erikson (Cambridge, Mass., 1980). On the midlife crisis, see also Daniel Levinson, *Seasons of a Man's Life* (New York, 1978).

14. The Lord

221 Paul Moore, Jr., *Take a Bishop Like Me* (New York, 1979), and in conversation with the author, May 1981.

222-223 The Vatican's declaration and Sonya Quitslund's critique are reprinted in Leonard and Arlene Swidler, *Women Priests: A Catholic Commentary on the "Vatican Declaration"* (New York, 1977).

223 Sister Theresa Kane, quoted in *Newsweek*, November 24, 1980.

Contemporary Jewish feminists include Rita M. Gross, "Steps Toward a Feminine Imagery of Deity in Jewish Theology," *Judaism*, vol. 30 (Spring, 1981); and Carol Christ, "The Liberation of Women and the Liberation of God," in *The Jewish Woman*, ed. Elizabeth Koltun (New York, 1976).

Islamic practices are discussed in Fatima Mernissi, *Beyond the Veil* (Cambridge, Mass., 1975), and in Lois Beck and Nikki Keddie, *Women in the Muslim World* (Cambridge, Mass., 1978).

The Buddha gave permission for establishing an order of nuns only after repeated requests from his women followers. When he finally consented, the Buddha told his disciple Ananda that his teachings would last half as long now that women had been included. According to some scholars, however, Buddhism seems less limited by a persistent anti-feminine bias than other Eastern religions. Concluded John Walters in *The Essence of Buddhism:* "The tradition of feminine freedom has been maintained until today, when in Ceylon the Burma women are proud, independent and influential. The Buddhist woman is an individual, not a thing; whereas, even in enlightened Moslem and Hindu communities, the woman is still regarded as an inferior being." See also Douglas A. Fox, *The Vagrant Lotus* (Philadelphia, 1973).

The spiritual pyramid, from goodness to evil, is examined in depth in Sheila Collins, "Exorcising the Patriarchal Demon," in *A Different Heaven and Earth: A Feminist Perspective on Religion* (Valley Forge, Pa., 1974). She described the hierarchy: "As God is the ruler and creator of his world, so man is to rule woman who is beneath him. She, in turn, rules children who are beneath her."

The sexual origins of the Devil figure are sketched in Marcello Craveri, *The Life of Jesus* (New York, 1967).

224–225   Estimates of the numbers of witches killed vary. Mary Daly summarizes some in *Gyn/Ecology* (Boston, 1968). In using the figure "a million or more," I am following the conservative reasoning outlined in Rosemary R. Reuther, *New Woman, New Earth* (New York, 1975).

225–226   Some of the sources used in discussing the European witch craze are: Daly, *Gyn/Ecology;* Amaury de Riencourt, *Sex and Power in History* (New York, 1974); and Barbara Ehrenreich and Deirdre English, *For Her Own Good: 150 Years of the Experts' Advice to Women* (New York, 1978). See also H. R. Trevor-Roper, *The European Witch Craze in the Sixteenth and Seventeenth Centuries* (New York, 1969).

De Riencourt, *Sex and Power.*

227   Jonathan Edwards's sermon is discussed in Perry Miller, *Nature's Nation* (Cambridge, Mass., 1966).

228   Phyllis Chesler, *On Men* (New York, 1978).

228–229   Paul Tillich, *Systematic Theology* (Chicago, 1957). Compare discussions by Patricia Martin Doyle, "Women and Religion: Psychological and Cultural Implications," and Joan Arnold Romero, "The Protestant Principle: A Woman's View of Barth and Tillich," in *Religion and Sexism,* ed. Rosemary R. Reuther (New York, 1974).

15. Heroism

240   The remarks cited are from Lester Brown, *The Twenty-ninth Day* (New York, 1978); Amory Lovins, *Soft Energy Paths: Toward a Durable Peace* (Cambridge, Mass., 1977); and "The Worldwide Loss of Cropland," *Worldwatch* Paper 24 (Washington, 1978). See also the writings of E. F. Schumacher, Wendell Berry, and Wes Jackson for similar comments.

243   "Fatherhood USA" is the tentative title of the forthcoming book by Levine, Pleck, and Lamb. Levine's comments, in conversation with the author.

248   Ury's and Fisher's comments, in conversation with the author.

251   Recent discussion of holistic perspectives can be found in Marilyn Ferguson, *The Aquarian Conspiracy* (Los Angeles, 1980); Willis W. Harmon, *An Incomplete Guide to the Future;* and Elizabeth Dodson Gray, *Green Paradise Lost* (Wellesley, Mass., 1981).

In her analysis of TV programming, Gray reached the hopeful conclusion that even the networks were encouraging diversity: "The name of the game is not 'rightness' anymore, or 'do you match the unattainable image of the hero?' The image has become broad enough to include almost all of us, black and white, Jewish and Puerto Rican and Italian."

For another perspective on the Colleague, see Michael Maccoby, *The Leader* (New York, 1982).

255   Brand, in conversation with the author.

256   Spock, in conversation with the author.

Afterword

263   Robert Moore and Douglas Gillette, *King, Warrior, Magician, Lover: Rediscovering the Archetypes of the Mature Masculine* (San Francisco, 1990).

269   Betty Friedan is quoted in "What Do Men Really Want?" *Newsweek,* June 24, 1991.

271   Carol Bly, "The Danger in Men's Groups," *Utne Reader,* November/December 1989.

273   The quote about smelly feet is drawn from Jon Tevlin, "Of Hawks and Men: A Weekend in the Male Wilderness," *Utne Reader,* November/December, 1989. The violation of trust to which I refer applies to both this article and one by Doug Stanton, "Inward Ho!" *Esquire,* October 1991. The failure of these articles is not that they are critical; of course the men's movement requires hard-headed scrutiny. The failure is that both authors lied and deceived other men to get their "scoop."

276   Sam Keen is quoted in Stephen Bodian, "Do Men Drive as to War?" *Yoga Journal,* May/June 1991.

277   Richard Musicant is quoted in *Newsweek,* May 27, 1991, p. 17.

278   To learn more about how to start and lead men's groups, see Bill Kauth, *A Circle of Men: The Original Manual for Men's Support Groups* (New York, 1992).

280   Ellen Goodman, *Boston Globe,* March 14, 1991, op-ed page.

280   The quote from the president of Bantam Books appears in Richard Zoglin, "Stormin' Norman: The Book," *Time,* July 8, 1991.

281–82   On the same day that reports appeared about the number of children dying in the devastated cities and countryside of Iraq, an interview with a Stealth fighter pilot was published. This American hero boasted at a Paris air show about the magnificent new "invisible" planes he flew; in hundreds of bombing sorties, he crowed, "We did not take one nick of battle damage." See Barry James, "Adventures of a Stealth Pilot," *International Herald Tribune,* June 21, 1991.

282   General Schwarzkopf is quoted in "Iraqi Troop Deaths Totaled at Least 100,000, U.S. Says," *Wall Street Journal,* March 22, 1991.

283   Details about the homecoming troops appear in Ray Wilkinson and Tom Mathews, "Return of the 'Wild Boys,' " *Newsweek,* June 3, 1991.

283   John Sedgwick, "The Men from DARPA," *Playboy,* August 1991.

283   Michael Meade is quoted in "There Is No Glory in Victory," *New Dimensions,* May/June 1991.

284   For a discussion of the connection between masculinity and violence, see Myriam Miedzian, *Boys Will Be Boys: Breaking the Link Between Masculinity and Violence* (New York, 1991). Sam Keen offers an equally compelling discussion in *Fire in the Belly* (New York, 1991).

About the Author

Mark Gerzon is the author of a best seller about the sixties generation, *The Whole World Is Watching,* and a portrait of the same generation at midlife, *Coming into Our Own: Understanding the Adult Metamorphosis.* He has lectured widely on gender issues in the educational, religious, and business communities and is featured in a series of videotapes called *Men in Crisis,* distributed by Concept Media, in Irvine, California. He lives with his wife, Shelley Kessler, and their three sons.